INTRODUCTION TO

International Education

International Schools and their Communities

MARY HAYDEN

SAGE Publications
London • Thousand Oaks • New Delhi

First published 2006

SAGE Publications Ltd
1 Oliver's Yard
55 City Road
London EC1Y 1SP

SAGE Publications Inc.
2455 Teller Road
Thousand Oaks, California 91320

SAGE Publications India Pvt Ltd
B-42, Panchsheel Enclave
Post Box 4109
New Delhi 110 017

British Library Cataloguing in Publication data

A catalogue record for this book is available from the British Library

ISBN 10 1-4129-1999-1 ISBN 13 978-1-4129-1999-9
ISBN 10 1-4129-2000-0 ISBN 13 978-1-4129-2000-1 (pbk)

Library of Congress Control Number 2006903705

Typeset by C&M Digitals (P) Ltd, Chennai, India
Printed in Great Britain by Athenaeum Press, Gateshead, Tyne & Wear
Printed on paper from sustainable resources

INTRODUCTION TO International Education

International Schools and their Communities

Contents

Foreword

Mary Hayden is arguably the most experienced researcher in her field – international schools and international education. She is acknowledged to be a distinguished writer and has published extensively in both journals and books. As many throughout the world will testify, she is also an accomplished teacher and has personally supervised the enquiry and research activities of literally hundreds of students at masters and doctoral levels – among them many teachers, administrators, curriculum developers and examiners – all of whom have benefited enormously from her dedication to their interests, her insistence on rigour in their work and their writings, and her particular way of motivating those with whom she collaborates. Her passion for the encouragement and promotion of the work of others, especially in the area of international education, has been evident in the many papers she has published jointly with students and colleagues and through the editorial roles she has taken over recent years in journal and book publications.

It is therefore fitting that, in writing a book on international education, she should draw upon the work of so many of those with whom she has collaborated over the years and, by including them in such a seminal volume, should pay tribute to their collective contributions to our understanding of the theory and practice of international education.

As may be expected of an experienced teacher, Mary Hayden has employed as her framework a number of underlying themes in constructing the *mélange* of knowledge, understandings and challenges that this book comprises. Among them are familiar dilemmas which those readers already engaged in teaching, administration and research in the field will recognise, and with which those contemplating involvement as teachers, students, parents and board members, for example, will rapidly become acquainted. By identifying international schools and their communities as the organising structure, the themes are woven through the account as the warp and weft of the fabric of the volume. They include a range of issues relating to, for example, pragmatism and ideology, which recur as unifying themes throughout the work. In constructing the book in this way, Dr Hayden will not only be satisfying the needs of those who seek greater knowledge and understanding of the field through the sheer quantity of information the book includes, she will also be challenging and encouraging others to generate implicit and explicit theories and explanations by reflecting upon their own practice.

This book deserves, and will surely command, a wide readership for it concerns a topic of crucial importance – the education of world citizens – explored in its historical and contemporary settings, which is so vital to the future for us all.

Jeff Thompson
Professor of Education
University of Bath

Acknowledgements

I have been fortunate in the course of my career to work in a number of different capacities with literally hundreds of inspiring professionals who have helped me to understand the context of international schools and the many issues and challenges that arise within them.

To these many colleagues and friends I owe a debt of gratitude for having helped to lay the foundations upon which this book is built. To some of them I am particularly grateful for not only having shared their ideas and experiences with me over the years, but for also providing particular assistance in the creation of this book. In addition therefore to thanking our helpful and supportive colleagues at Sage, I must extend a big 'thank you' to Jim Cambridge and Philippa Wheeler for sharing their technical expertise, and Gail Bradley, Ray Davis, Mary Langford, Peter MacKenzie, Edna Murphy, Bora Rancic, Coreen Sears, Wilf Stout, Ray Taylor and David Wilkinson for having been so willing to read early drafts of various sections of the manuscript and to highlight areas where improvement was needed. Extra special thanks must, as ever, go to my friend and colleague Jeff Thompson, without whose constant support, encouragement and chivvying the idea for this book would never have got off the ground.

To all of you, and to the international school community more widely, this book is offered as a contribution to further recognition and understanding of this important and rapidly growing field.

The author and publisher would like to thank the following for giving permission to use the figures in this book:

Nicholas Brealey Publishing for Figure 5.1, p. 70, TCKs and their peer groups, from D. Pollock and R.E. Van Reken (2001) *Third Culture Kids*.

Taylor and Francis Books (UK) for Figure 9.1, p. 139, Model of a learning environment for international education from M.C. Hayden and J.J. Thompson (eds) (1998) *International Education: Principles and Practice*.

CHAPTER 1

International Education: The Context

To many of those born and raised in the relatively stable, mono-cultural context of a country in the developed world of fifty years ago, where schooling was compulsory for a certain number of years prior to employment or further study, the concept of education was probably fairly straightforward. We went to school to be educated, to acquire the knowledge and skills which would be needed when we embarked on life in the adult world. If we gave any thought to the nature of our education (which most of us probably did not, other than when changing schools or if we went on to train as a teacher) we may have recognised that what we were being taught had been selected, either nationally, if in a country with a national curriculum, or locally (possibly by the school itself), as the basis for developing the knowledge and skills needed in order for the society in which we lived to be reproduced on a continuing basis. Lawton describes the curriculum (in the broadest sense, encompassing all the experiences offered within the school context) as 'a selection of the culture of a society' (1989) and in a slowly-evolving society, such a model can work well: if the society around us never changes very much, then the education we experience may not need to change very much either. There were changes of course, but for the most part children in the developed world experienced an education not majorly different from that of their parents, while most children in the developing world had little if any formal education at all.

Fast-forwarding to the early twenty-first century, the changes that have taken place in a relatively short period of time have been almost literally incredible. Advances in science, technology and engineering have led to greater comfort, increased ease of transportation and communication, and a growth in leisure for the privileged of the developed world and for some of those in the less developed world. They have also led to increased ease of violence and war, and presented us with enormous ethical dilemmas including how and when to preserve life (does the fact that we can, mean that we should at all costs?) and how to respond to the major challenges presented by the seemingly increasing gap between rich and poor, where some have plentiful if not excessive amounts to eat while others starve to death. Countries such as Yugoslavia and Czechoslovakia no longer exist, the notion of two superpowers has disappeared, and China is not only more open to tourism but is also increasingly seen as a major economic power on the world stage.

Sophisticated communication networks allow those who can afford to do so to keep easily and cheaply in contact with friends and colleagues across time zones and huge distances, and to have news beamed into their homes from the other side of the world as it is happening. Information is available via the Internet at the press of a button, though not without associated dilemmas about the credibility of the information accessed and whether such access is open to all (viz the recent opening up of a censored form of Google within China). The seemingly ubiquitous mobile telephone allows us to make contact with friends and colleagues at any time of the day or night, wherever they are, and has come upon us so quickly that an etiquette for its use – in meetings, during personal conversations, in schools – is only gradually being developed, while its use to send messages by text has led to the creation by young people of a new abbreviated form of language which causes great consternation to some adults (not least in an English examining board when it was used recently by a student to answer an English language examination question beginning 'Write a letter to your friend ...'). The role of the United States as the only superpower, the influence of the Internet and the colonial heritage of the British Empire have all contributed to the dominance of English as the world language (though in many different forms, and unpalatable as this may be to some) as increasing numbers of non-native speakers of English see it as a means of communicating not only with native English speakers, but also with speakers of different native languages than themselves.

The increased sophistication of communication systems has also led, again for the privileged minority, to increased ease of travel, both within countries and internationally. Frequent and cheap flights make international holidays commonplace, with barriers to travel seemingly more related to differences in language and culture than to travel itself, overcome (in some cases at least) by the latter-day colonisation of certain areas in other countries with better climates or more interesting architecture than our own to make enclaves of familiar language, food and activities available in a 'home from home'. Where once a young person embarking upon a career would have anticipated, unless they were becoming a missionary or joining the diplomatic service or the military, spending that career within one national context, it is now not uncommon to take up a post with a local company and to find oneself at some stage being asked to attend meetings in another country, if not to consider relocating internationally on a longer term basis. Nor is it uncommon to undertake one's nationally-based business via members of staff based on a different continent, because the business has out-sourced part of its operation to a location with lower employment costs; the regular telephone communications between call-centre staff in India and holders of telephone accounts or those enquiring about railway services in, for example, the UK and USA are just one example of such a phenomenon.

One clear consequence of all these changes, and particularly those in communication – whether in terms of travel, or of oral and written contact – is the highlighting of the artificiality of the borders that have been built around what we call countries. Wilkinson (2006: 1) describes attending a presentation by an astronaut who showed photographs of the earth taken from 300 miles up in space, and who highlighted the lack of borderlines or distinctions between countries visible from that distance. The same point can be made by taking a daytime flight across, say, Africa and Europe. The Nile is visible, the Alps can be seen, but the boundaries which are so important in terms of the way human beings relate to each other and the way in which political decisions are made are nowhere in evidence: a product of thinking at a particular point in the history of a geographical region which so often forms the basis of on-going conflict as to where exactly those borders should or should not lie. One need only consider the map of Africa, with its beautifully straight lines drawn by colonial administrators cutting across cultures, languages, tribes and families, to recognise the artificiality of the ways in which human beings have become divided, and to understand the root cause of some of the conflicts that have led to the borders and, literally in some cases, walls that have been built to keep people apart in the twenty-first century.

The artificiality of national borders, and the level of our interdependence, are no less highlighted when we become aware of issues relating to the environment which cannot be contained within those borders. When high levels of industry and individualised transport in developed nations are believed to contribute to the global warming which seems likely to lead to low-lying inhabited islands disappearing beneath the sea in the foreseeable future; when a chemical factory explosion in one country causes severe air pollution in another, or an oil tanker spillage in one country's shipping lane causes the destruction of wildlife in many other countries for miles around; when the threatened pandemic of Avian flu quite clearly cannot be contained within national borders and if it begins to spread will be no respecter of nationality, location or privilege in terms of who it will strike down; then again are we reminded of the artificiality of the boundaries we have chosen to place around ourselves.

Against this global backdrop, it is clear that even within the borders of a national system the concept of education is no longer straightforward. Where once the major purpose of education might have been to prepare young people for adult life in the relatively stable society of their childhood, it can no longer be assumed either that a young person will remain within that society or, indeed, that the society will be recognisable as having much in common with that of the child's parents or grandparents. Teachers in some, if not all, national systems are thus increasingly expected to teach transferable skills and to encourage young people to learn how to learn, rather than only to acquire knowledge which, of itself, may have little usefulness or relevance in twenty years time.

INTERNATIONAL EDUCATION

Given this overall context, the question of what we mean by the concept of 'international' and its use as an adjective to describe other concepts such as 'trade', sport' or 'education' can be seen to be problematic. It might be assumed that the word literally means activities between two or more nations, and in some contexts that may be so. In the case of education, however, definitions are not so straightforward.

The term 'international education' has, over a period of years, come to have a number of different meanings. Marshall (2006) provides a helpful overview of the different ways in which the term 'international education' is used. Development education, for instance, could be considered one such interpretation when focusing specifically on the promotion of awareness of development issues in schools, while comparative education is sometimes used interchangeably with international education – though Crossley and Broadfoot point out that 'comparative and international studies in education have evolved in different ways and there are significant differences in emphasis in approach that distinguish the two' (1992: 101). Crossley and Broadfoot go on to cite Postlethwaite's attempt to distinguish the two terms as follows:

> Strictly speaking to 'compare' means to examine two or more entities by putting them side by side and looking for similarities and differences between or among them. In the field of education, this can apply both to comparisons between and within systems of education. In addition, however, there are many studies that are not comparative in the strict sense of the word which have traditionally been classified under the heading of comparative education. Such studies do not compare, but rather describe, analyse or make proposals for a particular aspect of education in *one* country other than the author's own country. The Comparative and International Education Society introduced the word 'international' in their title in order to cover these sorts of studies. (1988: xvii)

Another dimension of international education is what has come to be known as global education, relating generally to the integration into national systems of educational considerations that go beyond national boundaries. Within the context of the USA, for instance, Clarke describes global education as 'the study of curricular perspectives and issues of cultural diversity, human rights, and prejudice reduction as they relate within the national context, and across national borders' (2004: 54). Within the UK, meanwhile, Marshall explains that 'Whilst education for global understanding has been an agenda for many non-governmental organisations (NGOs) for over half a century, recent UK government interest in global education is unprecedented. Government endorsed strategy documents and recommendations ... send a clear message to schools that incorporating a cross-curricular international or global dimension into the school curriculum is essential' (2007). Also arguably of relevance in any consideration of the concept of international education is that of cosmopolitanism, which Gunesch describes as 'a personal cultural identity form' (2004: 254) and which Hannerz argues 'tends ... to be a matter of competence, of both a generalised and a more specialised kind. There is the aspect of a state of readiness, a personal ability to make one's way into other cultures, through listening, looking, intuiting, and reflecting, and there is cultural competence in the stricter sense of the terms; a built-up skill in manoeuvring more or less expertly with a particular system of meanings. ... Competence with regard to alien cultures for the cosmopolitan entails a sense of mastery' (1992: 252–3).

Clearly then, there is no simple definition of international education to which all would subscribe. Perhaps it is most appropriate therefore to consider international education as an inclusive umbrella term which incorporates a number of other more specific interpretations, or as a Venn diagram in which different concepts overlap to varying degrees. A helpful summary in that sense is the following, taken from the editorial preface to the 1985 special issue on international education of the Harvard Educational Review: 'International, global, cross-cultural and comparative education are different terms used to describe education which attempts – in greater or lesser degree – to come to grips with the increasing interdependence that we face and to consider its relationship to learning'.

THE INTERNATIONAL SCHOOL CONTEXT

Given that the term 'international education' has to be used with caution, a book with international education in its title might conceivably be focusing on any one, or a combination, of the different interpretations referred to above. The focus for this particular volume, however, will be on a dimension of international education not so far mentioned: the context of international schools. Here again, the use of the term 'international education' is contentious, in that material generated within the context of, and/or written about, international schools seems often to suggest that international education is by definition the education experienced by those who attend such schools (and, by implication, not elsewhere). Writing about the international school context, Gellar pointed out the rather imprecise way in which the use of 'international education' as a concept had developed, whereby as the numbers of international or 'overseas' schools worldwide grew, 'for want of a better one, the term "International Education" gained currency – a term that meant all things to some people and meant very little to many – a good example of Wittgenstein's "bewitchment of intelligence by means of language"' (1981: 21).

The notion of a one-to-one correspondence between international schools and international education is rejected in this volume, in that international education is argued (as above) to be a broader, more inclusive, concept of which the education experience of those who attend international schools is just one form. One first year undergraduate included in a survey undertaken at the University of Bath in the UK, for instance, explained when asked about this issue: 'Both schools I have attended ... do not consider themselves as international schools, but I think they [offer an international education] for they offer you opportunities to develop an "international attitude" (for example by dealing with international issues or typical foreign issues, by offering trips abroad/ exchange programmes)' (in Hayden and Thompson, 1995: 341).

Conversely, the fact that a school describes itself as an 'international school' does not necessarily mean that whatever education it offers should be described as 'international education'. Another undergraduate involved in the same survey believed that, although she attended an international school, she had experienced a 'Western education, because everything I was taught was delivered in a Western point of view since all the teachers were from the West'. The same student did, however, believe that she had experienced an international education 'out of class' as, through clubs and societies at school, she was 'exposed to many different cultures and began to appreciate them, especially since some of my closest friends were not of the same culture as me' (in Hayden and Thompson 1995: 341).

Interestingly, the views of this undergraduate reflecting on the experience of international education are consistent with those of over 3,500 16–18 year old students in international schools who were asked in a different survey about their perceptions of the importance of a number of factors in the experience of international education. Three groups of students aged approximately 16, 17 and 18 respectively all rated most highly in importance their exposure to, and interaction with, students of different cultures within school (ahead of teachers as exemplars of international-mindedness, the formal curriculum, other informal aspects of school and exposure to others of different cultures outside school), a perception shared by international school teachers surveyed at the same time about the same issue (Thompson, 1998: 283–5). Such a view would seem to suggest a weakness in another one-to-one relationship sometimes implied in the context of schooling internationally: that international education is entirely related to the formal curriculum, usually in respect of one of the international programmes frequently offered in international schools such as those of the International Baccalaureate Organization (IBO, 2006) or Cambridge International Examinations (CIE, 2006). Again, such an implication is rejected on the basis that, as suggested by students and teachers, the international education experience within schools is a broad one of which the formal curriculum is just one – albeit very important – part.

CONCLUSION

In summary, then, it is argued that international education as a concept is inclusive, with many interpretations within different contexts. Within schools, international education has a number of facets including, though not exclusively, the formal curriculum. International education may be experienced in national schools, where suitable opportunities are built in to facilitate this experience for students, and may also be experienced (though not necessarily) within international schools.

It is international schools that provide the focus for this book. Beginning in Chapter 2 with a consideration of what it means to be an international school, the following chapters will go on to explore a range of issues relating to the different communities with which they are associated: the parents who send their children to these schools, the students who attend them, the teachers and administrators who work in them, and the Boards which oversee them. Further chapters on the curriculum, and on a number of external factors that impinge on international schools, will be followed by a final chapter which considers the future role of international schools and how they might develop as the twenty-first century progresses. In all chapters, a number of references have been made to relevant sources that have informed the developing arguments: in a still relatively thinly researched field, it is hoped that readers will find these references helpful signposts to sources of further relevant reading.

Throughout discussion in the various chapters one particular theme will be seen to recur. International schools in many cases are juggling to respond to the pragmatic demands of modern life (the very reason that many of them exist, as a response to increasing global mobility) and the more ideological and values-based issues which surely need to be central to any education offered to young people who will become adults throughout this century. The balance between pragmatism and ideology is not an easy one to strike, particularly when the two are sometimes in conflict. These, and other, issues will be raised and discussed in what follows. It is hoped that, while this book can only scratch the surface of the complex and multifaceted world of international schools and the issues faced on a daily basis by those who study and work in them, it will nevertheless make a contribution to raising the profile, and increasing understanding, of this still relatively little known but increasingly influential set of institutions.

CHAPTER 2

International Schools

Of the many books written on various aspects of education, few have devoted much space to the basic concept of a school. Why would they? We all know what we understand a school to be: there may be variations on the concept, encompassing those that are state-funded, those that charge fees, those that provide residential accommodation, those that cater for young children, those that cater for older students, those that cater for particular religious beliefs and those that specialise in certain areas of the curriculum. We don't feel the need to read what others think about how a school should be defined, or when a school can or should call itself a school, how many different types of school there might be, or what their characteristics are. Why, then, do we need a chapter in this book devoted to discussion of the concept of an 'international school' and what this term might or might not mean?

Part of the answer to this question lies in the fact that, unlike the more generic concept of a school in a local or national context, many people may not have come across the term before in the sense of having had to give any thought to what it might mean. They may know a family who moved abroad and whose child now attends an international school; they may peruse advertisements in a newspaper and fantasise about teaching in an exotic location where the sun always shines. But that's as far as it goes: international schools are, by and large, schools in other parts of the world in which others teach and learn. For some whose personal situation brings them into individual contact with such a school, their experience becomes first hand: the teacher who decides to move from a national school to an international school, or the parents whose work takes them to another country where an international school education is the most attractive option for their child, for reasons related to language, curriculum and perhaps university prospects. Such individuals may now know what they believe an international school to be: they have, after all, experienced it for themselves either first hand as a teacher, or vicariously through their offspring.

And therein lies the reason for devoting a chapter to the concept of international schools: because in moving on to another school in due course such a teacher or parent may, not unreasonably, make certain assumptions about the new school based on previous experience. Depending on the schools in question, these assumptions may be entirely justified. Alternatively, they may turn out not to have been justified at all, with the second experience being quite different from that of the first. This may not necessarily be a bad thing – perhaps they are pleasantly surprised by the differences – but the fact that they could make such inaccurate assumptions may give cause for concern. Next time they make such a move (if they do) they will know not to make assumptions, and to ask many questions in advance; indeed, the more moves they make over a period of their teaching career or their children's school career, the more questions they will probably ask.

Because in truth there are few assumptions that can be made with any confidence about a school that describes itself (or is described by others) as an 'international school'. Indeed the question of what is or is not an international school would seem to be one where the more one knows, the more complicated it seems to become. As Findlay points out,

> the nature of international schools can be puzzling. Most of us go to school within one education system. It is this experience that forges our educational beliefs. When families first explore expatriate education they discover a world of differences. The nature of the differences is confusing and can call into question some of the beliefs and values that families hold dear. (1997: 5)

DIFFERENCES AND SIMILARITIES

At the root of this potential for confusion is the fact that no one organisation internationally can grant the right to use of the term 'international school' in a school's title. It may be that within a national system a school has to meet certain conditions in order to be described as an international school, but even this is not necessarily the case in all countries and, where it is, the conditions may vary. In essence, schools describe themselves as international schools for a variety of reasons including the nature of the student population and of the curriculum offered, marketing and competition with other schools in the area, and the school's overall ethos or mission. In 1995, Hayden and Thompson wrote that 'for the most part, the body of international schools is a conglomeration of individual institutions which may or may not share an underlying educational philosophy' (1995: 332) and that, indeed, is where we still stand more than ten years later: more schools have opened, and a wider variety of such schools may exist than before, but there is no less ambiguity than there was previously.

Two major respects in which the schools may vary, for instance, are the curriculum (to be discussed in Chapter 9) and the nature of the student population, with the latter determined in part by whether or not the host country will allow its own nationals to attend international schools. If so, an issue may arise with respect to the optimal balance between expatriates and 'locals'. Some international schools, for instance, will always give priority to expatriates (perhaps when they are the only international school in the area, and local schooling may not be perceived as an alternative), while others – perhaps where expatriates have more choice of international school locally – would not prioritise expatriate applications, but will operate a quota system in order to preserve the 'international' flavour of the school. A useful summary highlighting the variation in a number of dimensions of international schools is provided by Blandford and Shaw, who point out that

> In terms of phase, size and sex, international schools defy definition: they may include kindergarten, primary, middle and upper, higher or secondary pupils, or incorporate all of these in a combined school; they may range in number from twenty to 4500; they could be co-educational or single sex. The governance and management of such schools might be determined by the school, the owner, the board, the senior management team or head of school or a managing agency. (2001b: 2)

While there is wide variation in international schools, it is true that many of them share a number of common characteristics. They are usually private and fee-paying, given that few countries subsidise education offered through anything other than their own national system. Other characteristics are neatly encapsulated by Murphy, who says that

> International schools serve the children of those international organisations and multinational companies whose parents are called upon to work in many different countries and to change their assignment at frequent intervals; the schools also educate the children of the diplomatic corps, and offer educational opportunities to children of host country nationals who want their children to learn English or who prefer the greater flexibility which an international school offers over the national system. (1991: 1)

While not all such schools would exactly fit this description (such as the international schools forbidden by law from accepting host country nationals as students), it provides a helpful mental image of the type of school which forms the backdrop to the discussion to come in the following chapters of this book. Attempts to define international schools are fraught with risks: almost any definition, other than the entirely vague and general, is likely to be contestable by someone familiar with an international school that does not quite fit the definition given, such as that of Chesworth and Dawe who claim that

> An international school is specifically established to cater for students from a wide variety of cultures who are likely to be internationally mobile as their parents move from country to country, often in the employ of UN organisations or private international companies. The staff also represent a mixture of nationalities, usually with no particular nationality predominating. Such schools normally teach an international programme of study or one or more national programmes (but not generally of the country in which they are to be found) or a combination of both. (2000: x)

Again, while encompassing most of what many would recognise as characteristics of those international schools with which they are familiar, this definition would exclude for instance the type of international school that caters largely for students from one national context.

In order to help to contextualise the lack of clarity in the current situation, the next section will focus briefly on how that situation arose. A number of different groupings and categorisations of international schools will then be considered, as the basis for what follows in future chapters.

EARLY DAYS

During 1996 a brief correspondence in *IB World* magazine (published for schools authorised to follow one or more programmes of the International Baccalaureate Organization) debated the issue of which might be the oldest international school in existence, the two possibilities under discussion being the International School of Geneva and Yokohama International School. Both were founded in 1924, following the end of the Great War (1914–1918), in a climate where the previously unimaginable horrors of conflict on such a large scale had focused minds on the importance of promoting international cooperation and understanding.

The outcome of this correspondence was a recognition that the two schools, both well established and highly respected institutions some eighty years on, had been founded literally within days of each other (Walker, 1996: 19–20; Stanworth, 1996: 53–4). In both cases, a more detailed account of the school's establishment exists in the public domain (Stanworth, 1998; Knight, 1999) and both make fascinating reading: in Knight's case of the need for a school in Geneva to cater for the children of expatriate employees of the recently formed International Labour Office and League of Nations; in Stanworth's of the need for a school in Yokohama to cater for the children of that city's 'foreign' community. Indeed both accounts of their early days are redolent, in purely practical terms, of similar stories to be encountered of earliest beginnings in many other international schools worldwide, often started by an enterprising individual or small group of expatriate parents who were prepared to take a risk to provide for an initially very small number of children. In the case of Geneva, it began with three teachers and eight children in a borrowed house (Knight, 1999); at Yokohama, with one teacher and six children in the local YMCA (Stanworth, 1998). More recently, in 1946, the Alice Smith School in Kuala Lumpur had its origins in the sitting room of the eponymous Alice Smith, with herself as teacher and two expatriate children including her own daughter (Alice Smith School, 1996). There are undoubtedly many similar stories - of pioneers, vision and risk - which sowed the seeds of what went on to become flourishing, well-established schools of the twenty first century.

The question of when the first international school was founded raises the question of what is meant by an 'international school'. The Maseru English Medium Preparatory School (MEMPS) in Lesotho, for instance, was founded in 1890 with one teacher for the children of officials of the British administration of the then Basutoland, traders and English speaking missionaries (MEMPS, 1990). Not in quite the same mould, perhaps, as the schools already mentioned, and not having the term 'international school' in its title, in catering for children of expatriates MEMPS was arguably - in an inclusive definition of the term 'international school' - a precursor of the higher profile schools that were to follow.

Again taking a broad interpretation of the concept of international school, Sylvester (2002) describes the background to what he argues could justifiably be described as the first international school: the International College at Spring Grove, London. Operating in premises not far from today's Heathrow International Airport, the 'Spring Grove School' was inspired by Richard Cobden, Thomas H. Huxley and John Tyndall and was open from 1866 to 1889, when Borough Road Training College took over its premises. The Spring Grove School catered for male students from at least ten different nationalities (Brickman, 1962) and its foundation was consistent with the views of many advocates of free trade during that era (Stewart, 1972) who 'hoped to realise their vision of international harmony by the creation of a new type of education which would enable the citizens of different countries to become international ambassadors' (Sylvester, 2002: 5). As Sylvester's research shows, the Spring Grove School grew out of a sustained interest on the part of a committed group of individuals (including, interestingly, the novelist Charles Dickens) in the notion of a number of international schools in Europe, catering for pupils (again all boys) from different countries and creeds in such a way that 'the pupils, in passing from one language and nation to another, would find no notable change in the course of study to retard the progress of their education'. Each student would 'acquire thoroughly several modern languages, each being learned with the others among school fellows of all nations, in the land where it is spoken, the arrangement of classes and method of study being precisely the same in each international school' (Dickens, 1864, in Sylvester, 2002: 8).

In fact, as Sylvester (2002: 6) points out, the very first organised attempt to establish international schools in the West may well have been an essay competition at the London International Exhibition of 1862 on the establishment of international schools. While others including Bibby (1959) and Brickman (1950) have argued that such a dawning was actually at the Paris 1855 Exhibition with an essay contest based on the theme of 'The advantages of educating together children of different nationalities', there would seem, either way, to have been considerable interest in the idea of international schools at that early stage – even if the idea was not transformed into sustainable reality until the twentieth century.

Arguably, depending upon one's interpretation of the concept of an international school, even in the 1850s the idea was not entirely new. In the early fifteenth century Prince Henry the Navigator of Portugal, for instance, reportedly brought young students from many countries to his Navigation School, and there are other examples from the nineteenth century and earlier of young people travelling beyond their home borders in order to be educated with others from different national backgrounds to their own. Whenever and wherever their origins, the most recent, and undoubtedly the most extensive, manifestation of international schools as a phenomenon has been in the period since the middle of the twentieth century. Through, arguably, a combination of two main influences – the pragmatic and the ideological – the number of international schools has grown markedly since that time to the present date. Because of the difficulties already identified in defining international schools, it is impossible to give a precise number at any one time. It would be safe to argue, however, even with this caveat, that the number in existence had increased to well over 1,000 in the late twentieth century (Hayden and Thompson, 1995) and is undoubtedly higher than this figure at the time of writing.

The growth has not been linear, having increased more rapidly in recent years than previously, with much of the gain in the past half century. Bereday and Lauwerys, for instance, referred in 1964 to 'a new concept – international schools founded with the specific purpose of furthering international education' (of which they estimated there then to be about fifty), observing that 'international education', as it was described, was at that time 'uncertain of its aims and fundamental premises', with 'only politicians, diplomats, missionaries and volunteer social welfare organisations' usually going overseas. This is in marked contrast to Storti's reference to Windham's (1999: 8) survey of 264 America-based multinational corporations of which two thirds expected their number of expatriate employees to increase (having already risen in previous years) by the year 2000: as Storti comments, with reference to the American business context, 'An ever-increasing number of companies (earn) more revenue from overseas than from domestic operations' (Storti, 2001: xvi).

That shift in balance of globally mobile professionals to include so many in business, linked in large part to the effects of creeping globalisation, could be seen clearly by the 1980s and 1990s. Jonietz and Harris, for instance, pointed out in 1991 how rapidly the number of international schools had grown since the 1960s (1991: ix), while Matthews in 1989 estimated that numbers had grown by that stage to the point where approximately 1000 international schools were in existence, catering for about half a million students and employing around 50,000 teachers (Matthews, 1989: 9). Indeed, whereas once the international school student might have been considered 'marginal (neither here nor there and always out of place), handicapped by being educated in a place different than their homeland' (Willis and Enloe, 1990: 175), by 1990 it was argued that 'international school graduates have become more and more attractive to universities and employers, [their] identity as "citizens of the world" [being] now viewed as more a benefit than a detriment' (Willis and Enloe, 1990: 175).

CATEGORISATIONS OF INTERNATIONAL SCHOOLS

There have been several attempts in recent years to bring some order to the long list of schools that might be considered 'international schools', either because they include that term in their title or because they seem to fit in some way the criteria associated with such a description. Leach (1969) was the first to attempt to do so by proposing a categorisation of international schools as follows:

- Those 'serving or being composed of students from several nationalities', a confusing definition, as he admits, when 'practically every school in such a cosmopolitan centre as London or New York includes a number of nationalities in its student body' (p. 7).
- Those 'overseas' schools which are set up in 'another nation [which] in most cases, serve only the expatriate community', including schools 'classified as French International, British International, American International, German International, etc' (p. 9).
- That relatively small number of schools 'founded by joint action of two or more governments or national groupings', such as the 'so-called binational schools of Latin America ... and, more recently, the John F. Kennedy School in Berlin' (p. 9).
- Those schools which 'belong to the International Schools Association (ISA), or could do so' (p. 10), though this was not a well-defined category as at the time the ISA accepted for membership schools which were working towards its criteria, as well as those which actually met them.

Leach argued that his own school, the International School of Geneva, was the only 'true' international school, and even that had 'too much Swiss influence, too many British staff, too many American students' (p. 36), a view which Peterson considered reflected 'an unrealistic purism ... about what an international school should be' (1987: 36). Sanderson (1981) later argued that there were in fact seven types of international school, before Pönisch (1987) went on to distinguish what she suggested were 11 types of such school. An alternative approach to making sense of the international schools growing up around the world, meanwhile, had been devised by Terwilliger (1972) who, rather than attempt to categorise them, cited four main prerequisites for a school to be classified as 'international':

- enrolment of a significant number of students who are not citizens of the country in which the school is located;
- a Board of Directors which should 'ideally, be made up of foreigners and nationals in roughly the same proportions as the student body being served' (p. 360);
- a staffing policy whereby teachers are appointed 'who have themselves experienced a period of cultural adaptation [and will thus] be better able to counsel those new students who have difficulty adjusting to the social and cultural atmosphere of their new school' (p. 360); and
- a curriculum which should be a 'distillation of the best content and the most effective instructional practices of each of the national systems' (p. 361) to allow maximum flexibility in transferring either amongst international schools or back into the home education system.

In practice, however, given the huge diversity of schools and the absence of any central authorising body, it is arguably of little value to discuss prerequisites – or even, perhaps, to attempt a categorisation. Matthews, in fact, pointed out that attempting to generalise about international schools is 'likely to produce little that is worthwhile, given the variety of institutions which describe themselves by that umbrella term' and instead identified a dichotomy between what he termed 'ideology-driven' and 'market-driven' international schools (1989: 12). Ideology-driven international schools, he argued, would include those schools founded for 'the express purpose of in some way furthering international understanding and cooperation', while market-driven schools would include 'all the other international schools which have arisen from the needs of particular expatriate communities. They may have been established, and may be operated by 'individuals, community groups, delegates of multinational companies or government agencies' (1989: 12).

While this dichotomy is helpful in moving away from attempts to categorise international schools or to define prerequisites for their status, it is arguably (and Matthews himself has made this point more recently) rather simplistic in seeming to suggest that each international school can fall into one or other category. In practice, it may be more realistic to envisage the grouping of international schools as representing a spectrum, with the ideological at one end and the market-driven at the other. Schools such as the United World Colleges may be placed as close to the ideologically-driven end of the spectrum as it is possible to be, while at the other end of the same spectrum could be those schools that are entirely market-driven in their approach (and possibly exist principally as businesses). The majority of international schools, meanwhile, would be likely to fall somewhere in between the two extremes, demonstrating in different proportions according to their mission statement and context the influence of both ends of the spectrum.

The notion of an ideological dimension to the education provided can clearly be linked in this context to the concept of international mindedness, and Hill recounts the foundation in 1951 with support from UNESCO of the Conference of Internationally-Minded Schools (CIMS), which was later subsumed by the International Schools Association (ISA) (Hill, 2000: 32). More recently, Hill (2006a) has addressed the challenge of categorising international schools and their students by including both national and international schools in a proposed typology, on the basis that both may have a mission to promote international education; he identifies four distinct school types based on the cultural experience from the students' perspective via the programmes of study, as follows:

- national school abroad and national programme of home country;
- national school in home country and international programme;
- international school and international programme;
- international school and national programme of one or more countries (and perhaps the host country).

It is with Hill's last two school types that this book is chiefly concerned, and the next section will consider some of the groups of schools that may be found in this context.

GROUPINGS OF INTERNATIONAL SCHOOLS

United World Colleges

Arguably this grouping of colleges do not belong in any discussion of international schools, since some would claim that they are not international schools at all. Where international schools are generally founded in response to a pragmatic need, and are therefore 'service schools' in some sense, United World Colleges (UWC) are not. From the founding in 1962 of the first UWC, Atlantic College in South Wales, based largely on the philosophy of Kurt Hahn (Peterson, 1987), the colleges continue to be ideologically focused. Promoting international understanding and peace through education, they bring together young people from many different countries, providing a practical response to the question asked by the then Prime Minister of Canada, Lester B. Pearson, in his 1957 Nobel Peace Prize lecture, 'How can there be peace without people understanding each other, and how can this be if they don't know each other?' (Lester B. Pearson College of the Pacific, 1982: 9).

Funded by scholarships raised by national committees worldwide, students at all but one of the colleges (Simon Bolivar UWC, Venezuela, which focuses specifically on agriculture) follow the IB Diploma programme, while also engaging in challenging outdoor pursuits and service in the local community. Students attend for just two years (age 16–18) at all the ten colleges except for the UWC of South East Asia in Singapore and the UWC Waterford KaMhlaba in Swaziland, both of which offer education to a wider age range having been pre-existing schools granted UWC status as opposed to being founded as a UWC. A new UWC has recently opened in Costa Rica, and plans are in hand to open new UWC in Bosnia and Herzegovina, and in Kenya (UWC, 2006). Though in one sense entirely ideologically-driven, since they have no reason to exist other than for the promotion of an internationalist ethos, a pragmatic dimension enters the frame for the UWC in that they can only continue to exist for as long as funding is found for the scholarships upon which their students rely. It is already the case that some UWC need to fill a number of places with fee-paying students: continuing to secure sufficient funding to fill all the places at existing and proposed colleges seems likely to be an ongoing challenge to them for the foreseeable future.

European Schools

In 2003 this group of day schools, of which there are now 12, celebrated 50 years of existence. Intended primarily as a means of educating the children of employees of what would now be described as European Union organisations, to varying degrees they also make up their numbers by accepting fee-paying children from the local community. Whether or not these schools should be described as 'international schools' is a moot point. Undoubtedly ideological in mission in addition to serving a pragmatic purpose ('Without ceasing to look to their own lands with love and pride, [the students] will become in mind Europeans, schooled and ready to ... bring into being a united and thriving Europe': words sealed into the foundation stones of all European Schools, cited in Gray, 2003: 315–16), the schools are overtly Eurocentric rather than more widely international in emphasis. They also differ from most international schools in the high level of importance they place on the development of language, including a requirement that by the time students reach the stage of study for the European Baccalaureate (the pre-university school-leaving qualification: see Chapter 9) they should be studying through the medium of at least two languages including their mother tongue (Baetens Beardsmore, 1993: 121–3).

Not surprisingly, given the changing nature of the European Union in which they are so deeply embedded, the European Schools face challenges and uncertainties in their future. As Gray points out, the initial commitment to each child studying through the medium of their first language was made when six countries and four major languages were involved. As the European Union expands, increasing numbers of first languages are spoken by students, with a suggestion that by the year 2010 as many as 22 language groups may need to be supported, some of them in relatively small numbers (Gray, 2003: 324–6). How the European Union will manage to square this particular circle of ideological commitment versus pragmatic issues of viability and organisation remains to be seen.

The English Schools Foundation

Set up in 1967 by the colonial government of Hong Kong, this prestigious group of schools catered largely for expatriate British families in delivering a British-style curriculum. As their environment has been changing since the 1997 handover of Hong Kong to China, so too have the ESF schools. The phasing out of the original government subsidy is leading to greater financial constraints than previously, while the schools are now attracting greater numbers of Hong Kong Chinese students, and a decision has been taken to replace A levels with the International Baccalaureate Diploma by 2008 (ESF, 2006; Luck, 2005).

Yew Chung International Schools

Also based largely in Hong Kong and China, this group of schools grew out of the establishment of a first school in 1932 which led to the creation of a network with an emphasis on a bicultural education philosophy integrating Eastern and Western cultural elements. Schools operate a co-teaching system, with one Chinese and one Westerner in the classroom using Chinese and English dual language teaching, while all schools are run by two co-principals, one Chinese and one Westerner of equal status arriving at decisions through consultation and consensus (YCEF, 2006).

Other Groupings

As the number of international schools grows, so too does the number of networks or groupings operating in this context and based on varying philosophies: those mentioned briefly above are just some of the more well established among them. Others include, for instance, the Dutch international primary and secondary schools which are state-subsidised and linked closely in each case to a mainstream Dutch school (Koopman, 1991), while those such as the Japanese schools found in a number of countries (Yamada-Yamamoto and Richards, 1998) cater for particular national groupings. An interesting variation on the theme of international schools established to cater for expatriates away from home is that of those established to cater for expatriates returning home, again as in Japan (Yamada-Yamamoto and Richards, 1998), when children would find it difficult to cope with returning to schooling within the national system.

Also among national groupings are those which Sears describes as having been founded by groups such as missionaries or rich benefactors for the education of students in a third country, including 'the famous schools in Turkey founded during the Ottoman Empire by American Christian organisations' which have evolved to offer 'a bilingual programme to local students in the local language and English' (1998: 10). Other groupings of schools internationally include the Round Square schools, based – as are the UWC – on the philosophy of Kurt Hahn (Round Square, 2006), and those run primarily for the employees of particular companies such as the Shell Schools (2006) as well as those run by, for instance, more commercial enterprises such as the Nord Anglia Group (2006) and Global Education Management Systems (GEMS, 2006).

Equally of note, though not groupings in the same sense, are the large numbers of international schools that have grown up in the relatively recent past in areas of high economic development such as Hong Kong (Yamato, 2003; Bray and Yamato, 2003) and Shanghai (Bray and Yamato, 2006). A recent development too has been the establishment of schools in, for instance, China and Thailand, with links to 'parent schools' from the independent school sector in England, including Harrow, Dulwich, Shrewsbury and Repton.

CONCLUSION

So what are international schools? Are they an enlightened set of institutions with a vision of global peace and an ideology based on promoting internationally-minded values among their students? Are they essentially private institutions whose main aspiration is a business-focused profit margin? Or are they rather organisations that have responded to the growing demands of a global socio-economic elite: members of what has been referred to as the 'transnational capitalist class' (Sklair, 2001: 8), for whom the imperative to maintain a competitive edge in the labour market leads to the desire for their offspring to obtain globally recognised qualifications (Lowe, 2000: 24–5)?

In truth, there is no simple answer, because for each of these questions the answer is 'yes – in some cases': there are schools that fit each, and schools that fit more than one, of these descriptions. The following chapters will consider a range of issues arising in this complex and varied set of institutions.

CHAPTER 3

International Schools and Parents

Any book about international schools and their communities must surely include reference to one community about which relatively little has so far been written: the parents of the children who attend them. Parents wear many hats, and some may also belong to one of the other communities discussed in this book. They may be expatriates or local nationals, spouses or ex-spouses, Adult Third Culture Kids (ATCKs) or otherwise. They are customers (of the school attended by the child) and may be employees or employers, teachers or governors.

This chapter will focus on those aspects of the role of parent which have most relevance to the international school context. It will begin by discussing some characteristics of individuals who find themselves in that role, before going on to consider a number of areas in more detail. It will not include discussion of parents as ATCKs or parents as governors, both of which roles will be touched upon in other chapters of this volume.

INTERNATIONAL SCHOOL PARENTS: WHO ARE THEY?

Parents of children attending an international school are clearly an important group of stakeholders. The roles they play, however, their degree of influence in the school, the extent of the choice they have in relation to the school their children attend, and the factors central to their exercising of that choice all vary according to the complex pattern of events that brought them to the point where an international school education was a likelihood for their child. In the majority of international schools, the parent body will consist for the most part of well-educated, professional people who value education and have the high expectations of their children and their children's school that would generally be associated with those of such a background. In some cases their child may attend an international school with a residential facility: in most, the child will attend a day school within daily travelling distance of the family home. Parents in the former case, while not involved on a daily basis, may be influential from a distance. For day schools, parental involvement is likely to be more immediate: whether from expatriate parents for whom the child's school assumes a higher prominence than it might do in the home country, or from local professional parents who are used to playing an active role in their child's education.

In some cases both expatriate and local parents will pay school fees themselves. Local parents will generally be from relatively affluent backgrounds if they are able to consider the international school as an alternative to the local system for their child. For many expatriates, however, school fees are paid by the employer for whom one or other parent has relocated with their family, as part of the 'package' associated with their contract. The affluence of expatriate parents may vary: perhaps from the regional director for a large multinational organisation at one end of the spectrum to, in some schools such as the International School Moshi described by Garton (2002: 46), the missionary at the other end. And somewhere along that spectrum as parents may well be the international school teachers and administrators themselves, from classroom teacher to Principal or Director, whose children are attending the same school with fees paid as part of their employment package.

Clearly then, the parent body in international schools in general, and possibly even in an individual school, is fairly heterogeneous: in the context of just one international school MacKenzie et al. (2001: 63) were of the view that 'parents are a constituency no more homogeneous than the international schools that their children attend'. There are, however, a number of characteristics that may well be shared by international school parents in a range of settings; the following sections of this chapter will focus on some of these characteristics.

PARENTS AS INDIVIDUALS

The parents of whom the staff of an international school may be most aware are those whose children attend school on a non-residential basis and who live within reasonable proximity to the school. Often (though not always) such families are expatriate, temporarily based locally as a consequence of one or other parent's employment. Aside from those families where parents are employed by the school, who will be considered below, the characteristics of such families are often similar. It would be inappropriate to over-generalise: as Gordon and Jones point out, 'There is no such thing as a characteristic expatriate situation, or even characteristic expatriate situations, despite the fact that some elements will be common to all of them. Each varies according to the individuals and circumstances that compound it' (Gordon and Jones, undated: 19).

The same authors go on to suggest that there are 'three main types of international moves: the 'one-off', usually fairly short move; the frequent, shortish type of move commonly associated with diplomatic life, business transfers and international experts; and the lengthier open-ended or indefinite move which certain international civil servants like the EC fonctionnaires are called upon to make' (Gordon and Jones, undated: 31). Those who experience any of these moves may be recognisable in some of the following categories.

The Breadwinner Father

The 'typical' expatriate family is generally of the traditional Western type including mother, father and children. In some cases only younger children of the family will have accompanied the parents while older siblings are elsewhere, at university for instance, or completing their secondary education within a national system. In most cases the main breadwinner, whose employer has precipitated the family move, will be the husband/father: as Langford et al. point out, 'in international schools it is probably still most common to find a traditional family where the father is the professional 'assignee' on overseas assignment' (2002: 41). For that father, the move to a new location will involve the demands of settling into a new job, meeting new colleagues, becoming familiar with new contexts, systems and ways of working and the possibility of regional and international travel with long periods away from home.

Though having to deal with the demands of work as well as with the responsibilities of resettling a family, the husband's adaptation process may be eased by the support structure provided by his employer: '[My] husband ... moves from one familiar structure to another. ... He moves from one office to another office. ... He has lunch with this person, coffee with that person, and a definite job to do ... He won't have this total floundering that I have every time I get to a new place' (Gordon and Jones, undated: 41).

The Trailing Spouse

The so-called 'trailing spouse', on the other hand, is the partner who effectively follows the main breadwinner on an international posting, because he/she does not – or sometimes may not – work, or has a lower earning potential. Or, if both parents have professional careers, it may be impossible to arrange international postings at the same time to the same place: as Meyer points out, though the 'dual career couple' is becoming increasingly familiar as a phenomenon, this is presenting increasing challenges where international postings are concerned (1996: 17–18). While little systematically-gathered evidence exists in relation to the role of the trailing spouse, what evidence there is suggests that such spouses respond in different ways to the contexts in which they find themselves. Some undoubtedly see it as a positive experience ('[M]obility's fantastic if you open yourself up to it ... you've got to be flexible. I've enjoyed all my moves ... I've met people I'd never have met and done things I'd never have done' (Gordon and Jones, undated: 32)).

Many manage to cope by accepting that there will be negative as well as positive aspects of the experience, as recounted in Keenan's entertaining stories of life as the wife of an ambassador: 'When I read the section (of a report on a new posting) on "Opportunities for Wives" and found the usual exhilarating list (bridge, amateur dramatics, Scottish dancing, madrigal singing etc) I was plunged into gloom' (2005: 201), as opposed to her overall very positive reflection at the prospect of retirement: 'For most of our travelling lives I have been vaguely looking forward to [her husband's] retirement. Yesterday, for the first time, I realised that it would be closing the door to adventure, and that, once closed, that door might not be easy to open again' (2005: 288). For many, experiencing such moves can be challenging and difficult, faced as they are with having to adapt to the new environment and the culture shock, language barriers and unfamiliarity with support systems that may ensue, while at the same time being primarily responsible for supporting their children who may be experiencing the same difficulties while looking for parental help and reassurance.

Culture shock in relation to children is discussed in more detail in Chapter 5, but it is undoubtedly the case that culture shock affects adults too, both teachers (as noted in Chapter 6) and parents. As Langford et al. point out, it is commonly recognised that some of the main sources of stress in life are changing job, moving house, separation from parents or adult children and major purchases such as a new car. 'With an international move', Langford et al. say, 'they come all at once' (2002: 39). Little wonder, perhaps, if parents – and children – find such moves stressful, however willingly they have been negotiated; if an element of reluctance has been involved, no doubt the stress is exacerbated. As Storti points out.

> When all is said and done, expatriate families usually go overseas because of an opportunity that became available for either the husband or the wife, but only rarely for both. ... one spouse is almost always less enthusiastic

> than the other and likewise has to give up more than the other ... at-home spouses typically make the greater sacrifice and also face more – and more difficult – adjustments than do employees. (2001: 17–18)

In the scenario described above, it may be that the father is less directly affected by culture shock if his working environment embodies an organisational culture not too different from that experienced previously. For the mother, however, the impact of culture shock can be severe, exacerbated by the need to 'cope' for the sake of the children. 'Generally it is still the father who is posted to an exciting job abroad', according to Langford et al., 'and he will be immediately whisked off on a tour of local operations. This leaves the mother, who is missing friends, family, colleagues and career, to establish a home in a strange society in which she is a fumbling novice. And still everyone leans on her for emotional support!' (2002: 35–6). The experience of culture shock has been well documented by, amongst others, Paige (1993), but the fact that such experiences are well documented does not mean that they are well disseminated. Some expatriate families, depending on previous experiences, the new environment and also, perhaps, the extent of support provided by the employer or 'sponsor' (the organisation by which the parents are employed: Finn Jordan, 2002: 212), may be taken aback by just how hard culture shock can hit.

When the mother finds herself in such a situation, the child's school may assume a more central role in her life than would ever have been the case 'back home'. This may be particularly the situation where a language barrier exists, and the international school is one of the few places where the mother can usually interact with others (possibly through English, if this is the only common language) who have had similar experiences. Depending upon her cultural background, she and her husband may either be extremely reluctant to participate in school issues beyond that point – despite encouragement by the school to do so – or, perhaps where she has previously had a professional career but is not permitted to work in the new context (either because visa restrictions prevent the issuing of a work permit, or because the husband's employer – such as is the case with some diplomatic services – formally forbids or strongly discourages it), her close interest in the child's schooling and the organisation of the school itself can be a mixed blessing.

On the one hand, as demonstrated in the review of literature relating to parental involvement, parental support and family education undertaken by Desforges and Abouchaar in the UK context, parental involvement in its many forms (including 'at-home good parenting', contact with schools to share information and participation in various aspects of school life) is an important dimension of encouraging pupils to 'maximise their potential from schooling' (2003: 1). On the other hand, the demands placed on the school may be perceived as unreasonable, however understandable they may be in terms of the parents' feelings and concerns about their children.

Pollock makes a point about 'missionary parents' that could well have application to expatriate parents more widely: '(they) often struggle with a sense of guilt. They fear their decision to move overseas will have a negative or even destructive impact on the lives of their children (and) this guilt may become "educator directed". Parents may make high, perhaps even unreasonable, demands for special, individual attention to their children. Occasionally anger accompanies these demands' (1998: 389). Langford et al. reinforce this point in noting that

> Many parents experience high levels of anxiety about the predicament in which they have placed their children. After all, it is generally a parent's career move that has precipitated the overseas move. This can be a source of guilt for many parents who have uprooted their children from familiar school surroundings and moved them into a strange and possibly foreign environment where they may face tremendous challenges. (2002: 39)

Again, the different cultural backgrounds of parents may mean that their demands (with respect to, for example, the amount of homework seen) are inconsistent and thus difficult to satisfy.

International schools may come into conflict with demanding parents. Some, as recommended by Ezra (2003: 141), provide counselling and other forms of parental support: indeed many have taken upon themselves more roles and responsibilities than would ever be considered reasonable to expect of a school in a national system, in terms of support for the wider family as well as for the child. Recognising that supporting the mother in such circumstances indirectly supports the child (and there is much anecdotal evidence to suggest that the extent to which the mother is settled and content in the new environment is the strongest single indicator of the extent to which the child will be settled and content), some actively encourage the involvement of mothers in the school. Not only do parent committees and parent teacher associations usually exist; in some cases a parents' room is provided at school where parents may meet informally during the day for social contact.

It needs to be noted, of course, that despite such generalisations, not all expatriate main breadwinners are husbands and not all trailing spouses are wives. Indeed, as might be expected given the increasing numbers of professional women to be found in many parts of the world, growing (though still relatively small) numbers of expatriate family units will include a male trailing spouse. As Meyer (1996: 58–64) points out, while some husbands are content with this role and others less so (just as would be the case for trailing wives), the trailing spouse experience for men can be particularly challenging because of the 'high profile role reversal' involved and the relative absence of support facilities such as the International Women's Clubs designed for the trailing wife. As relatively short-lived as the apparent 'strangeness' of the male trailing spouse phenomenon may perhaps be, with female breadwinners becoming more commonplace on international circuits as well as in national contexts, no doubt the challenges faced in some cases are no less daunting for all that.

The Trailing Spouse as Teacher

Recognising the difficulty of coordinating equally acceptable moves to the same place at the same time for two careers in, say, business or the diplomatic service, not a few trailing spouses (again generally wives) have turned to teaching as a career that is relatively portable. Linguistic barriers and other legal or social constraints may mean that teaching posts can only really be considered in international rather than local schools. The nature of the contract available in international schools, though, may well be restricted (as discussed in Chapter 6) and further challenges can arise in terms of the qualifications and experience required. In those schools accredited by the Council of International Schools (CIS, 2006), for instance, recognised teaching certification will be required; recognised certification may also be insisted upon by the Ministry of Education of the country in which the school is located. For those not already qualified to teach, obtaining appropriate certification can be difficult for a spouse based at some distance from the context in which relevant training is offered. For those who manage to obtain work on the strength of, say, a degree alone, a later frustration can be the non-recognition of their teaching experience on return to a national context. Challenges facing teachers returning 'home' will be discussed further in Chapter 6.

A variation on this theme is that of the spouse with teaching certification from a national system which is not recognised at an international school because it is not considered to be at an appropriate (possibly degree) level. Even more frustrating perhaps for the spouse in question than the situation described above, there is again often little that can be done locally to 'upgrade' the qualification and thus allow the spouse to teach.

PARENTS AS TEACHERS

Chapter 6 focuses in some detail on a range of teacher-related issues including how individuals come to find themselves as teachers in international schools. As in many schools elsewhere, the teaching staff will generally cover a range of ages and experiences. What might be more common in many international schools than in schools nationally, however, is a relatively high number of teaching couples: usually expatriates who have decided to move away from home together and to look for postings in the same school. Among such couples will be those who have school age children. Often it will be part of the teacher's contract for the fees of their offspring to be either waived completely or substantially reduced (Hardman, 2001: 124). For expatriates it may also be that, as noted above in relation to expatriate parents more generally, the international school provides the only realistic means of educating their child, while for local teachers the international school may have a prestige (and, through the language of instruction, a perceived link to higher education in 'the West') which makes attendance for their child attractive. Thus it may well be the case that international schools have a higher proportion than would likely be found in most national systems of teachers whose own children are pupils in the school. Zilber estimated that around five per cent of enrolment in an international school may be children of staff (2004).

Teacher-parents are an interesting phenomenon in any context but, surprisingly perhaps, little research appears to have been undertaken on any aspect of the link between their practice and parental status. 'One of the most important yet under-discussed influences on how teachers teach and how they approach their teaching', writes Hargreaves in more general terms, 'is their own experience of being parents' (Hargreaves, 1997). If this is true in national contexts, it is certainly true that the role of teacher-parents (a term used here to encompass administrators as well as classroom teachers) has been barely considered in the context of international schools. Writing in the UK context, Sikes reinforces the perception that the notion of teacher as parent 'has not traditionally been seen as a significant and important factor influencing how teachers teach' (1997: 11). Sikes's own study (the main focus of which was 'if and how becoming a parent had affected other teachers' perceptions and experiences of their professional lives') touched upon some experiences of being a teacher in the same school as one's child, such as the point made by one of her interviewees that 'I was lucky because I saw the kids in assemblies and things and I was lucky because they were in my school' (1997: 64).

And it is in this area, perhaps, that there may be most overlap with the experiences of teacher-parents in international schools. One systematic study undertaken in this context focused on the perspective of such parents and their colleagues – through focus groups, through online interaction and through international school conferences (Zilber, 2005) – investigating with participant teacher-parents the perceived advantages and disadvantages of raising their own children as pupils within the same international school community. Among advantages frequently cited were the pragmatic free school tuition which a number believed enabled their child(ren) to access a higher quality education than could have been available 'back home'; the social network of support and the feeling that 'the staff becomes like an extended family for each other, like aunts, uncles, cousins, etc'; the sense of security and perceived higher status for the child(ren) because of their parents' role as teachers; and the relationships such children develop with other teachers whom they learn to perceive as friends of the parents, and see in social situations as well as in the more formal teacher/student classroom context.

Having ready access to one's own child during the school day, if needed, was also an advantage cited by some. The close bond often developed by such families because of the additional time spent together, and the shared experiences not normally open to other families (expatriate or otherwise) were also noted, linked to deeper understanding by parents of the child(ren)'s educational experiences and a better understanding by children of their parents' work. Interestingly, as Zilber (2005) points out, in a study by Cottrell (2002) relating to career choices of American Adult Third Culture Kids, the highest number of children following in parents' footsteps were those whose parents were teachers.

Teacher-Parents: Some Challenges

Not all aspects of such a situation, however, are positive. The advantage of being much more familiar with the education experienced by the child may bring with it the disadvantage, highlighted by some in Zilber's (2005) study, of increased sensitivity to and awareness of the quality of teaching offered by colleagues, and the challenge of knowing how to deal with a situation where the teaching of one's own child is not all the parent might wish it to be. The positive aspect of the status which comes from being the child of a member of staff could be counterbalanced by a perception that being treated differently from other children is a hindrance (particularly where this leads to teaching colleagues having unrealistically high expectations). Indeed, some parents felt that being the parent of a child in school 'impacted negatively on their teaching' and, if a child's behaviour were less than ideal, that this presented a particularly stressful situation.

Some parents in Zilber's (2005) study reported experiencing suspicious reactions from colleagues if their child was particularly successful in some dimension of their schooling and, while frequent feedback on the child's performance from colleagues could be seen in a positive light, immediate feedback about often minor infringements was viewed as disheartening and often inappropriate. A reluctance to 'lobby' for their children, in a way that non-teaching parents might well do, was lamented by some as a drawback to this situation which could lead to feelings of guilt. The need to exercise caution in home conversations was also noted as a challenge, when children would not normally be privy to otherwise confidential information about other students and teaching colleagues.

A general concern about either real, or potential, conflicts of interest in the two roles of parent and teacher was noted by some, as were the complex multiple roles (parent, teacher, teacher of friends' children, teacher of children's friends) and the generally unpopular situation of having your own child in class. The role in the community as teacher was also noted as being particularly difficult sometimes – perhaps more so in expatriate communities – where friendships could be abused by friends whose children were taught by the teacher in terms, for instance, of seeking inside information. Some parents also felt that having mother and/or father easily contactable at school all day could be detrimental to their child's developing independence, while many of the disadvantages attributed to the children and parents sharing the same home/school experience could be described as 'family overload' (Zilber, 2005), summed up by Dehner and Dehner observing that 'They say overseas life brings families together, but this might be too close for comfort' (2001: 24).

Where one or both parents is an administrator, this may exacerbate the situation even further if the parent has difficulties with colleagues or children who are teachers or friends of their son or daughter. Interestingly, a similar point is made by Evans and Evans in the case of 'missionary kids' and the 'dorm parents' with whom they may live in residential schools:

> Having emphasised the importance of nurturing a team spirit between teachers and dorm parents, we must also stress the importance of maintaining the separation and distinctiveness of these two groups. Separation between the academic world and the dorm is essential so the child can have a safe haven. Teachers need to establish their own discipline and authority in the classroom, so students can return to the dorm without fearing that they face 'double jeopardy'. (1998: 396)

For children whose 'dorm parents' are actually their real parents, and these parents are also teachers in the school they attend (if not of their class itself), no such separation is possible.

Despite numerous references to the difficulties and disadvantages of the parent-teacher situation, parents in Zilber's (2005) study were generally of the view that the benefits far outweighed the challenges which, given the numbers of teachers who devote more than a short period of their professional lives to contracts in international schools worldwide, should perhaps not be surprising. It is of course true that within schools in national systems a parent may teach his/her own child. In some residential schools nationally it may also be that children live with parents in school accommodation. It is almost certainly the case, however, that international schools provide a higher incidence than any other school context of both parents teaching in a school also attended by their children. Further research into this under-explored area would almost certainly be of interest both to the parents themselves and to the schools that employ them.

PARENTS AS CUSTOMERS

One difficulty with the notion of parents as customers is that the concept of customer brings with it an associated implication of choice, whereas not all parents of children attending international schools have choice in any real sense. There may, for instance, be only one school in the vicinity of the parents' employment and accommodation that offers what is considered appropriate schooling while allowing the child to live at home. Where choice does exist, it is interesting to consider similarities and differences with such issues in national contexts. UK-based research, for instance, suggests that in general parents are in agreement about the characteristics of schools they would actively avoid for their child; perhaps not surprisingly these include apparently uninterested teachers, low academic standards, and evidence of racism and bullying (Ellison and Davies, 1993). Overall, too, parents place high in the list of factors affecting choice of school the desire for their child to be happy, tending to base their choice on 'process' criteria (related to human relationships) rather than 'product' criteria (including, for example, examination results) (Petch, 1986).

Of particular interest in any discussion of parental choice of international school is the fact that, when reasons for choice by middle-class professional parents (likely to be similar in socio-economic status to many international school parents) were considered in such national studies, very clear messages came through as to what is valued by these 'active choosers' (a term coined by Farley, 1993): high standards, good examination results, a well-disciplined atmosphere and special support for the particularly able. While parents in general tended to allow their child a major say in the choice of school, with parental input ranging from a certain degree of influence through to indifference (West and Varlaam, 1991; Walford, 1991), in families of higher socio-economic status parents were far more likely to play an active part in school choice and to make decisions jointly with their child (Yorke and Bakewell, 1991).

Of relevance too is the fact that parents of children in international schools are often from many different ethnic and cultural groupings, a factor which may influence both the basis of their school choice and the expectations they have in relation to interactions with the school during the course of their child's studies. In a UK-based 1995 study, for instance, Osler and Hussain highlighted the fact that Asian parents generally favour single-sex education for their daughters, as well as supporting the preservation of cultural identity and traditional values. The emphasis on expatriate Japanese children attending either full-time or Saturday Japanese school (Yamada-Yamamoto and Richards, 1998: 3), meanwhile, is indicative of a similar concern that not only language but also cultural identity should be preserved during periods away from the home country. Different expectations between expatriate and local parents may be in evidence in relation to a number of factors including the nature of the curriculum, especially perhaps if local parents are paying fees personally and are less enthusiastic about, for instance, the resource-intensive sports programmes and school trips than might be the expatriates whose children's fees are being paid by an employer.

There may also be a range of different expectations between those from a variety of cultural backgrounds (including different groups of expatriates) with respect to issues such as the amount of homework judged appropriate. For many parents, particularly perhaps those native English speakers for whom the international school may not at first glance appear as different from schools at home as it would to those from other cultural and linguistic backgrounds, assumptions may be made initially about cultural and educational similarities between the international school and schools of their previous experience that turn out not to have been justified. Murphy, an experienced international school head, in referring to enrolling new children at an international school highlights how such differences can manifest themselves:

> I sometimes tell parents that they enrol their children at their peril. The children will be learning different things and in a different way from anything in their parents' experience. The values they learn may not be identical to their [parents'] values. Children may change. They may become independent. They won't just be the same Japanese or Arab children who have learned to speak English. They will become a mix of nationalities. That is what makes it so hard for the parents. (Murphy, in Langford, 1998: 39)

Parental Priorities

So why do parents, where there is more than one international school option open to their child, opt for one school rather than another? Anecdotal evidence suggests that one factor influencing newly arrived expatriates can be what they hear from their compatriots or colleagues who have been in the country for some time: this can lead to 'clusters' of children of particular nationalities or groups of employees being found in particular schools. International schools can be attractive in some situations also to those families where one parent is expatriate, one local, and the school provides a means for the children to have exposure to the cultures and languages of both. It also needs to be remembered that, as noted in Chapter 2, a certain amount of confusion may be experienced by globally mobile parents who, having experienced an international school in one location, assume that international schools elsewhere will share the same characteristics when in fact the term 'international school' is not, in itself, any guarantee of a particular ethos or philosophy of education.

Two systematic studies of international schools in Switzerland, as well as one in Sri Lanka, one in Thailand and one in Saudi Arabia, have highlighted a number of pertinent issues, as has a study conducted at bilingual schools in Buenos Aires. One study in a Swiss co-educational and English medium international day school, broadly representative of those found in many European cities with approximately 700 students from K-12, from commercial, academic and diplomatic communities locally, representing 40–50 nationalities, offering all three IB programmes and with other well-established international schools in the area, elicited completed questionnaires from 89 parents, closely mirroring the representation of the whole parent body, with nine follow-up in-depth interviews (MacKenzie et al., 2001). Asked about their reasons for choice of school, one intriguing finding was the importance attached by parents to their child experiencing education through the medium of English: 'the language of the future', as one non-native English speaking parent described it, 'that will provide (my children) with wonderful opportunities later on in life' and, from an American parent, 'English is the lowest common denominator of language, at least perceptually, and the most useful'.

As MacKenzie et al. (2001) note, 'An English language education was consistently cited by sub-groups of parents ... as the principal reason for choosing the school'. The most important factor for parents of both primary and secondary school children, it was ranked highest in importance by both native and non-native English speakers. In analysing responses by sub-group, 40 of the 42 respondents who were non-native speakers of English ranked 'learning English' as either 'very' or 'extremely' important as a necessary part of an 'international education', while British and North American parents showed relatively little interest in the experience of international education as a reason for their child attending the school. A similar division was noted in relation to the fact that the school offered the IB Diploma: as MacKenzie et al. point out, 'Parents from continental Europe appear to have valued it very highly when choosing the school, parents from the UK very much less so and those from North America hardly at all' (2001).

The Role of English

One query arising from this study therefore relates to the place of English in international schools; as MacKenzie et al. ask, 'Is there a suggestion here that some parents perceive an "international education" and an English language education to be one and the same thing?' (2001), a question that has echoes in one of the conclusions of a study undertaken by Deveney at an international school in Thailand, which on the basis of Deveney's findings 'could be viewed as being – for many of its clientele – a proxy language school' (Deveney, 2000: 36). Deveney's school offered the English national curriculum and the option of boarding facilities, catering for children aged 2–18 from both expatriate (largely British, Australian and Korean) families, and Thai families who had chosen to pay to send their child there rather than to have them educated in the free, state sector. It was in competition with three other international schools locally (one American and two British).

Deveney's survey elicited 210 completed questionnaires and also involved 13 interviews. Most notable of the findings was that, for all groups of parent respondents, learning English was the highest overall ranked factor for choosing the school. Though of importance to all, it was rated of greater importance by the Thai community than by expatriates, for whom a range of other factors – none particularly marked in importance over others – was also influential in their choice. Although Deveney's study was not in the end able completely to prove or disprove a number of initial hypotheses, two of them are perhaps worth noting or modifying (given that they arose in one particular national context) as the basis for possible further research in the context of British-type international schools more widely:

- 'Non English speaking Europeans have no home system school therefore choose between UK or American system international schools, although the acquisition of English is a principal aim. (The same can be said for Japanese or Korean expatriates.)'
- 'English speaking nationals such as Australians, New Zealanders, Indians and Pakistanis have a cultural leaning towards an English curriculum. This leaning may be the result of the lack of availability of a home national school and/or antipathy/neutrality towards an American curriculum school'. (Deveney, 2000: 11)

In another study of a British-type international school in Saudi Arabia offering the English national curriculum to around 500 pupils, approximately two thirds of whom were British (Saudi nationals are prevented by law from attending international schools in that country), Gould (1999) developed a typology of three groups within the school population which he described as follows:

- the 'natives' (as in native to the school education system): children of British expatriates;
- the 'captives': children of non-British expatriates with no national school available locally (for example, Canadians, Japanese); and
- the 'electors': children of non-British expatriates whose national education system is available locally (for example, Egyptian, Pakistani) but who nevertheless elect to be educated in a British-type international school.

In focusing particularly on the group of 'electors' and noting the complexity of the decision-making process, Gould concluded that parental choice was based on aspects of the following, linked in part to issues related to increasing globalisation:

- the maintenance of national and ethnic cultural identity;
- the development of multiple or alternative identities;
- education for personal survival in relation to the economic situation of developing countries;
- global employment structures, and job opportunities in a global economy;
- the global mobility of highly skilled personnel;
- education as the cultural capital investment of a global elite. (Gould, 1999: 18)

An influencing factor here, Gould believed, was the 'kudos of private, English-medium education', available to a limited number in Pakistan, where English language proficiency is valued 'partly because it is tied to the structure of labour market incentives [as] a prerequisite for career advancement in both private and public sectors' (p. 18). The same point applies in Egypt, where 'access to university places and thereby employment opportunities is linked to higher levels of academic ability associated with the purchase of educational opportunities ... including the private sector, English medium schools' (Arabsheibani, 1988, paraphrased by Gould, 1999: 10).

In two quite different geographic contexts, then, from that of the MacKenzie et al. (2001) study, the very same message came through in Deveney's and Gould's research about the importance to parents of an English-language education. Indeed, in a follow up study of parental priorities by MacKenzie et al. (2003), undertaken with three unconnected but comparable international schools (including the school from the 2001 study) in three different Swiss cities, the same message emerged. All three schools cater for the entire K-12 curriculum and are well-established day schools, offering the IB Diploma programme and catering for 'the expatriate commercial, diplomatic and academic communities' as well as 'small numbers of local Swiss students', with similar teaching faculties made up largely of American, British and other English-speakers. Completed questionnaires were returned by 238 parents, of whom 76 per cent rated a desire for their child to be educated in the English language either as 'very' or 'extremely' important, with no real difference between responses from parents of primary and secondary age children. The existence of the IB Diploma programme was rated highly as a reason for choice by parents even, perhaps surprisingly, by as many as 42 per cent of the 106 parents of primary school children who – given the relatively short mean duration of stay in the school – were unlikely still to be in school by that stage of their schooling. Perhaps, as MacKenzie et al. speculated, those parents perceive the existence of the IB Diploma Programme in school 'as some guarantee of quality in the institution as a whole' (2003: 305).

Other features of note in this second Swiss study which would be worth investigating in further research include significantly higher levels of importance attached to a number of items by mothers than by fathers (not, of itself, explained by the fact that mothers 'are more likely to be involved in their children's education than are their husbands', according to the authors), and differences in response by geographical group: only Swiss parents, for example, did not rank an English language education as most important. It is the importance attached to the place of the English language overall that is the most striking aspect of this study: a finding that verifies, as Murphy points out in relation to international schools more generally, 'the anecdotal evidence of many school heads – that the acquisition of English is the main attraction' (2001: 9), to which 'and the maintenance of English' could no doubt be added.

This finding is not inconsistent with Wijewardene's (1999) study of ten international schools in the centre and suburbs of Colombo, Sri Lanka. Of three different types (very high fees, moderately high fees and lower fees), all were open to Sri Lankan as well as expatriate families and mainly attended by local students. Questionnaires were distributed both to teachers (94 completed questionnaires were returned from across the ten schools) and to parents (from whom 46 completed questionnaires were returned), face-to-face interviews were conducted with two heads, and telephone interviews were conducted with five teachers and five parents.

By far the most frequent reason cited by questionnaire respondents for the popularity of international schools in Sri Lanka (of which there were 47 at that time) was the fact that they offered an English-medium education. As Wijewardene points out, bearing in mind that national schools since the late 1950s had used two indigenous languages, Sinhalese and Tamil, as their medium of instruction, 'it is through an English medium education that foreign universities become accessible to Sri Lankans, it is the ability to speak good English that earns prestige/status in Sri Lankan society and it is people who are fluent in English that get good/better paid jobs' (1999: 55). Other reasons cited by respondents for the popularity of international schools included poor standards in national schools, and the fact that international schools offered equal opportunities to those of any race or religion, and are co-educational (unlike the single sex national schools in and around Colombo).

Clearly the context of international schools in Colombo (largely Sri Lankan students, state schools not held in high esteem by a number of parents, ethnic sensitivities) is different from that of the international schools in Switzerland that formed the basis for the two studies reported by MacKenzie et al. Different again is the context in which the study described by Potter and Hayden was carried out: two Buenos Aires bilingual schools which, given that schools registered as bilingual (English/Spanish) in the Argentine educational system 'generally offer international examinations such as International GCSEs (IGCSEs), or one or more of the International Baccalaureate (IB) programmes, or a mix of these' (Potter and Hayden, 2004: 90), would be considered as 'international schools' in the inclusive use of the term discussed in Chapter 2. Based on questionnaires and interviews with parents in two unconnected but comparable bilingual schools, 50 and 59 questionnaires were returned from the two in question, while six parents were interviewed from one school and five from the other. With 95.4 per cent of parents who completed the questionnaire rating 'desire for a bilingual education' as very important, 88 per cent wanted their children to speak English fluently and 86.2 per cent wanted them to learn English.

Parents also rated highly other academic factors, with certain aspects overlapping with the language issue as pointed out by one interviewee, who argued that such schools 'give students a wider vision. They often employ expatriate teachers who help to inform students about other cultures and customs which are very different to their own' (Potter and Hayden, 2004: 98). As Potter and Hayden point out, 'all parents ... implied that choosing a bilingual (English/Spanish) education for their children was an investment that would pay off later on in the world of work' (Potter and Hayden, 2004: 107), implying support for Adler's (1997) suggestion that increasing numbers of parents 'view education as a route to economic and social success and (that) finding the "right" school for their children is seen by many parents as a way of giving their children a good start in life' (1997: 305).

The importance attached by parents to the use of English as a medium of instruction in all schools referred to in these studies may well be a dispiriting finding for those committed to the ideological notion of international education as a force for promoting global understanding. Are international schools for many parents really simply the 'proxy language schools' referred to by Deveney? Such a finding might not, however, surprise those with long experience of the international school sector. Richards, for instance, an international school head with teaching and management experience in a number of different international schools, noted that 'It is (the) alchemy of idealism and pragmatism that determines the individual characteristics of international schools around the world; their clients are not all imbued with a sense of mission, other than to do what is best for their children within the locally imposed limits' (1998: 174).

Consistent with Adler's perception of the strongest factor governing parental choice of school – giving their child a good start in life – Richards' realism about the priorities of parents of international school children helps to explain why such importance is attached to the use of English. In a world where, for better or worse, English is becoming the *lingua franca* for international business, travel and employment, it is hardly surprising that so many parents should value achieving fluency in English as one means of giving their children a good start in life.

CONCLUSION

The topics touched upon in this chapter, while all relating to parents in some way, have been varied and do not easily lend themselves to generalised comments or summary. What *is* clear, however, is that there is a rich vein of research still waiting to be mined in this particular area, whether in relation to parents as choosers of international schools, to parents as teachers in international schools, or indeed to any one of a number of areas relating to international school parents which have either been omitted entirely from this discussion or skimmed over fairly briefly. Further research can only be helpful to those schools, and indeed to the families themselves, in helping to ensure that the relationship between school and parents is based on mutual understanding and becomes as productive as possible.

CHAPTER 4

International School Students: Who They Are

Given that international schools, as noted in Chapter 2, come in all shapes and sizes, it is entirely consistent that the population of students who attend them should not be homogeneous in any sense. This chapter will focus on the community of students that is the raison d'être of an international school, beginning with a consideration of who they are and some of their characteristics.

Not only does the population of international school students vary in terms of cultural, national and linguistic backgrounds and previous educational experience, there is also considerable variation in the reasons for students attending an international school in the first place. Students at United World Colleges, for instance, are generally there after experiencing a nationally-based education and then successfully achieving a UWC scholarship; the majority of this multicultural population will be between the ages of 16 and 18, living in school accommodation in a location other than their home country. The nature of the student population of international schools more broadly will depend in part on the countries in which they are located. In some countries host country nationals are forbidden by law from attending an international school. In others, the student population of some international schools might appear at first glance to be much like the student population of a national school in the same country. In Thailand, for instance, some international schools may cater principally for host country nationals who are generally from 'the economic elite of the local country who believe that such an education will lead to higher education possibilities in North America or Europe' (Langford et al., 2002: 48).

Such students have generally been placed in an international school by their parents as an investment for the future, quite possibly because of the English-medium education offered (as noted in Chapter 3), and therefore illustrating the reference by Lowe to growing numbers of schools offering international qualifications as

> a response by local elites to a stiffening of the local positional competition on the one hand and a globalisation of that competition on the other. As more people gain local educational qualifications, those who can afford to do so seek a new competitive edge by taking qualifications that they hope will give them a local advantage. At the same time, it is hoped that these international qualifications will give access to a labour market that is becoming increasingly globalised – for the most advantageous occupations, at least (Ilon, 1997). (2000: 24)

Among the host country nationals attending an international school may also be the children of host country employees of a particular industry who have been granted the right to attend such a school (Langford et al., 2002: 48). And also to be found in many international schools are repatriated host country nationals who, having been educated for a period outside their own national education system, find an international school in their home country more appropriate than attempting to fit back into the national system (though the relatively high level of fees charged by many international schools might rule out this option for at least some families). Depending on a number of factors, argue Langford et al., host country national students attending an international school

> may feel isolated and different, living on the local economy rather than enjoying the many benefits shared by their expatriate classmates. Alternatively, they may represent the economic elite of a country and in fact may seem to be more privileged than the expatriate families in the school. Or they may dominate the community to the extent that the school has to adjust its practices to suit their interests and the expatriates are made to feel like outsiders. (2002: 48)

Deveney, in describing a study of Thai students attending an international school in Thailand, highlights the challenges that may be faced by host country nationals in such a context, which is 'not their home system, not a foreign system in a foreign land and not an international school abroad, but an international school in their home country which does not represent their native culture and beliefs' (2005: 161).

Another notable group of international school students are the children of expatriate parents who, for whatever reason, are away from their parents' 'home' context during their school years. Indeed in many international schools the student population is a mix of these main groups: expatriates and host country nationals attending the international school for different reasons. The nature of the balance between the two groups (whether host country nationals or expatriates are in the majority and how the two are integrated) can be crucial to the smooth running of such a school, and it is not unusual for international schools that accept both groups to operate some sort of quota system, official or unofficial, in order to achieve what is perceived to be an optimal balance between them. The relative transience in school terms of those described here as 'expatriates', and their repatriated host country national peers, has led to the increasingly recognised concept of the globally mobile child.

GLOBALLY MOBILE CHILDREN

> They are perpetual outsiders, millions of children around the world, born in one nation, raised in others, flung into global jet streams by their parents' career choices and consequent mobility. Some move often, from place to place, country to country. Others establish semi-permanent lodgings on foreign soil, returning to the place their parents call home for vacations or family events. Their parents are educators, international businesspeople, foreign service attachés, missionaries, military personnel. The children shuttle back and forth between nations, languages, cultures and loyalties. They live unrooted childhoods. (Eidse and Sichel, 2004: 1)

The notion of rootlessness, as described by Eidse and Sichel, is not one to which all would subscribe: some would argue that such a childhood has actually resulted in their feeling rooted to several places rather than to one. The concept of globally mobile children, however, is certainly well established. Children have moved from country to country, generally with their families, over many years and for many reasons. Walker's (1998) analysis of a number of fictional literature sources relating to what are referred to as 'disoriented children' provides a moving account of a range of situations – in fiction but often based on fact – in which the child's notion of 'home' has been severely challenged.

A number of these situations relate to temporary displacement arising from war or illness, but it has often been the case that children with their families have made more permanent moves. Murphy-Lejeune describes a number of different types of migrant in terms of their 'status upon entry', including 'political refugee, asylum seeker, labour migrant, professional expatriate, international student or foreign resident' (2003: 101). The notion of what is often referred to as 'economic migration' tends to be applied to 'people that are considered economically or politically deprived and seek betterment of their circumstances' (Bryceson and Vuorela, 2002: 7–8). Such migrants generally aspire to a reasonable level of permanence in another country which can offer them a better way of life.

Indeed, some who might be referred to as 'asylum seekers' or 'refugees' seek not only an improved way of life but also the safety and security denied to them in their own homeland. Such immigrants may aspire to assimilation by adopting the language, habits and patterns of behaviour of the new cultural context and refraining from the use of their primary language, habits and patterns of behaviour, or to adaptation by modifying their patterns of behaviour in order to function effectively – while not absorbing or incorporating the new behaviour and thus preserving their original cultural identity (Fennes and Hapgood, 1997: 32). And indeed some children of such families may attend international schools, though the number is relatively low: in part because the fee-paying nature of many international schools may rule out such a possibility where state-provided education is free, and in part because the desire to assimilate points to education within the national system as the preferred option.

For the most part though, the globally mobile children who attend international schools are not those whose families make a permanent move to a new country where they can put down roots and establish a new home. They are, rather, the children of families whose moves are more transient, who generally do not expect to remain indefinitely in their new location. Bryceson and Vuorela refer to 'Transnational families at the higher end of the income scale, who tend to move for financial or status reasons ... bestowing their presence and skills on the receiving nation as opposed to other migrants who are imposing or even inflicting their needs on the receiving country'. Transnational elites, they suggest, 'are perceived as "mobile" rather than "migrant"'. As cosmopolitans – people who have entered international careers – transnational elites seem to move more by choice and be in a better position to negotiate their connections, their nationalities, and benefits associated with their choice of a national residence. The symbolic capital of education and language enable them to move freely, offering relatively easier access to border crossing and citizenship' (Bryceson and Vuorela, 2002: 8).

Sears describes the major characteristic of the children of such families as their mobility: 'Although a proportion of international school students experience only one posting outside their home country', she says, 'many experience a series of moves every two or three years. These moves are the result of their parents' relocation to take up a first overseas job, or a fresh assignment in a series of postings' (1998: 6). Such internationally-mobile children, the offspring of 'international ... communities of employees ... characterised by a high degree of mobility [whose] ... job demands (frequently) require that they and their families move to other international centres or back to their countries of origin at short notice' (de Mejía, 2002: 4) may be variously described as 'Global Nomads', 'Third Culture Kids' (TCKs), 'Military Brats', 'Preacher Kids' (PKs), 'Missionary Kids' (MKs) and no doubt other terms in particular contexts. Willis et al. refer to them as 'the New Diaspora' of what they describe as 'transculturals' or 'transnationals'. 'Unlike the children of immigrants or refugees, who have been forced by political, religious or economic difficulties to migrate', they say, this New Diaspora are those 'whose move overseas was based on opportunity (economic, educational, social, cultural) [who represent] a privileged elite. ... They, and other highly mobile groups like them, are an essential feature of our contemporary world, especially as more and more people are mobile or are dreaming of the next move' (1994: 29). Such a description, while clearly applying to some of the globally-mobile children who spring to mind in the context of international schools, serves to highlight the differences between the various terms that are employed in this context and to accentuate the need for clearer definition.

Some such terms are more obvious in their meaning than others. 'Missionary Kids', as the term suggests, are the children of missionaries whose work has taken them to other parts of the world. Where once such children may have remained in their parents' country for education, a more recent trend has been for many of them to accompany their parents, attending either national local schools, mission schools, International Christian Schools, or 'secular international schools' (Bowers, 1998: 269). Indeed some international schools, for historical and location-related reasons, have a tradition of catering for missionary children among their student population: the International School of Moshi in Tanzania, for instance, is a 'boarding school with a substantial enrolment of Scandinavians from missionary and aid worker backgrounds' (Garton, 2002: 146). 'Military Brats', meanwhile, are the children of military families, the term possibly originating as an acronym for British Regiment Attached Traveller, or, as defined in Webster's Dictionary, relating to the child whose father was a colonel in the Army (Ender, 2002a: vii). According to Segal, the term 'brat' is preferred over others by many who might be so categorised, despite its apparently pejorative connotations (2002: xvii).

Children of the military, whether or not referred to by the colloquial 'Military Brat' soubriquet, are an interesting case in terms of the educational provision made for them. Tending, when away from their home country, to be clustered in larger groups than might often be the case for missionary children their education has, in the case of at least some national military systems and for some of their schooling, been catered for by schools set up for that particular purpose. Ender points out that after the Second World War, 'American and other First World countries expanded their political, military, corporate, and humanitarian responsibilities outside their national borders ... with families in tow, service people began to move and live, in increasing numbers, outside the borders of their host country. ... Military and other service agencies in the United States and abroad imposed organisational demands on members, their spouses, and children [including] out-of-country service and residence', estimating that 'about two percent of the US population grew up in a service-organisation family' (2002a: xxvii). The British Service Children's Education organisation (SCE, 2006), as another example, runs schools in British army bases such as those in Cyprus and Germany. Children of US military personnel, meanwhile, may be educated in Department of Defense Education Authority schools in '13 foreign countries, seven states, Guam and Puerto Rico' (DODEA, 2006).

Occasionally MKs, PKs and Military Brats might be found in international schools, and the recent closure of some US bases, for instance, has led to higher numbers of Military Brats attending international schools than might previously have been the case. The majority of the globally mobile student population of such schools, however, do not belong to these groupings, and it is this majority on whom the remainder of this chapter will largely focus.

THIRD CULTURE KIDS

There would seem to be little doubt about the origins of the term 'Third Culture Kid', which is recognised as having grown out of the work of the Michigan State University sociologists Ruth Hill Useem and her husband John Useem. As explained by Rader and Sittig (2003: 2), in the 1950s Useem and Useem spent time in India researching expatriate families (Americans and others), concluding that such families were neither a part of the 'host culture' (India) in which they were then based, nor of their 'home' culture with which they interacted only occasionally, but shared a 'culture' with other expatriates of similar experience to their own. Following later research with the children of such families when they returned to the USA for university study, which suggested that the characteristics of such young people were different from those of their contemporaries raised in the USA, Ruth Hill Useem coined the term 'Third Culture Kid' and described them as follows:

> Although they have grown up in foreign countries, they are not integral parts of those countries. When they come to their country of citizenship (some for the first time), they do not feel at home because they do not know the lingo or expectations of others – especially those of their own age. Where they feel most like themselves is in that interstitial culture, the third culture, which is created, shared and carried by persons who are relating societies, or sections thereof, to each other. (Useem, 1976)

More recently, Norma McCaig (1992) coined the term 'Global Nomad' which has been used widely since by others, including Schaetti, who defines Global Nomads as:

> Individuals of any age or nationality who have spent a significant part of their developmental years living in one or more countries outside their passport

> country because of a parent's occupation. Global Nomads are members of a world-wide community of persons who share a unique cultural heritage. While developing some sense of belonging to both their host culture(s) and passport culture(s), they do not have a sense of total ownership in any. Elements from each culture and from the experience of international mobility are blended, creating a commonality with others of similar experience. Global nomads of all ages and nationalities typically share similar responses to the benefits and challenges of a childhood abroad. (Schaetti, 1993)

While it might be tempting to search for differences in the two definitions, it is clear from consideration of their usage that as noted by, inter alia, Rader and Sittig (2003: 2), Langford (1998: 30) and Zilber (2005: 7), the terms 'Third Culture Kid' and 'Global Nomad' have come to be used interchangeably. Clearly many feel there is no need to make a distinction: Pollock and Van Reken, in pointing out how much more complex the situations of globally mobile adults and children have become since the days of the Useems' initial research, explain that Ruth Useem when asked in 1994 whether she felt the term 'TCK' still applied, was of the view that the concept needed to be flexible to reflect the changing world. Useem went on to give a more recent definition of the third culture as 'a generic term to describe the lifestyle created, shared and learned by those who are from one place and are in the process of relating to another one' and of Third Culture Kids simply as 'children who accompany their parents into another society' (Useem, in Pollock and Van Reken, 1999: 21). Pollock and Van Reken actually propose another variation on the definition, stating that a TCK

> is a person who has spent a significant part of his or her developmental years outside the parents' culture. The TCK builds relationships to all of the cultures, while not having full ownership in any. Although elements from each culture are assimilated into the TCK's life experience, the sense of belonging is in relationship to others of similar background. (1999: 19)

Others have embellished and modified the definitions over time. Tokuhama-Espinosa (2003a: 165), for instance, says that the term TCK 'is used to describe a child who has parents of two different cultures, and they are "abroad" in a third ... Or it may apply to a child with parents from the same culture who lives in a country other than his or her own, and attends a school in a third culture', while Pascoe suggests that 'A Third Culture Kid – or a "trans-cultural kid" as the term is now also being defined – is a child who spends a significant part of his life in a country or countries which are not the same as the one stamped on his passport. The child is not, as the term might lead you to believe, the product of parents of mixed cultures' (1993: 162).

It is not the intention here to undertake a detailed analysis of the various definitions used to describe the globally-mobile child, and it may well be that it is most appropriate to stick with a generalised definition such as Useem's most recent reference to the concept of 'Third Culture' as a generic term. Purists may argue that any detailed definition cannot hope to apply accurately to the myriad 'types' of such children now to be found in international schools. Take, for instance, a child with two British parents who continue to refer to the UK as 'home' and with grandparents in the UK who are visited for long holidays each year, who watches BBC World News on television and attends a British international school largely staffed and attended by expatriate British. This child is certainly a Global Nomad and is in one sense a TCK, but is arguably very different in terms of identity from another child whose parents are of two different nationalities and first languages, who does not keep in regular contact with either set of grandparents, who attends an international school with no particular national affiliation, and whose best language is English because that is the language of his or her school.

Whether or not the terminology currently used is adequate to describe and distinguish between the many variations among children who follow their parents' career around the world, it is clear that such children may share to differing degrees a number of characteristics which will influence their personal development as individuals and their educational achievement both during their school years and later. Rader and Sittig (2003: 3) point out that some of the characteristics of such children are likely to be similar to those of children who move within one national context (referring to research by Jason et al. (1992) and Jasper (2000) as of relevance in this respect). This is an important point to bear in mind, while at the same time acknowledging the additional layers of complexity that may be added for a TCK in terms of distance from the passport country, lack of clarity about a national identity, and the challenges of living in a place where the language is different from any previously spoken.

IDENTITY

Pasternak describes a scenario which may not be atypical of a child in an international school, who

> begins her day with a news report on a war somewhere in the world, graphically illustrated with explicit scenes provided by a CNN International camera. As she munches her international breakfast of products from far-off places she may switch to Euro News for an update on the latest decisions taken at the European Parliament. But not for long: a quick flick of the wrist and a Japanese cartoon, dubbed into English, will hold her attention for a

> fleeting ten minutes. As she sits on her German-built school bus some fruity chewing gum, straight from friends in the USA, is passed around. ... Back home, in the evening, 15 minutes French homework is quickly completed to leave time for a computer game, set in 'darkest' Africa. ... The evening meal pizza ... provides focal time for a discussion on the forthcoming holiday in the Caribbean. A final 30 minutes TV, an adventure film in Urdu, and another international day comes to an end. (1998: 253)

Who is such a child? What is her identity? Where does she belong? It would be difficult to find clearer or more thorough accounts of issues relating to identity in TCKs than those written by Pearce (including 1998, 2002 and 2006). 'Identity', says Pearce, 'is seen as the perception that subjects have of their own properties, applying to themselves the value system that they have constructed by interactions within their social group' (2002: 150). Pearce goes on to refer to the work of, inter alia, Bowlby (1969) in describing the strong mutual attachments formed between children and their carers prior to the developing of 'lesser attachments' with a number of other individuals which form the 'framework' referred to by Vygotsky (1962) and the 'scaffolding' described by Bruner (1985). Such individuals may be referred to as 'significant others', 'referent others' or 'reference groups' (Keats et al., 1983, in Pearce, 2002: 152).

Relationships with all such individuals contribute to the child's development of self: while for the child who experiences a reasonably stable upbringing the notions of 'self' ('the principal element of identity', according to Pearce), and 'alterity' ('the "otherness" of people or values beyond the cultural horizon of the self') (1998: 54) may be clear, for a globally mobile child the development of identity is likely to be more complex. Strength of attachments to parents may be as strong as for a less mobile child (though the case of military children is interesting, when one parent may be absent for long periods of time), but attachments to others may be more ephemeral (Pearce, 2002: 152). Add to the transience of the relationships with 'others' of the globally-mobile child the variation in cultural, national and linguistic background of the 'others' with whom such relatively transient relationships may be formed, and the additional complexity of the TCK's identity formation becomes clear.

Schaetti, discussing in relation to Global Nomads a number of issues relating to 'attachment theory' – the development of a relationship between a child and his/her caregiver – highlights the issue of what she refers to as the 'host national caregiver': the amah, ayah, nanny, who in some instances 'become not simply additional caregivers but in fact take primary responsibility for the infant's or child's well-being' (2002: 111). While noting the potential benefits of such a relationship, including the opportunity for the child to develop fluency in the host culture language, Schaetti notes two concerns: the potential for cultural dissonance with the passport country culture, and the 'inevitable loss of the attachment relationship when the child moves away' (2002: 111). Indeed there are anecdotal accounts of difficulties that can arise in relation to children's developing language if they spend (relatively) so much time with the host country caregiver that they are able to communicate far more fluently in the host language than in the language(s) of their parents, with whom communication may prove problematic if the parents do not also speak the host language. The child's already complex linguistic development can be further complicated if the language of the international school attended (which is probably English) is different from the carer's mother tongue, and also possibly from the mother tongue(s) of the parents.

A related issue encountered in some international schools, possibly less so in the context of global nomads than with privileged host country students, arises where the host country caregiver is expected to do everything for the child long after the age at which the children of less privileged families would have been expected to learn to do things for themselves. Bathing, dressing, carrying bags and remembering to bring homework may all continue to be a caregiver's responsibility, providing challenges for the teacher more used to a child having developed such skills and responsibilities at a younger age. The notion of what might be described as 'learned helplessness' (Soraci et al., 1986) is also one that would cause concern to many teachers (if not, perhaps, to the parents) in terms of the child's potential for growing into a self-reliant and responsible adult. Langford et al., in referring to 'those affluent families who seem to leave matters of child-rearing and education to their nannies, governesses, private tutors, drivers, maids and secretaries' (2002: 41), highlight the frustration that can be felt by an international school teacher in not being able to engage in discussion with a parent about the child's education (and, indeed, not being clear about the acceptability of discussing such issues with 'employees' of the family).

The Concept of 'Home'

Nette suggests that at the heart of the dilemma of the internationally mobile individual are the questions 'Who am I?' or 'Where do I belong?' (2000: 25–6), referring to Bauman's statement that 'one thinks of identity whenever one is not sure of where one belongs' (1996: 19). What does the concept of 'home' mean to a child who has moved country every two years since a baby and has not returned to grandparents in a 'home country' on a regular basis? In a study conducted in Botswana with 9–11 year old students who held passports from other countries, Nette concluded that their sense of belonging was strongly influenced by the friends and family with whom they currently lived, and that they only appeared to begin to identify Botswana as their 'main home country' after living there for at least two years. The notion of home country was clearly not straightforward, with children variously identifying their country of birth, passport country and parents' countries of birth as their home country and not necessarily, as Nette points out, linking the notion of having a home country with the idea of actually belonging to it.

The concepts of home and nationality have also been discussed from the perspectives of an expatriate wife and mother by Pascoe, who describes separating the two concepts so that, for her children, 'home is where we are living together as a family at the moment; our nationality is Canadian' (1993: 168). She and her husband, she explains, deliberately bought a house in Canada that is rented out while they are away and to which they return after each foreign assignment, the children re-establishing links with the same peer group who live nearby (and also returning to the family dog, who is rented out with the house). During summer vacations the family rent a cottage nearby to encourage the renewal of friendships and the reinforcement of some sense of 'permanence': 'the smartest thing we ever did' she says (1993: 168).

Children, of course, naturally do their best to adapt to their surroundings – and most globally mobile children make four adaptations to their mobility, according to McKillop-Ostrom:

> They show forced extroversion by going out of their way to get to meet new people and form friendships quickly. They tend to mesh and mimic, which cuts down on the need to gain acceptance. They travel lightly, entering relationships that are typically short-term and intense, and they develop ease in saying goodbye, leaving very few people from whom they cannot walk away. (2000: 74–5)

Arising from characteristics such as these, Chapter 5 will go on to consider some of the issues and challenges likely to be faced within international schools by this group of globally mobile children.

CHAPTER 5

Globally-Mobile Students: The International School Experience

Following discussion in Chapter 4 of some of the characteristics of children attending international schools, this chapter will consider the school experience of one group in particular: the so-called Global Nomad or Third Culture Kid (TCK). At first glance, many TCKs appear privileged. They 'generally have parents who are successful in their sphere of work and who have high educational expectations for their children' (Sears, 1998: 18) and tend therefore to be relatively affluent and well educated, with international travel a regular occurrence as well as access to all the latest technology and other attributes of a prosperous professional lifestyle. And indeed they are privileged, in many respects. It would be dangerous to assume, however, that such children do not also face challenges that may not be faced by their more rooted contemporaries; within the context of international schools, it is clearly important that teachers who work with them are aware of these challenges. This chapter will focus on a number of issues arising with respect to the TCK school experience, before touching briefly on what is known of some of the longer term effects of such a childhood. The first such issue, one of the most central to TCKs, is that of transition.

TRANSITION

In recent years the issue of transition has become increasingly well researched, whether in relation to the military, international schools or national contexts. A study by the Migration Research Unit at University College London, for instance (Dobson et al., 2000), pointed out that pupil mobility, defined as 'a child joining or leaving a school at a point other than the normal age at which children start or finish their education at that school, whether or not this involves a move of home' (Dobson and Henthorne, 1999: 5) is not a new phenomenon, with various UK-based studies having been undertaken previously in relation to the homeless, refugees, service (or military) children, travellers and children in care. Undoubtedly there are some areas of similarity between such studies and the context of international schools, though there are also differences, and none of these groups coincides closely with the profile of the Global Nomads to be found in so many international schools. Superficially privileged, TCKs often live in what Pascoe refers to as a 'jumbo jet culture, where pint-sized travellers flash their passports in exotic airports, or smoothly exit in chauffeur-driven airport limousines or embassy cars' (1993: 163). Rader and Sittig refer to some of the less material benefits of such a lifestyle including 'an expanded view of the world, adaptability, cross-cultural skills, social skills, observational skills and linguistic skills' (2003: 3) while being communicative and having social confidence – 'the aptitude to connect easily with individuals one encounters [taken with] the desire to communicate' – were highlighted by Murphy-Lejeune as attributes of students who have travelled (though not necessarily in the context of international schools) (2003: 106–7). Davis groups under a number of headings the positive characteristics attributed to TCKs by several authors: 'linguistic awareness and ability, adaptability to new environments, relationships, international perspective and preparedness to travel, cross-cultural skills, increased maturity, strong family bonds and positive contributions to society' (2001:12).

Such children are clearly privileged materially, socially (in terms of social and communication skills developed) and educationally (through first-hand experiences of history, geography, religions, languages and cultures that other children might learn about only through books or the Internet). But it would be simplistic not to scratch below the surface of their life histories to investigate the potentially less positive effects of such a lifestyle. The relative instability of their upbringing, for instance, can have an impact. Rader and Sittig note 'confused loyalties, a sense of rootlessness and restlessness, a lack of true identity, and unresolved grief' (2003: 3) as some of the likely characteristics of such a childhood, while Pollock refers to the 'residue of unresolved grief, anger and depression' (1992: 73) that can follow as a result of the many separations of a nomadic lifestyle, as well as stresses in personal relationships including reluctance to form close emotional bonds. 'All global nomads are not alike' says Pollock, 'They do not fit perfectly into a mould' (1992: 73), and clearly every Global Nomad's experiences will in a sense be unique, as the many varied factors relating to family, locations, schools and friends combine to influence their development. In general, they are likely to become in some senses 'cultural chameleons', a term used by Pollock to describe how 'after spending a little time observing what is going on, they can easily switch language, style of relating, appearance, and cultural practices to take on the characteristics needed to blend better into the current scene' (in Pollock and Van Reken, 1999: 92).

Pollock and Van Reken point out that life for everyone consists of a series of transitions – some expected (from infancy to childhood or from school to university) and some sudden and unexpected (loss of a job, serious injury, untimely death of a loved one). TCKs, however, go through major transitions far more frequently than do those born and raised in one area, and their relocation usually involves changing not only places but also cultures, leading to 'culture shock' in addition to the normal stress involved in any transition (1999: 61–2). Pollock and van Reken go on to propose what they describe as the five predictable stages of transition from the perspective of one who is leaving:

- *Involvement*: before any notion of leaving has been raised;
- *Leaving*: from when the idea of leaving is raised as a certainty, to the point of departure;
- *Transition*: beginning with leaving one place and ending when, as Pollock and Van Reken put it, 'we not only arrive at our destination but make the decision, consciously or unconsciously, to settle in and become part of it' (1999: 66);
- *Entering*: where the individual has decided to become part of the new community, but is still figuring out what that means;
- *Reinvolvement*: where the individual once again becomes 'part of the permanent community' (1999: 62-71).

In the context of this book, the central question would seem to be 'what is the role of the international school in supporting such students?' Langford, following an excellent review of a range of literature sources relating to TCKs and Global Nomads, points out that 'It is in the international school community's own interests to understand why families sometimes fail to adjust and how they as educators can help improve the transition process for their pupils' (1998: 37). In order to arrive at a better understanding of what international schools were doing to accommodate the needs of such students, she undertook a survey of 287 international school teachers and administrators working at 41 international schools worldwide, as well as interviewing ten experienced international school administrators. Langford's study showed that the international school educators in question felt that their schools were most successfully addressing issues relating to the adjustment of internationally mobile pupils in two areas – orientation of new pupils on arrival, and acknowledging the educational needs of internationally mobile pupils in the school's philosophies and objectives – while also feeling their schools were successful in offering a curriculum that serves internationally mobile pupils. Seven areas these educators agreed should be given greater attention were pupil counselling; in-service training for teachers; development and maintenance of a 'profiling' portfolio to accompany pupils between schools; classroom activities to facilitate the arrival of new pupils; parent counselling; providing the family with practical local information; and incorporating classroom activities that facilitate the pupils' departure (Langford,1998: 38).

Davis, an experienced international school head in Kuala Lumpur, accessed eight international schools in Malaysia to investigate the views of parents of TCKs with respect to the value placed on different types of school support, and the views of administrators (headteachers, principals and superintendents) in the same eight schools as to the levels of school support provided. Responses from the 73 parental questionnaires and ten follow-up parental interviews, plus eight administrator questionnaires and three follow-up interviews, led Davis to conclude that 'The gap between the levels of support that are available in schools and the level of support required by parents is wide. International schools can, and should, do a lot more to provide specific support for internationally mobile students and their families' (2001: 127), before going on to recommend that international schools should do more to:

- celebrate the positive characteristics acquired by internationally mobile students;
- demonstrate their commitment to supporting internationally mobile students and foster an understanding of the difficulties associated with mobility;
- provide programmes of support for departing students;
- supply written information in languages other than the language of instruction;
- place emphasis on the school being a community centre for parents and building strong links with expatriate support groups;
- clarify the types of support valued by parents and students and ensure such support is provided;
- provide a specific transition education process to assist globally mobile students with the moving on process;
- provide counselling support for both new and departing students as well as counselling facilities for parents of globally mobile students. (Davis, 2001: 127)

Increased attention to such points would provide support for the psychological needs of international school students, which McKillop-Ostrom argues 'are as critical to their success at school as are the academic needs' (2000: 73). McKillop-Ostrom refers to 'sojourner adjustment' as 'the psychological adjustment of relatively short-term visitors to new geographic areas where permanent settlement is not intended, and where assimilation into the host culture is not expected (Berry et al., 1992; Church, 1982)' and to various models of transition and adaptation. McKillop-Ostrom goes on to refer to the development of transition programmes at schools such as her own at that time, the United Nations International School of Hanoi (UNIS–Hanoi), and the potential effectiveness of transition resource teams (of 7–10 teachers, administrators, counsellors, parents and students) to deliver such programmes, which can include activities such as the following:

- consolidation of transition efforts;
- increased transition expertise (including transitions-related professional development for team members and then other staff members);
- transition education and cultural awareness (for teachers and for students);
- transition-related activities (including orientation for new students and departure programmes for those who are leaving, as well as activities to support 'those students who must continually adjust to the comings and goings of those around them');
- customised transition services (learning from programmes used at other schools, but ensuring they are adapted to ensure sufficient relevance);
- institutionalised transition programming (supported by board policy and proper budgeting);
- year-round transition support. (McKillop-Ostrom, 2000: 80–2)

Building in such activities in order better to support students undergoing transition experiences will, McKillop-Ostrom argues, help them to become better-adjusted individuals. It is too easy, says Akram, to emphasise the 'rubber band type' flexibility of children and to overlook the level of support they may actually need from teachers and administrators at their international school, as they are being asked to 'stretch' in terms of separation both from those left behind in the previous location and from newly made friends who subsequently move away (1995: 39). Children are also expected to cope with the effect on intra-family relationships of relocation – and all this even if the child is a native speaker of the language of both countries and both schools: how much more elasticity is required in the rubber band when a variety of languages is involved? Ezra, in discussing issues relating to the globally mobile child, suggests 16 points for support that should be provided by international schools for such children and their families, a number of which overlap with the suggestions made by McKillop-Ostrom and by Davis (2003: 141–4).

Not to be forgotten in any discussion of transition and the globally mobile child should be those children in international schools who do not move so frequently, but who regularly lose friends who move on to another location. 'This group of students suffer psychologically in the process of ending friendships as others move on' said the mother of one such student in one of the international schools studied by Davis. '[They] are continually suffering from something I have come to recognise as close to the grieving process. Eventually many stop the hurt by not getting so close to others. This may last some time, depending on the circumstances and the individual' (2001: 112).

In the growing, if still relatively limited, research and literature on the effects of global mobility on children (those who move and those who are left behind), one voice is infrequently heard. While it is essential to draw on the experience of teachers and administrators and to listen to the views of parents, it is rarely the case that the thoughts of the children themselves are actively sought in any systematic way. Dixon's (2004) study is unusual in setting out to discover how upper primary age (10–11 year old) children at an international school in Thailand felt about moving from one culture to another, before going on to discuss the implications for international school educators. Using an online child-friendly questionnaire, 30 recently-arrived expatriate children from 13 countries (and a wider range of previous locations) responded to a number of questions, based on Pollock and Van Reken's five stage model, asking how they felt about relocating before and after the move, about the process of settling in, and about changes more generally.

One interesting feature which may not be unusual among TCKs was that seven of the 30 had moved internationally four or more times already, by the age of 11 years. Settling in had clearly been easier for some children than others, as had the sense of loss felt about leaving behind relations and pets. Losing and making friends, however, was a concern that ran through all responses, though those who had already moved more than three times appeared to worry less about leaving friends behind than did others, supporting Pollock's view that such children develop strategies to cope with parting and that after multiple moves they learn strategies for developing less deep friendships (in Pollock and Van Reken, 1999). Among several detailed conclusions in Dixon's (2004) study, a number likely to be of more generalised interest are the importance of having a formalised induction programme for incoming students, of ensuring that any buddy system in operation is as effective as intended (only by asking the students did it transpire, for instance, that some aspects of the buddy system at this school were not effective at all) and the importance of schools developing some form of transitional support teams along the lines proposed by McKillop-Ostrom.

CULTURE SHOCK

Though arguably somewhat dated as a concept, and with limitations in describing the experiences of many Third Culture Kids, the term 'culture shock' will be used here in the absence of a better description of one characteristic of their situation. The well-documented U-curve used by, inter alia, Lysgaard (1955) and Sewell and Davidson (1956) to describe 'culture shock', a term coined by Dubois in 1951 (Paige, 1993), consists of three stages: initial enthusiasm; disenchantment when the 'sojourner's' knowledge has advanced sufficiently to be aware of the limitations being experienced; and a period of recovery when the sojourner becomes more competent in the host culture. Gullahorn and Gullahorn's extension (1963, 1966) to a W curve incorporated two further stages for those who return to the home culture: a stage of re-entry crisis and a final readjustment period.

It needs to be noted, of course, that not everyone moves successfully through the three or five stages; some effectively 'get stuck' part way through and either remain 'stuck' (in, for example, a state of disenchantment) or decide to surrender and return to the home context where greater security beckons. Such choices are not usually, of course, open to the child, who will have moved to the new location either willingly or unwillingly and who is likely to be there for the duration of the parents' stay, like it or not. If the child has moved unwillingly, then even the first U-curve or W-curve stage of initial enthusiasm may not apply. It should also be borne in mind that a number of the culture shock models are based on the notion of a cycle of approximately three years, whereas often globally mobile families move on after a shorter period. Arguably, therefore, the traditional culture shock models will not apply in all such cases and an updated version of such a model is needed for this context.

Culture shock, say Fennes and Hapgood

> can be experienced when we realise that the behaviour we consider to be 'normal' or 'natural' is not perceived as appropriate or is possibly rejected by another culture; when what has always been self-evident does not seem to be so any more; when we do not understand the behaviour of members of another culture; when we get the impression that they do not behave in a 'normal' way' (1997: 29).

In the case of many international school students then, and TCKs in particular, it is likely that on arrival at a new international school and for some time afterwards (the duration depending on a number of factors), at least two types of culture shock will be experienced: in relation to the culture of the host country and in relation to the culture of the new international school. The former may be more obvious. It is an experience likely to be shared with other members of the student's relocated family, and there may be school systems in place to assist the family in adapting to local cultural norms. The latter may not be obvious to an observer at all, and in that sense could be potentially more problematic.

To a child whose first international school experience this is, for instance, and whose previous educational experience was in a more traditional teacher-centred environment, the new school may at first appear to have no rules as the subtle cues understood by those familiar with the relatively liberal child-centred approach found in many international schools pass them by. Such children may very quickly find themselves in contravention of the school's accepted norms of behaviour through misreading, or completely missing, the behavioural cues understood by their peers. They will also need to become acculturated to the 'culture' of the new school, in terms of all sorts of other aspects of the way things are done (such as raising hands, or not, in order to ask questions) which would be experienced by any child moving schools, or even classes, nationally or internationally.

It is also possible, depending on the nature of the experience and the training of the teachers with whom the student interacts, that the student may experience culture shock in relation to the different cultural backgrounds of the teacher and the student him/herself. 'I have witnessed a Japanese student being told by a teacher to "Look me in the eye when I speak to you!", says Poore, 'with no concept of how abhorrent that is in Japanese culture. I have seen teachers pursue the moral high ground from a Western perspective when a student did something wrong, rather than proceed so that all involved could save face, a cultural imperative in much of our world' (2005: 354). Such lack of sensitivity on the part of the teacher may well be the cause of another form of individualised culture shock which could potentially manifest itself, in different ways, with every teacher with whom the child interacts during the school day.

And then, of course, there is the issue of culture shock in relation not only to the host culture, to the overall school culture, and to individual teacher culture(s), but also to the various cultures of the other students in the child's class and other parts of the school with whom he/she interacts on a daily basis. Heyward describes as 'intercultural literacy' the successful cross-cultural engagement which it is hoped such students will develop. Intercultural literacy, says Heyward, requires cross-cultural experience and develops in response to the experience of confronting another culture: 'It is the shock of cross-cultural contact, the crisis of engagement, that stimulates the learning necessary for intercultural literacy' (2002: 18–19). Similarly,

Allan refers to what he describes as the cultural dissonance experienced by students in international schools, which are

> areas where different cultures operate within the same environment, where there is often a dominant cultural ethos, both among the faculty and the students, and where the culture of the host country can impinge on the school culture to varying degrees and in various ways, producing a school culture with individual and specific characteristics. (2002: 77)

The 'cultural borderlands', says Allan, are where the students' experience of the school will take place (2002: 78).

In the study on which Allan's writing was based, set in an international school with a culture largely Anglo-American in nature (and therefore not atypical of many international schools), it was students from East Asia and Japan whom Allan felt to have suffered particularly from cultural dissonance and culture shock. 'Cultural dissonance' he says, 'was seen to be both the means and the medium of intercultural learning, in that students had to learn from and through this in order to negotiate the minefield of cross-cultural personal interaction' (Allan, 2003: 89). Intercultural learning was noted by Allan to take place mainly in students from outside the predominant student national cultures. For those from that majority (Anglo-American) student culture, 'the prevailing norms and values of the school culture were found to be so similar to their own that there was little cultural dissonance and they were rarely seen to move further than an awareness of other cultures' (2003: 89–90). The nature of the learning taking place in international school students, both academic and social, is clearly complex.

LANGUAGE ISSUES

Many international schools offering an English-medium education (which is by far the majority of such schools) provide language support for non-native speakers of English. Depending upon the nature of the school and its location, the extent and nature of the support required will clearly vary. In those many international schools that cater for highly mobile Global Nomads, the question of language support can be complex and sometimes fraught with difficulty. Grosjean points out that at least half the world is bilingual but only in oral skills; multiliteracy skills are the exception, not the rule (1994, in Tokuhama-Espinosa, 2003a: xiii). This distinction serves to highlight the inadequacy of the term 'bilingual' as it is often used in perhaps less complex contexts. 'Is someone bilingual' asks Baker, 'if they are fluent in one language but less than fluent in their other language? Is someone bilingual if they rarely or never use one of their languages?' (2001: 2), before going on to discuss the many factors that need to be considered before such questions could begin to be answered. Suffice to say that issues relating, inter alia, to the four basic language abilities (listening, reading, speaking and writing), to the balance of fluency between the two languages (and indeed the four basic abilities in each), the uses to which each language is put in different contexts and the extent to which an individual can exercise choice in use of language are all complicating features. In a situation such as the international school environment in which many globally mobile children are educated, issues are further complicated by more than two languages being involved, by the relatively short period of time for which a child may have been exposed to at least one of the languages he/she can 'speak', and by the fact that the child's parents might each have different 'mother tongues'.

A childhood such as that described by Allemann-Ghionda (2003) would not be entirely atypical in this context: Italian father, German mother, brought up until the age of 3 years old in Rio de Janeiro speaking Portuguese with her 'tata' or 'nanny' and parents, then moving to Italy for two years and learning to speak fluent Italian before relocation to the French-speaking part of Belgium and a French-speaking kindergarten and school; learning to communicate during this period in German as well as French in order to speak to her maternal grandmother, before relocating with her family to Colombia and a bilingual French-Spanish school, and then to a bilingual Italian-Spanish school in Peru two years later, followed by a move to Rome after three years (and still only 13 years old). Despite fluency in Italian, education in the national system proved not to be possible because she had not reached the required level in Latin and she was therefore enrolled at an international school for three years, before relocating to Germany to complete her Abitur after another three years and then moving with her family to Switzerland, where she attended university (2003: 171–88).

While perhaps more extreme in the number of moves, countries and languages than would be the case for many international school students, this sort of lifestyle, with its fragmented approach to language development and usage, is not as uncommon as might be imagined. Allemann-Ghionda does not give any impression of having done other than take all the different language experiences in her stride, but not all Global Nomads cope as well as she appears to have done. Baker refers to the concept of what he describes as 'semilingualism', where an individual has some, but not 'sufficient', competence in two languages and demonstrates the following profile in both: 'displays a small vocabulary and incorrect grammar, consciously thinks about language production, is stilted and uncreative with each language, and finds it difficult to think and express emotions in either language' (2001: 9): a definition which, it needs to be acknowledged, does not attract universal acceptance.

English and the Non-Native Speaker

Invariably in the international school context one of the languages in which the student will be aspiring for fluency (if they are not already a native speaker) is English: it has already been noted (see Chapter 3) that for many parents of non-English speaking children the international school may serve as a 'proxy language school' (Deveney, 2000: 36), with English providing an additional tool likely to be used throughout their education, at school and university level in many cases. Murphy suggests that, very often, the non-English speaking child

> has been enrolled in the school to learn English, or to have what the parents perceive to be a superior, western-style education, or both. Furthermore, the parents hope to achieve some measure of continuity in the child's schooling abroad by enrolling the child in an international school in each location. They also hope that such an education will equip their child with some knowledge of how the world works, so that a measure of success may be ensured in the future. All the child has to do is learn English. (2003: 26)

Garner points out the distinction between the various types of English teaching likely to be encountered, explaining that 'English as a Second Language' (ESL) is generally the term used to denote the learning of English in addition to the student's mother tongue (1991: 2–3). In a context where terminology is regularly changing and being updated, it is arguably now the more recently fashionable term 'English as an Additional Language' (EAL) that would describe the situation of many international students who, as with Allemann-Ghionda above, speak more than one other language in addition to English. Murphy (1991) includes consideration of a range of issues relating to the provision of ESL support in international schools, as does Sears (1998) who points out the variety of approaches taken in different international schools, from the name given to it (sometimes ESL, sometimes ESOL – English to Speakers of Other Languages), to the teaching support made available (for example, an ESL department with a head of department or ESL coordinator who represents the needs of ESL students in in-school discussions), and to the very nature of the programme. As Sears explains,

> In some schools, the basic provision takes the form of a pull-out programme of classes for learners at different levels of competence. In many cases, three levels of classes are offered, equating broadly with beginner, intermediate and advanced level learners. The classes themselves may comprise students of mixed ages or serve the students of one year level. In many schools, the ESL provision consists of support within the homeroom for individual students or small groups. The role of the ESL teacher in this

> instance is to offer language support to the student related to the specific language needs of the curriculum. Many schools offer an ESL programme that combines pull-out classes with classroom support. (1998: 53)

Clearly in many international schools a good deal of support is provided for students who are not first language speakers of English. So why is there concern about the effectiveness of this provision? Sears says, for instance, that 'There is considerable debate about the effectiveness of the different models of ESL programme' (1998: 53), including the relative advantages and disadvantages of the 'pull out' and 'home classroom support' programmes described above. In addition to differences of opinion about such issues are the concerns expressed by some practitioners experienced in working in international schools with younger children. Kusuma-Powell coined the term 'Functionally Multi-Lingual' (FML) to describe 'children who are multi-lingual at a surface level of conversation but who appear to have difficulty developing abstractions and higher order thinking skills' (2004: 158), a small but growing number of international school children, she says, who 'despite being multi-lingual, are unable to take full advantage of the curriculum on offer' (2004: 158).

Ezra describes two different types of language it is suggested are acquired by young children (2003: 132–3). Basic interpersonal communication skills (BICS), it is argued, allow for effective interpersonal communication when used with other contextual cues such as eye contact, facial expressions, intonation and gestures which also communicate meaning (Cummins, 2000). It is argued that to reach what Cummins describes as 'cognitive academic language proficiency skills' (CALPS), however, which require knowledge of the language of text, complex vocabulary and grammatical structures, and make greater demands on memory, analysis and other cognitive processes, can take five years or longer (Ezra, 2003: 132–3).

If young TCKs spend two or three years in an international school before returning for a short period to a local home-language school during a parent's home posting, and then move to a different international school during another international posting (possibly repeating this pattern more than once), it may well be the case says Ezra (2003: 133) that the child will develop basic interpersonal communication skills, but may never remain long enough in one language environment to acquire academic proficiency. His/her mastery of spoken languages 'is not sufficiently robust in any language to support highly conceptualised academic learning ... [and his/her] facility with linguistic abstractions does not appear to follow the same developmental trajectory as it does in other students. For many of these students, as evidenced by their speech and writing, their actual thinking remains "stuck" at a concrete level' (Kusuma-Powell, 2004: 160).

As Kusuma-Powell further points out, one of the difficulties associated with such a student is delay in diagnosis. Teachers tend to assume that any academic difficulties experienced arise from a poor facility with English, and may assume that there is another, stronger language in which the child has much greater facility to manipulate ideas – when in fact the poorly developed English the teacher observes may actually be the child's most highly developed language. Kusuma-Powell acknowledges that many children in international schools experience the type of linguistically unsettled childhood described and yet succeed academically with no difficulty. She suggests therefore that there may also be other factors involved, possibly relating to underlying learning disabilities which may thus be disguised (2004: 161). Delays in diagnosis can clearly present a real problem when the result is a lack of awareness of underlying developmental difficulties until the child is well past the age at which support can most effectively be provided. But diagnosing learning difficulties effectively is only really possible when the child has sufficient competence in a language (probably English) in which any assessment is likely to be undertaken: a 'Catch 22' situation indeed.

Language Support Provision

Language, then, is clearly an issue in international schools and particularly, perhaps, for the young child in terms of the cognitive development processes to which language development is so closely linked. What can international schools do in order better to support such students? Murphy argues for greater provision of support for the child's first language (ideally through the operation of a bilingual curriculum) in order to support cognitive development in that language which, as Collier and Thomas (2002) point out, would make the second language less difficult to acquire and lead to better academic performance (in Murphy, 2003: 36–7). As Murphy herself acknowledges, there are resource and other implications of such provision, a point echoed by Carder in stressing the importance of maintenance of the mother tongue for international school children. 'Certainly there are administrative problems in scheduling and finding mother-tongue teachers', he says, 'there are financial difficulties about whether to add them to the payroll or get parents to pay extra; and there is the challenge of persuading and cajoling parents into understanding that it is one thing to speak your own language well, and quite another to write it well enough to get good grades in school subjects' (1993: 24–5). Murphy also argues for such issues to be given a higher profile within international schools and not to be 'left entirely to chance or to ESL departments, knowledgeable and effective though many of them are' (2003: 39).

Kusuma-Powell makes a similar point, urging all international school teachers (and not only ESL specialists) to see it as part of their role to become knowledgeable about expected progression of language development, so that they can provide support in the diagnosis of difficulties and the development of areas of weakness (2004: 166–7). Sears, meanwhile, proposes that there are now three agreed aspects to the effective support of second language English speakers in international schools, about which their teachers across the school should be aware:

- mother tongue maintenance and development (in which the school's role varies);
- an effective and integrated programme of specific English language teaching in whatever form; and
- the training of mainstream teachers in second language learning and culture issues and in the strategies necessary to give ESL students access to the mainstream curriculum. (Sears, 2006)

while Murphy argues that international schools have a moral commitment, when admitting second-language children, to recognise

> throughout the school, in the curriculum, in admissions, in testing and assessment, in counselling, in the learning disabilities department, as well as in the library, the lunchroom and the boardroom, that we are more often than not looking at children who are struggling with language, culture and ultimately understanding, without the benefit of support from their own culture, and with far too little help from the school. (2003: 39)

Anecdotal evidence suggests that student rolls in many international schools are gradually changing, with increasing numbers of bilingual students who in many schools are now in the majority. In such a situation it is the second language English speakers who are becoming the 'norm', and it could be argued that it is the first language English speakers in fact who are disadvantaged in missing out on the experience of being bilingual (Montet, 2005). Clearly the increasingly complex linguistic situation in many international schools is one that none of the schools' constituencies – teachers, administrators, boards – can afford to ignore.

SPECIAL NEEDS

As Bradley points out, 'For families with children who fit the "norm", confronting the whole issue of global mobility and the difficulties that often accompany it can be a daunting task. For parents of a child with special educational needs, however, problems are manifold' (2000: 30). The very term used to describe such needs is itself potentially controversial and can seem to change regularly within one national context, let alone across the host of cultures, nationalities and languages in which international schools operate. A number of once-used descriptions would today be considered offensive and it is difficult to be sure, unless one is an expert in this area, whether the terminology being used is currently considered appropriate and has not been superseded by more recent developments.

For the purposes of this chapter, the term 'Special Needs' will be utilised, while making clear that this is not used in the sense sometimes applied of referring only to those with learning or other difficulties. Haldimann and Hollington assert that 'By definition all international children have Special Needs. However, within an international school there are certain groups of students, eg ESL, learning disabled, gifted, with additional educational needs who require instruction beyond what the regular classroom curriculum can provide' (2004: 9). This section will discuss, briefly in each case, issues relating to identification of special needs, giftedness and learning difficulties, before describing the case of one international school which offers an inclusive education incorporating provision for a range of needs.

One issue in considering Special Needs is whether provision is actually made for such needs in international schools. Such schools are not required to accept a child with Special Needs (however defined), but it would be unreasonable for a school to accept such a child and then not provide the support needed, a practice which Haldimann and Hollington describe as 'unethical': 'All students at international schools', they argue, 'should be expected to succeed whether or not they require additional support to meet their educational needs' (2004: 9). Indeed accreditation agencies such as the Council of International Schools (CIS) may require, if accreditation is to be given, that provision is made for the initial identification of the learning needs of students and for the subsequent addressing of those needs (CIS, 2003: E 62–6). One approach adopted in a number of international schools is the Optimal Match Concept, whereby curricula are 'fine-tuned' to match an individual student's level and ideal pace of learning (Haldimann, 1998: 134), so that 'all students receive the "best fit" of the curricula to the student rather than a "one size fits all" approach' (Haldimann and Hollington, 2004: 9). Such an approach can of course be resource-intensive, and whether or not it is implemented is likely to be at the discretion of the school head or board (Haldimann and Hollington, 2004: 10).

Given the 'skewed' nature of international school populations arising from the well-educated professional nature of the parents and the particularly high proportions of students who go on to university-level study (Matthews, 1989), those who might be described as 'gifted' may be potentially relatively large in number. But the very notion of 'giftedness' is, of course, complex and covers a range of dimensions of development in which a particular child might excel compared with the 'norm'. Neihart suggests that

> It is not uncommon for a seven-year-old gifted child to be cognitively similar to a twelve-year-old, socially similar to a nine-year-old, and physically just like other seven-year-olds. These developmental discrepancies present challenges for parent and child alike, but they are especially difficult to deal with when the child has limited access to true peers. Therefore, one of the most beneficial things we can do to support the healthy adjustment of our gifted children is make sure they have time to learn and play with others like themselves. (2003, in Haldimann and Hollington, 2004: 150)

Foreman (later Foreman-Haldimann) cites a quotation from Rice (1980) to the effect that gifted and talented children demonstrate achievement and/or potential ability in one of the areas of general intellectual ability – specific academic aptitude, creative or productive thinking, leadership ability and ethical or moral development, visual and performing arts – before going on to discuss a number of issues that can arise in the context of international school provision for such children, including challenges presented to the child him/herself, the parents and the teachers (1983: 65).

Increasingly, support for schools is becoming available in national systems with some transferability to the international school context. The Schoolwide Enrichment Model, for instance, identifies a 'talent pool' of 15–20 per cent of 'above average ability/high potential students' through various means, including teacher nominations, achievement tests, assessment of potential for creativity and task commitment, parent nomination and self-nomination. Students identified for the talent pool are then eligible for three 'services'; interest and learning style assessments, curriculum modification and three types of enrichment experience (Carber and Reis, 2004: 343–4).

Clearly, providing the diagnosis and support required if every gifted child is to reach his/her potential is quite a task. More obviously challenging to all concerned, perhaps, is the diagnosis and support provision for children who may be described as having 'learning difficulties', not least because, as Sears points out, parents can sometimes be reticent about providing the new school with full details of their child's previous educational history if there have been difficulties. 'They hope that their child can make a fresh start', says Sears, 'free from the labels of "difficult student" or "special needs child". Teachers who suspect the presence of specific learning difficulties may have a challenging task in persuading parents that action needs to be taken in their child's interest' (1998: 87). When developmental, medical and behavioural histories are only available if provided by the parents, since no contact exists between the current school and the child's previous school or family doctor, precious time can be lost in diagnosis if parents do not cooperate: in particular (and as noted earlier), in the case of a child in an English medium international school who is not a native English speaker and where underlying learning difficulties are mistakenly attributed to problems in learning to speak English (Kachirskaia, 2002: 70).

Parental response to a diagnosed learning difficulty can also be culturally determined and may result in the child being punished or ostracised, rather than supported, by other family members. Other challenges relating to diagnosis include the inappropriateness of some of the diagnostic tools that might be available in national systems: perhaps because of language differences, or because of the relatively temporary effects of transition, or because tests were standardised in a different context where norms would be other than those in an international school.

Waldron highlights the resource-intensive demands of the provision of support systems for children with learning disabilities, which can cause difficulties for the family if, as in a case he cites, the multinational organisation that is the parental employer refuses to pay the additional fees involved (1991: 71). Difficulties and challenges are also presented to the international school (such as the International School of Brussels, which Waldron commends for establishing a special unit) in relation to resourcing a need which is difficult to predict in terms of numbers and type of need. Aside from giftedness and learning difficulties, the term 'Special Needs' can of course relate to physical disabilities. Tokuhama-Espinosa, for instance, raises a set of interesting issues in relation to special needs in the form of Down's Syndrome, deafness or dyslexia, and how they might relate to the learning of more than one language: an issue potentially of relevance in many international schools (2003b).

A notable, if unusual, example of an international school responding positively to these and other challenges is that of Dover Court Preparatory School, an international school in Singapore which specifically 'opens its doors to all' (Bradley, 2000: 30), with 12 per cent of the student population having 'special needs', including

> physical disabilities, specific learning difficulties, and mild, moderate or severe learning difficulties. Those with special needs could include the hearing impaired, children with Down's Syndrome or autism, students with speech and language disorders, students with epilepsy, gifted or talented students, those with cerebral palsy and those with difficulties related to a variety of syndromes. (Bradley, 2000: 30).

Clearly unusual among international schools, which often do not provide much support other than in the area of English as a Second Language (Haldimann, 1998: 132), the Dover Court commitment to inclusive education arises from a belief that, while many international schools actively welcome diversity in the student population in relation to cultural and linguistic attributes and utilise such diversity to enrich the curriculum, little attention is paid to diversity in ability or achievement. In emphasising the fact that a child with special needs in one area of the curriculum may excel in other areas, Bradley stresses the benefits that inclusive education can bring not only to the international school child with special needs, but also to 'mainstream students' who are presented with additional learning opportunities and encouraged to face challenges rather than to run away from them. As Bradley states,

> Familiarity and associated tolerance reduces fear and rejection and as a result inclusive schools better prepare mainstream children for living in an inclusive society. The system provides a range of learning opportunities, develops emotional intelligence and fosters qualities of tolerance, empathy, respect, generosity, self-confidence, compassion, caring and responsibility – all necessary ingredients for the adult of the twenty-first century. (2000: 37–8)

One last point of relevance to the issue of special needs concerns the nature of specialist expertise available externally to support the school when skills are required beyond those available internally. For administrators in a school in a developed country it might be quite clear where to turn externally for support for a child with serious emotional problems, for instance. For some international schools, however, there may be little if any external support available (either with or without the advantage of a common language to ease communication), thus putting more pressure on the school and, ultimately, on the shoulders of the teachers.

ADULT THIRD CULTURE KIDS

Given all that has been written about the potential psychological effect on children of a globally mobile (whether or not multi-lingual) upbringing, it would be surprising if those effects did not spill over into their adult lives. As yet, little systematic research has been undertaken into the nature of those effects, though anecdotal evidence exists in a variety of sources. Useem et al. coined the term 'Adult Third Culture Kid' (ATCK) to describe those who had experienced such a childhood, whatever the mobility or otherwise of their adulthood (1993a). In a study based on a 24-page questionnaire completed by 680 American ATCKs aged from 25 to 80, Useem et al. highlighted the wide variation in types of adult lives, though with the majority having been academically highly successful (perhaps as might be expected, given the nature of international school students already noted).

Socially, however, the majority reported having felt (sometimes very painfully) differences from their peer group 'back home' in the USA: a phenomenon apparently more problematic in their late teens and twenties and of lessening import with increasing age. Two thirds of those surveyed felt it important to continue to have an international dimension to their lives, even though they preferred to establish their homes in the USA

(Useem, 1993a, b and c; Cottrell, 2002). One of the examples given in the fascinating collection of accounts arising from 13 interviews with ATCKs conducted by Bell (1997) sums up such an ATCK lifestyle: that of Tony, an American who lived in four other countries before entering an American boarding school for the last three years of high school, and at age 37 lives in California, working for a large multinational company that requires him to travel to Europe several times annually.

The 11 in-depth interviews undertaken by Fail (2002) with TCK alumni of the International School of Geneva tell similar stories, though of different experiences. For the most part positive in their reflections on their mobile childhood and subsequent adult experiences, a common theme running through these accounts as well as through those gathered from a study of adult 'Overseas Brats' (children of US military personnel who had been based overseas during their childhood: see Williams and Mariglia, 2002) and another of adult Americans primarily (but not entirely) with military globally mobile childhoods (Ender, 2002b) is a lack of any real sense of 'rootedness' or 'belonging' (Fail, 2002; Fail et al., 2004). While such experiences can foster resilience, tolerance and worldliness, says Ender, they can also contribute to feelings of rootlessness (2002b: 96).

Noted, too, in a number of writings related to the ATCK is the notion of unresolved grief: it is the second greatest challenge faced by TCKs, say Pollock and Van Reken, after the sense of personal identity, even though people frequently ask 'What do TCKs have to grieve about? They've had such exciting lives' (1999: 165). The grief, say Pollock and Van Reken, is often related to what they call 'hidden losses' (loss of their world, when relocating; loss of status in starting anew; loss of lifestyle; loss of possessions; loss of relationships; loss of role models; loss of system identity; loss of the past that wasn't; loss of the past that was): losses for which they may not ever have been able to grieve (1999: 167).

Finn Jordan recounts a phenomenon also noted in a number of other writings, including Van Reken's, of the sense of relief that can be experienced by ATCKs on first encountering a description of the TCK concept, having previously experienced a lack of belonging and of it being 'my fault for being so "out of it"' (Van Reken, in Pollock and Van Reken, 1999: xxiv–xxv). As one respondent in Finn Jordan recounts, 'It was like this enormous thing opened up and I could understand again what was going on ... until then I just thought I was an oddball ... then I discovered there's many other oddballs out there and there's a term for it and that it is really an OK thing' (2002: 226).

Transition From School

The issue of transition has been discussed earlier in terms of TCKs moving between schools, cultures and languages, and in terms of the support

Foreigner Look different Think different	**Hidden Immigrant** Look alike Think different
Adopted Look different Think alike	**Mirror** Look alike Think alike

Figure 5.1 TCKs and their peer groups (Pollock and Van Reken, 1999: 53)

which will ideally be provided by their international school not only on an ongoing basis, but also in relation to arrival and departure. Departure at the end of the schooling process is an experience shared by everyone, TCK or otherwise, and in many contexts various rituals (parties, proms, graduation ceremonies) exist to mark this particular rite of passage. Moving on to college or university is also an experience shared by many and, depending on the national system and the individual student, may also involve moving away from home to live in the college/university community. For the international school student the move will often include moving to another country. For those from the host country of the international school for whom an international school education was seen as a means of facilitating entry to an English-medium university, such moves may well be to a country never previously visited – with all the challenges such a move presents. For many others – the TCKs – moving on to university could well involve returning to the home country and a process of 're-entry'. Similar in some respects to the experience of a child re-entering their home country at an earlier stage (and with all the challenges that scenario presents), returning to university is different in that the student is not accompanied by his/her closest family members, who may still be based in another part of the world.

The matrix generated by Pollock and Van Reken to categorise the various relationships between TCKs and those peers in their surrounding (home or host) culture is helpful to consider here, as shown in Figure 5.1.

Those TCKs who have spent relatively short periods of time away from their home country and/or had 'overseas' experiences that were relatively encapsulated (based on a British compound abroad, perhaps) may fall into the 'mirror' category in this matrix and have transition experiences similar to those of their peers who have never left the home country. New undergraduates in the 'Foreigner' category may be obviously 'different', and in the case of many universities particular provision will be made for supporting them as they adjust to their new lives. Those who have spent longer, perhaps more formative, periods away from their 'home country', however, may well fall into the 'hidden immigrant' category, where 'they appear like those around them, but internally [they] view life through a lens that is as different from the dominant culture as any obvious foreigner. People around them, however, presume they are the same as themselves inside, since they appear to be the same outside' (Pollock and Van Reken, 1999: 54).

The example given by Deveney of her British TCK daughter's concerns on anticipating return to a UK university after schooling entirely in the Middle East and Southeast Asia sums up the unease undoubtedly felt by many such students and their parents: 'How will I fit in with other English people at university when I've never been part of their culture? Will I be able to make friends? Will everyone think I'm weird because I don't know what they know?' (2004: 2). After spending so many years negotiating different cultural contexts away from her own country, Deveney notes that her daughter's first task 'back home' will be to 'successfully negotiate the obstacle course presented by her own national culture' (2004: 3).

More generally (whether or not university is part of the re-entry picture), the re-entry process can be stressful because of differences in skills and experiences from those of the peer group (use of slang and idiom, familiarity with popular television programmes, films and music, ownership of/familiarity with the latest telephone, music and computer technology, and so on). Some returners become frustrated and angry with their 'home' peer group, while others withdraw or despair (Pollock and Van Reken, 1999: 250–1). Those whose international education has been particularly ideologically-focused (such as those who have attended United World Colleges, for instance), can sometimes find it difficult to adjust to the harsher realities of the wider world and to know how to respond to them: should they be tolerant or critical, for instance, of the intolerance they find around them?

Other transition processes that can be particularly challenging are those arising when the cultural gap between 'home' and international school environments is particularly marked. How does a child who grew up in the mountains of Lesotho before winning a scholarship to an international school re-adjust to his/her home environment, if at all? Can a girl brought up in a society where women have relatively few rights, before moving to an international school where far more liberal views on women's rights were encouraged, ever hope to re-enter successfully her home culture? In the case of these two examples, and others like them, it could be that re-entry will never be entirely successful and that the initial departure from the home context will turn out to have been more permanent than was envisaged at the time.

As increasing numbers of families adopt a globally mobile lifestyle, it is clear that greater understanding is needed not only of how their children can best be supported during their school years, but also of the longer-term effects of such a lifestyle as those children move into adulthood.

CHAPTER 6

Teachers

There is no shortage of literature available from many different national contexts about the multiple roles for which the teacher has responsibility and the factors that affect these roles. This chapter will focus on just some of these roles as they affect particularly the context of international schools, beginning with the individuals who find themselves as 'international school teachers'. Issues relating to those whose school role is principally administrative/managerial will be considered in Chapter 7.

INTERNATIONAL SCHOOL TEACHERS: WHO ARE THEY?

Given the diversity of schools operating under the 'international school' umbrella (see Chapter 2), it would be surprising were it not the case that the teaching population in such schools is also varied. Depending on a range of factors including, inter alia, national and local government requirements, work permits and school employment policies (Garton, 2002: 147), not to mention the formal curriculum and the national affiliation – if any – of the school, the composition of the teaching staff in international schools can vary quite markedly. Cambridge suggests that in many international schools a 'tripartite' organisational structure has grown up 'consisting of a long-term administrative core ..., a fringe of relatively highly paid professional expatriates ... on shorter-term contracts, and local staff hired at lower rates of remuneration who are likely to be longer term' (2002b: 159), drawing an analogy with the 'shamrock organisation' proposed by Handy (1991). A similar set of groupings is suggested by Garton as the categorisation of teaching staff in many international schools: host-country nationals, 'local hire' expatriates and 'overseas hire' expatriates (2000: 87).

In referring to those in the last of Garton's three categories, Sutcliffe suggests that

> Few teachers in international schools are from countries in which teachers are civil servants. The only regular exceptions are teachers in national schools abroad (the French Overseas lycées, the German Auslandsschulen), whose international aspects are secondary to the national emphasis, and the schools of the European Community. The difficulties are the lack of freedom to move and respond to openings as they occur, the national career and pension structures, and the general bureaucracy. Most teachers on the international circuit are therefore either British or American. (1991: 175)

Anecdotally, it would certainly seem to be true fifteen years on that many expatriate teachers in international schools are from the UK or the USA which, given the high proportion of British and American-type international schools, may not be surprising. Canterford, in a (2003) study of nationalities of teaching staff in international schools, highlighted the difficulty of finding relevant statistical data to prove or disprove such impressions: of three major agencies recruiting such teachers, for instance, only one (International Schools Services (ISS)) routinely published such data, in their annual Directory, whilst neither the European Council of International Schools (ECIS), nor Search Associates, kept such data centrally. Nevertheless, given the very high proportion of international schools that offer English as the medium of instruction (Richards, 1998: 175), Peterson's point that 'one would expect ... a high proportion of the teachers in international schools to come from English-speaking countries' (1987: 37) makes eminent sense.

Issues relating to the different types of basis on which international school teaching staff are hired will be discussed in more detail below in the context of recruitment. Here we will focus on the nature of the individuals who teach in international schools and how they came to choose that job: for the purposes of this discussion, the terminology of Garton's three part categorisation will be used. Host country national teachers may be attracted to international school employment by conditions of service that are (in developing countries at least) better than would be available in the national system. While such employment may be attractive in the short term, however, it may become a problem in the longer term for both teacher and school if it means that the teacher then has 'nowhere to go' career-wise, since moving back into the national system is an unattractive option. Local-hire expatriates, meanwhile, will often include 'trailing spouses' (referred to in Chapter 3), who have 'spouses or partners who work for embassies, aid agencies or multinational companies in that particular country' (Garton, 2000: 88) or who, perhaps following marriage to a local national, are 'host country nationals or residents of the country in question' (Garton, 2000: 88). The 'overseas hire' teachers, on the other hand, are generally those who have moved to the country in question specifically for the purpose of taking up the teaching position at that particular international school. They may be young and with no commitments, moving away from home for the first time, or they may have had previous international teaching positions and be effectively making a career of international teaching. They would normally have at least some experience of teaching 'back home' before taking up an overseas post: indeed at least one teacher placement service, that operated by the Council of International Schools (CIS), requires at least two years recent full-time experience of teaching through the medium of English (CIS, 2006) before registration will be accepted.

What prompts an individual to dip a toe into the water of international school teaching for the first time? Perhaps they are among the growing number of adults who had globally mobile childhoods in international schools and seek to recreate that type of lifestyle (Cottrell, 2002). Perhaps they simply want to see the world, while unattached and with no commitments, with no thought as to what might happen later in life; perhaps they have every intention of seeing the world for two or three years (maybe with a partner in a similar situation) before returning to 'settle down' in the national system back home. There has certainly been more than one international school teacher whose main impetus for moving was the relentless greyness of a British winter in a challenging school, compared with the prospect of life in a warm climate with motivated students and ocean views.

There will have also undoubtedly been more than one teacher whose move has been prompted by problems – professional or personal – back home, for whom the prospect of a fresh start with new friends and colleagues seems enticing. In that sense the international school sector has the potential to be the French Foreign Legion of the education world. Which is not to say, of course, that many teachers have not embarked upon an international school career without a clear long-term plan and been highly successful. As always when discussing international schools, it is impossible to generalise.

Hardman's research led to a useful categorisation of overseas teachers applying for posts in international schools as follows:

- childless career professionals;
- mavericks ('free and independent spirits');
- career professionals with families;

and among the more senior members of the teaching staff:

- senior career professionals;
- senior mavericks;

- senior 'Penelopes' ('faithful to the country they had adopted', based on the character of Ulysses' wife in Homer's *Odyssey* who remained faithful to her husband during his twenty years of absence). (Hardman, 2001: 132–3)

Anyone familiar with the world of international schools will no doubt recognise in these categorisations colleagues and ex-colleagues who had a myriad of different reasons for finding themselves in a particular school at a particular time, and for staying there for a short, medium or long period. The school's location cannot be overlooked as a contributing factor, of course, with some environments proving more conducive to long-term residence than others; nor can the fact that a travelling teacher may enter into a long-term relationship with a local resident and thus form a stronger bond with the host country than would otherwise have been the case. All these factors, and many more, are influential in determining the make-up of the teaching staff in an international school, and it is within this context that those responsible for recruitment, the area to be considered next, have to operate.

RECRUITMENT

Blaney, an experienced head at the United Nations International School (UNIS), New York, argued in the context of international schools that 'Staff should be carefully recruited so as to represent, without an unreasonable financial burden being placed upon the schools, the major cultural areas of the world and as many nationalities as feasible' (1991: 203). Earlier, Terwilliger had suggested that the teaching faculty should include those who 'have themselves experienced a period of cultural adaptation' since they 'will be better able to counsel those new students who have difficulty adjusting to the social and cultural atmosphere of their new school' (1972: 360). As will be seen below, recruiting what might seem to be an ideal balance of national, cultural and linguistic backgrounds of teaching staff is fraught with difficulties and challenges.

Some Constraints

Garton points out that the aim of having a multicultural mix of teaching staff 'can be significantly affected by the policies of the government in which the school is located, as regards both work permit requirements and the potential personal taxation liabilities for such employees' (2002: 151). Some international schools, for instance, face quite severe restrictions on the number of non-nationals who may be appointed or the length of time they may remain in the country. Equally challenging, and perhaps more difficult to deal with for a head or school board, is the pressure which may be put upon English-medium international schools to recruit native English speakers as teachers. As Garton points out, 'it is often the case that a number of parents would "prefer" their child to be taught by a native-English-speaking "Western trained" overseas-hire expatriate, for reasons that may be founded rather more on prejudice than on a well-informed evaluation' (2000: 87).

The existence of such 'customer discrimination', as it is described by Canterford (2003: 54), is reinforced in the study of parents' views undertaken by MacKenzie et al. which also summarised the dilemma faced by various heads and boards, in a quote from one parent who on the one hand supported strongly the suggestion that an international school should have 'a policy of recruiting teachers from a diversity of religious, ethnic, racial and linguistic backgrounds' while on the other hand proposing that 'the goal would be to have English native speakers from as many countries as possible' (2001: 60). Indeed one study undertaken by Walsh in an international school suggested that parents would accept non-Western trained, non-native English speaking local teachers only if they were to teach 'local' subjects such as 'local' languages (1999). Interesting in relation to this finding is that it was not only expatriate parents who held this view, but also local nationals.

Perhaps such parental pressure arises from prejudice, as suggested by Garton. Undoubtedly it is linked, as proposed by Canterford (2003: 56), to Matthews' point regarding the nature of the often 'affluent high achieving' parents whose children attend international schools and the fact that such a high proportion of international school students go on to study at university (approximately 90 per cent at that time, according to Matthews), with many of those aspiring to university-level study in English medium locations such as the USA (1988: 47). Either way, there may often be a tension between the more ideologically-focused wish of at least some teachers and administrators to have as culturally diverse a teaching staff as possible (notwithstanding the challenges this may bring in terms of differences in practice and expectations) and the more pragmatically-focused desire of many parents.

Also a constraint in recruitment, and aside from any attributes of the individual applicant, can be the issue of whether they are single, married or in a long-term relationship with a teaching or non-teaching spouse, and whether they have children of school age. The relevance of such issues in recruitment will depend in part on whether accommodation is provided by the school and, if so, on the nature of that accommodation: if the outgoing teachers were all single and living in single staff accommodation it may not be possible to appoint as replacement for one of them a married person with two young children, however suitable they would be for the post, because the only accommodation available is not appropriate. It may also be impossible for an international school to appoint an openly gay or lesbian couple in a country where homosexuality is illegal. And perhaps more widespread as an issue is that of expatriate heterosexual couples both wishing to teach in a context where the international school is the only realistic employer. In such a situation the school may be faced with having to appoint both or neither, and real complications can occur when contracts are due for renewal and the school wishes to renew one contract but not the other.

The Recruitment Process

To anyone used to recruiting in a national system where jobs are advertised, applications are submitted, shortlisting and interviews follow and eventually a post is offered to the successful candidate, the recruitment processes followed by many international schools can at first seem unusual, if not bizarre. One challenge faced by such a school is deciding where to advertise: in a national context there may be an obvious publication, while in an international context the very decision as to whether to advertise in an Australian, American or Canadian newspaper, for instance, pre-determines to some extent the cultural, national and linguistic background of successful applicants. Some national newspapers have a wide international readership and regularly have pages of international school advertisements competing for attention. A recent advertisement for a goalkeeper for the staff football team (with the ability to teach secondary mathematics) stood out in such a list. And there are, of course, publications produced for the international school sector itself: *The International Educator* (TIE) and *Newslinks* (produced by ISS) are just two examples, but are also illustrations of the fact that such publications invariably have a particular national affiliation (in these two cases, the USA). Organisations such as CIS allow a school to advertise year round vacancies on the website, as do some regional networks of international schools.

Increasingly sophisticated websites generated by many international schools over recent years also have a part to play, both in highlighting job vacancies and in providing information about the school: not least importantly, as Garton points out, 'so that inappropriate candidates have a chance to filter themselves out of the process' (2000: 89). Garton actually provides a helpful overview of what he perceives to be the three main phases of recruitment for international schools: the preparation and advertising phase, the interviewing and contract-offering phase, and the follow-up and settling in or orientation phase. The latter, which Garton argues 'should be regarded as an important aspect of the overall recruitment process' (2000: 89–90), will be discussed below. Just deciding where to advertise, however, as noted above, can be challenging and one experienced recruiter, Peter Gummer (Director of Gabbitas Educational Consultants, writing in Garton, 2000: 89), points out that

> We need constant new blood in the international sector, so schools should be trying to access as wide a range of potential candidates as possible, rather than dipping only into the pool of existing international staff. This means the press, the web, and probably several agencies, as well as any recruitment fairs you may choose to attend.

Perhaps should be added to this list 'word of mouth', since anecdotal evidence suggests that within the network of international schools worldwide there is an effective 'bush telegraph' which communicates a myriad of information relating to international school teachers' experience, including which are the good and not-so-good schools to work in, which teachers are likely to be moving on at the end of the year, and so on. In fact at least one prestigious international school comes to mind which eschews recruitment fairs and agencies, and concentrates almost entirely on selectively placed and rather discreet advertisements, a good website and word of mouth, hoping to attract teachers who actively wish to work at that particular school rather than those who are interested in international schools teaching more generally.

In order to recruit non-overseas hire teachers, international schools will generally have 'local' systems in place in which word of mouth may play a part, in terms of availability of 'local hire' trailing spouses known within the expatriate community. For overseas hire recruitment, some international schools make use of telephone interviews and/or videoconferencing as at least part of the selection process. Many make use of agencies, as Garton points out, as a means of filtering out from the large numbers of applicants and enquiries a smaller number of potential appointees (2000: 90). Well-known agencies include Gabbitas, Search Associates, ISS and CIS. CIS is one example of an agency which organises much of its recruitment through a number of recruitment fairs, 'the largest of which, the London fair in February, attracts around 150 schools and 1000 teachers' (Canterford, 2003: 50). The advantages of such a fair are summarised by McKay as including the fact that 'an international school Head can screen and select from hundreds of candidates, all of whom have a minimum of two years previous teaching experience in the subject areas they are applying for, current teaching certification and three highly supportive references' (1999, in Garton, 2000: 91).

Undoubtedly such recruitment fairs can prove advantageous to both recruiter and applicant (particularly when a good deal of preparatory work has been completed in advance), although the spectacle of a large hotel full of applicants being interviewed in the recruiters' own bedrooms – since the sheer scale makes the provision of any other form of private space impossible – can seem strange to the recruitment fair novice, as can the sight of applicants being interviewed by recruiters from a number of different schools in succession before deciding on offers from a range of locations. Equally strange to those who have not previously witnessed such a scene can be the difficulties faced by recruiters who interview a strong candidate early in the proceedings, in deciding whether to risk waiting until all applicants have been interviewed before making an offer, with the possibility that the strong candidate will accept a post with another recruiter at the same fair later in the same day. It is perhaps not surprising, therefore, that Garton refers to interviewing and contract-offering as 'the most stressful and critical phase' (2000: 90) of recruitment.

No less strange – to anyone more used to a national recruitment process whereby applicants for even relatively junior teaching positions will generally be interviewed by a panel including at least the head, possibly a head of department and a governor, and may be observed teaching as part of the interview process – is the fact that in many such cases the interviews will be conducted on behalf of the recruiting school by the head or principal alone. For pragmatic reasons it is understandable that only one person should travel across the world to participate in recruitment fairs (or indeed to interview applicants in other contexts, where fairs are not used). Whether it is reasonable to expect one individual, however senior and experienced in such matters, to make such important decisions without the opportunity to discuss with colleagues in advance the relative strengths of various applicants, bearing in mind that the director of a large school may, for instance, be secondary trained but recruiting primary teachers (or vice versa) is debatable (J. Lewis, 1993: 171). When it is remembered that decisions being made will often involve a new recruit moving to a country never previously visited, possibly with spouse and children in tow, it is perhaps surprising that as many appointments made under such circumstances are as successful as they appear to be.

Recruitment fairs and use of agencies generally relate, of course, to the recruitment of expatriate teachers from outside the country in which the school is based. As has already been noted, in addition to the 'overseas hire' expatriates within the teaching staff of an international school are often the 'local hire' expatriates and host-country nationals, which raises the issue of the different bases on which appointments are made within the international school context.

CONTRACTUAL CONDITIONS

As ever, it is impossible to generalise about the situation with respect to international school contracts. The tripartite situation described above by Cambridge and Garton, for instance, tends to apply in developing countries, whereas in some other countries there is little if any discrimination in salaries between different 'types' of employee, and salaries for all are lower than they would be in the national system (and may be lower than expatriate employees would be paid 'back home'). Host-country nationals may thus not be motivated to teach in an international school, unlike the situation in, say, an African country where host-country national teachers would find an international school teaching post in their own country better remunerated than teaching within the national system, even though the salary scale is somewhat lower than the scale for expatriates teaching in the same school.

At the other end of the salary spectrum in such schools are the 'overseas hire' expatriates who move to that country in order to teach in that particular international school: they may well have had previous experience of teaching in international schools elsewhere or (which may be important in nationally-affiliated international schools) have 'recent and relevant' experience of teaching in that national system. Alternatively, they may have experience of teaching particular international programmes such as those of the International Baccalaureate or IGCSE. Their experience, their 'international' qualifications (which may be considered more prestigious than those awarded locally) and possibly, as noted earlier, their fluency in English are all factors contributing to what is often a relatively generous 'package' of salary and other benefits (such as health insurance, flights 'home', professional development, waiving of school fees for offspring, and accommodation), not all of which will necessarily be available to the host-country national.

And somewhere in between may be the 'local hire' teachers, the expatriates who are not recruited from outside the country to take up the post. Often a trailing spouse of an expatriate, or possibly the spouse of a local national, these teachers may have all the qualifications and experience of those appointed on 'overseas hire' contracts. Market forces, however, dictate that as 'captive' recruits they need not receive the same package of salary and benefits as their overseas-recruited colleagues. In such a situation tensions can and do arise between colleagues as a result of such a structure, which are highlighted when, for instance, a local hire or host-country head of department is paid less than an overseas hire classroom teacher in his/her department. Again, the tension between the ideal situation and the pragmatic (of market forces, balancing books, parental demands) comes to the fore. And such situations can be complex in terms of the local context as in the case, for instance, of one prestigious school which had among its host-country national teachers the wife of the prime minister.

It is an unfortunate by-product of the apparent hierarchy of staff arising from the different contracts in such situations, and thus the implicit relative value of their contribution, that host-country nationals may appear to be not as valued as their colleagues. Richards, in highlighting a passage from the promotional material of a major international school which claimed that 'Over 70 teachers ... share (a) broad international experience, coming from such countries as Australia, Canada, France, Germany, Great Britain, Holland, Ireland, New Zealand and the United States', asks the question 'Can we infer from the above that no teachers are employed (or employable?) from so-called less developed regions of the world? Or merely that advertising such teachers would not be a positive selling point for the school?' (1998: 174). Such issues need to be handled with sensitivity and wisdom, as the head and board tread a fine line between respecting the contribution of all colleagues, supporting the school's mission (if it has such a mission) of promoting respect for all regardless of cultural, national or linguistic background, and providing appropriate role models for a multicultural student population, but at the same time responding to the (perhaps sometimes unpalatable) wishes of the parents whose fees finance the running of the school.

INDUCTION

Any teacher in a national system who moves from one school to another within that system could reasonably expect some form of induction, or orientation (a word often used in American literature, while 'induction' tends to be used in the British context) in at least the early stages of a new appointment. Indeed, many schools would have an expectation that such a programme is necessary if the new recruit is to achieve his/her potential in the shortest possible time. If this is true for a teacher moving between two similar schools, offering the same national curriculum with children from similar cultural backgrounds, how much more necessary is a good induction programme in an international school where the new recruit may be new not only to the school, but also to the cultural mix of students, the curriculum offered, the country in which the school is located, and the first language of that country? With the best will in the world on all sides, and however thorough the recruitment process, the first experience of teaching in an international school may be, as J. Lewis points out, 'completely overshadowed by the inability to settle into both the new school and the new culture' (1993: abstract), involving not only adjustment to a new country but also possibly 'to a very different style of management, curriculum and parental involvement' (1993: 2).

Most schools in national systems would be surprised to think of their responsibilities for induction of new teachers as extending beyond the immediately school- or department-specific. International schools, however, may find that a consequence of not taking on such extended responsibilities is that new recruits fail to settle or to achieve their potential as teachers, not because of difficulties arising within the school context but because of an inability to settle into life in the new environment. Even schools with a national affiliation, while perhaps providing a more familiar environment to new recruits from that context than would some other types of international school, will face such a challenge. Many international school teachers and administrators will have heard stories, or had first-hand experience, of new recruits who have broken contract and taken the first flight home after only a few days in the new school. From a purely pragmatic viewpoint, therefore, it is incumbent upon the international school to do everything it can, after what may have been a lengthy and expensive recruitment process, to protect its investment.

Storti, writing in the context of business organisations, points out the high costs to an organisation of what is referred to as 'assignment failure', including the costs not only of recruitment but also of training, moving, 'and all the costs associated with lost opportunities, damaged relationships, low morale, reduced productivity, and perhaps even damage to the ... organisation's reputation in the country or region' (2001: xvi–xvii). The costs of failure for the individual, meanwhile, may include 'financial, professional and emotional costs; and costs to one's own career prospects, to one's self-esteem, and to one's marriage and family' (2001: xvi–xvii). The fact that the three leading causes of 'assignment failure' cited in Storti are partner dissatisfaction, family concerns, and the inability to adapt (2001: xvi) highlights the additional level of challenge placed on a recruiting head, and on the recruit himself/herself, when he/she is accompanied by spouse/partner and family.

The question of how best to support new recruits in a new cultural environment is by no means an easy one to answer, and is shared by multinational commercial organisations. The fact that, as Brein and David point out, the extent to which an individual is able to assimilate into a foreign context depends to a large degree upon 'the sojourner's relationship with himself' (sic) (1971: 215) means that it is impossible to devise a 'one size fits all' induction programme which will cater for the needs of every new member of staff. And one hopes, of course, that the careful preparation and planning put in by a school to the advertising and recruitment process will mean that new recruits are as well prepared as they might be prior to arrival for differences in climate, language, religious practices and other non-negotiables. The new appointee will also, it is hoped, have done his/her homework before setting off. There is little a school can offer by way of induction to a teacher who cannot bear heat and humidity but has accepted a post in Singapore, while the anecdote of a teacher who accepted a post in the Falkland Islands (prior to the 1982 Argentina–UK war, admittedly) in the belief that she would be living somewhere off the north coast of Scotland, highlights the risks of a less than thorough approach to job-hunting.

Storti makes a helpful distinction between what he describes as 'country shock' (relating to differences in the attributes of a country, such as climate) and 'culture shock' (2001: 3–25) (relating to differences in culture, or 'the shared way of life of a group of people': see Berry et al., 1992). It is perhaps in relation to the latter that the school can be most supportive following a teacher's appointment. Much has been written about the concept of 'culture shock', a term initially developed in the 1950s and commonly represented in the U-curve three stage model (Lysgaard, 1955; Sewell and Davidson, 1956) of initial enthusiasm, disenchantment and recovery. Gullahorn and Gullahorn's (1963 and 1966) extension of the model into the W-curve, adding a period of re-entry crisis followed by final re-adjustment, and a further extended adjustment cycle such as that shown in Fennes and Hapgood (1997: 31) have also attempted to model the stages which many, if not all, individuals experience when moving into a new and unfamiliar cultural context (See Chapter 5).

What may be most important to the teacher arriving for the first time at an international school situated in a new cultural context is to understand that the experience of some form of culture shock is entirely normal, that he/she is not the only person in the world who goes through phases of depression, homesickness and finding it difficult to cope, and that for most people the dip of the 'U' is followed by the rise to 'recovery'. In this sense publications such as that produced by Langford et al. (2002) provide invaluable forms of support. Analyses such as that outlined by Joslin of some of the key attributes desirable in those teaching in an international school are also helpful, summarised in the acronym MEASURE UP, which incorporates the following: mental flexibility to reframe fields of reference; ethnorelativist view of the world; awareness of one's own cultural heritage; sensitivity to different cultures; understanding of the nature of the range of international schools; respect for other cultures (not just tolerance); emotional balance; understanding of education in an international context, and professional/technical expertise (2002: 52–3).

Stirzaker's (2004) review of literature relating to induction in international schools makes the point that the majority of, if not all, texts relating to induction in the context of education refer exclusively to the induction of what might be referred to as 'beginner teachers'. While some of the problems faced by a relocated experienced teacher may be similar to those of a beginner teacher, however (new school structure, new ways of doing things, new colleagues and students), 'a very common cause of stress to experienced but relocated teachers ... is feeling unexpectedly "de-skilled" in a new school because an unfamiliar set of pupils react to them differently' (Stirzaker, 2004: 32). Such a situation is described by Deveney as happening when, following a move to a different cultural context, some teachers may find that 'lessons that worked before no longer seem effective; letters sent home to parents appear to be ignored, and seemingly simple requests to local administration staff are met with a smile but no action' (2005: 155).

Such an experience might not only arise in a new country or cultural context, of course, but could also arise as a result of a move within a country. Gamwell, for instance, explains in the context of Papua New Guinea, where 'citizen teachers' are recruited from the state schools to International Education Agency (IEA) schools – independent schools catering for expatriate families – that 'Despite the fact that most of the citizen teachers being recruited are experienced in the state sector, there is still a tremendous amount that needs to be done to smooth the transition to their new environment if they are to settle well and become effective members of staff' (1999: vi).

The benefits of an induction programme are not simply related, Stirzaker argues, to the provision of information which might anyway have been assimilated by the individual in due course; without such a programme the information might be assimilated 'slowly and probably with omissions (Seyfarth, 1991: 162), which can lead to great frustration and errors', whereas 'with a carefully planned and well executed orientation programme the process can be faster, more coherent and, as Skeats (1991: 9) suggests, offer other positive benefits to the organisation such as improved "goodwill, morale and work efficiency among both new and established staff members"' (Stirzaker, 2004: 34).

The case for having an induction programme of some kind in international schools would seem to be clear, though its form will vary according to the country in which a school is situated (and how 'alien' its culture and language are likely to be to expatriate teachers), the nature of the local environment, the type of school, make-up of the student population, and so on. Such variations notwithstanding, there would appear to be several key features likely to be common to any effective form of teacher induction in an international school, as follows:

1 The induction phase should be seen as an integral part of the recruitment process, with newly appointed teachers provided with accurate and comprehensive information at the point of accepting the post (Hardman, 2001: 131; Stirzaker, 2004: 41).
2 Induction should be recognised as a process that not only begins prior to arrival but also continues beyond 'the often customary three day

orientation period' (J. Lewis, 1993: 172) as part of ongoing professional development (Gamwell, 1999: 72).

3 It is important to recognise that a 'one size fits all' approach to induction (that runs the risk of being 'boring to old-timers and confusing to beginners': Seyfarth, 1991: 163) is less likely to be effective for all new teachers than one that acknowledges their differences in professional experience, cultural background and personal situation, as well as being sensitive to the fact that the same 'problem' can affect different people in quite different ways.

4 Similarly, what is an effective induction programme in one international school may be less effective in a school elsewhere with a different make-up of staff and students. Lewis categorised the adjustment problems facing expatriate teachers embarking for the first time on an international school post as falling into three broad categories: cultural, professional and personal, and it would seem that the induction programme should include support in relation to all three in order to facilitate the process of settling into the new environment (1993: 124). Hardman, among others, gives suggestions as to what might be included in such a programme (2001: 134), but clearly it is for the individual school to decide on the detail and the balance in relation to their own particular circumstances.

5 The school's induction programme should, ideally, be a whole-school project which draws on expertise from a wide range of sources including teachers, other staff, administrators and parents. While several authors stress the importance of responsibility for the induction programme resting with a relatively senior individual within the school (to give it status), the benefits to a school of shared ownership of such a programme – Meighan's argument that 'providing induction for new staff can have a positive effect on present staff' (1995: 27) – are also widely stated.

6 The process of settling in for the new teacher, and of induction for the school, can be greatly facilitated by the identification of a 'mentor', 'supportive facilitator' (Wilkin, 1992: 56), or more informal 'buddy', who can provide a certain amount of emotional and personal support in addition to the more formal aspects of the induction programme. Whereas in a national context a buddy system may be entirely work-related, in the context of an international school it is likely that support provided will extend into other aspects of the new teacher's life. It goes without saying that the buddy should be carefully selected: for their interpersonal skills, knowledge and understanding of the context, positive perspective on that context, and their ability to empathise (which may be more likely to be found in relatively recently-appointed colleagues than in those for whom the experience of arriving is a dim and distant memory).

TEACHER APPRAISAL

No less important than recruiting the right teachers at the outset and providing suitable induction for them is ensuring that these colleagues continue as effective contributors to the school's mission during their time in post. One important dimension of what might be referred to as 'quality assurance' is teacher appraisal. It needs to be acknowledged in any discussion of teacher appraisal that, as Dimmock and Walker point out, 'Teacher appraisal is a contentious and divisive issue regardless of the context within which it operates' (2005: 143). Highlighting the fact that debate and publications about appraisal have largely emanated from the English-speaking 'Western' world, they point out how little note has been taken of the place of societal culture in appraisal developments to date. Many international schools operate appraisal systems that are 'borrowed' from a particular national (invariably 'Western') context and are thus derived from a series of culturally-based assumptions that may be alien to at least some members of the teaching staff. Dimmock and Walker suggest that 'It is not unusual for educators around the globe to openly and/or covertly resist involvement in appraisal schemes for a multitude of reasons, ranging from a fear of negative information becoming public to a complete lack of trust in the appraiser or supervisor' (2005: 143). If this is true in national contexts, how much more potential is there for division and resistance in an international school with a multicultural teaching staff, who bring with them a range of previous experiences and assumptions about what lies behind the process?

Many of the issues that might surface in an international school as a result of such cultural differences will be familiar to those who have introduced appraisal systems in different national contexts. Some such issues are discussed in a collection of case studies from a number of countries edited by Middlewood and Cardno (2001) which highlight how differences in culture can lead to areas of contention. Dimmock and Walker's account of the introduction of an appraisal system in Hong Kong in the 1990s argues that, while there are universally acceptable principles underpinning any appraisal system (all teachers should be accountable for what they do and need feedback to help them to perform well in the classroom; schools need a means of determining which teachers should be promoted or have their contracts renewed), such principles tend to become less straightforward as cultural differences are highlighted during the implementation stage, and manifest themselves in issues such as 'whether the scheme focuses on individuals or groups of teachers; who should be the appraisers; the relationships necessary for appraisal to be successful; the skills required by appraisers; or the need for open communication' (Dimmock and Walker, 2005: 145).

It is undoubtedly the case that, while appraisal is a difficult and contentious issue in some international schools (as in some national schools), there are other international schools in which it has been made to work well. Dimmock and Walker point out that 'the key to a culturally sensitive teacher appraisal system may involve a model that separates judgemental and developmental purposes' (2005: 158). Since these purposes are in some senses quite distinct, it could be that they should be handled in different ways in different cultural contexts in order 'to meet different needs in different ways while taking full account of culture', since 'the continued penetration of Anglo-American teacher appraisal policies and practices into different cultural contexts may well result in failed attempts at implementation' (Dimmock and Walker, 2005: 158).

Indeed, Matthews suggests in relation to appraisal in international schools that, while most have a system in place, 'few have been able to spend the time to develop a fully effective process, with the result that appraisal in international schools is a mélange of good ideas which are all too rarely consolidated into an effective structure' (2001a: 3). In going on to describe an appraisal model he has developed specifically for international schools, Matthews argues (2006: 13–14) that the need for an effective appraisal system is highlighted as a result of certain characteristics shared by many such schools, as follows:

- high teacher turnover (which leads to schools facing a 'constant challenge in establishing and maintaining a consistent educational identity': 13);
- diverse professional backgrounds (which means that an appraisal system is needed in order to 'ensure that the disparate approaches of individual teachers are blended into a coherent and consistent school educational philosophy': 13);
- lack of systemic 'norms' (since international schools do not have their educational programmes defined by, for example, national requirements their choices require 'continual re-affirmation or modification': 13); and
- professional isolation (international school teachers may feel out of touch with the 'mainstream of educational thought', and an effective appraisal system can help with identifying appropriate areas of professional development).

Matthews' model is based on similar principles to those of the accreditation process which many international schools undergo (see Chapter 10) and he argues that the familiarity of many international school teachers with accreditation systems of this type will give the model credibility. It is encouraging to see an appraisal model developed specifically for international schools and it is to be hoped that the model in question, by being tailored for this culturally diverse community, will be successful in overcoming some of the challenges identified above and highlighted particularly by Dimmock and Walker.

One other issue, raised by Matthews and arguably also of relevance in contexts other than that of international schools, is that of who should actually undertake the appraisal of teachers. In many situations it appears to be taken as given that the appraiser should be one of the school's senior administrators but, as Matthews points out, few administrators have had any training in the appraisal process (2006: 25). If not administrators, though, then who? Again referring to the recognised model of external accreditation (conducted by visiting teams of practising teachers), Matthews proposes that schools consider appointing a panel of appraisers, 'selected from volunteers for their experience and aptitude, who could receive specific training' and 'implement the appraisal system from a truly collegial perspective', having been given appropriate release from teaching to make time available (2006: 25). Certainly a novel idea, it will be interesting to see how such systems work in practice when sufficient time has elapsed to allow the model to be properly evaluated.

MOVING ON AND RETURNING HOME

While teachers or others might expect to experience some form of culture shock when moving to a new and unfamiliar context, it seems still to be the case that many are unprepared for what might be termed the 'reverse culture shock' potentially to be experienced if and when they return to their home country. The 'if' is important here, because not all international school teachers do actually 'go home'. Some, in fact, never leave the location of their first international school posting: whether because they meet and marry a local national and effectively make their new location 'home', or because the location is so attractive that it is practically impossible to envisage moving elsewhere. International schools in locations such as Geneva and Vienna, for instance, are well known for having had many expatriate teaching staff whose stay has been far longer than the two to three years common to many other international schools worldwide. Others do move on, but to posts within the international school world, effectively becoming career international school teachers with no intention whatsoever of returning home before retirement (if, indeed, then). Reasons for such a choice of long-term career may vary, but are likely to include some or all of the following:

- a deeply-held philosophical commitment to a particular curriculum which may not be as available 'back home';
- a belief that the skills and experience developed in international schools (such as working with classes of children from many different cultural and linguistic backgrounds) are best capitalised upon by continuing to work within that context;
- a concern that moving out of the international school world to return to a national system will lead to a loss of status and drop in quality of life for the individual and his/her family.

The latter point will apply to differing extents in different contexts, depending on the location of the international school and the country which is 'home'. Someone who has worked in Thailand, for instance, may be used to the perception in Thai culture, according to Mulder (2000), of the teacher as a 'representative of moral goodness who bestows the gift of knowledge on his/her pupils ... creating a moral debt [which] is repaid by students being respectful and behaving appropriately' (in Deveney, 2005: 156). And it is undoubtedly the case that many international school teachers, while committed, hard-working and professional in every sense, enjoy a lifestyle that they could not hope to emulate 'back home'. As a member of the expatriate community, the lifestyle and status of a teacher may be far removed from that of the semi-detached suburbia more familiar to many teachers, however senior or experienced, in a national context.

For those who make a career in the international school world, one decision looming on the horizon from mid-career onwards (if it has not been made much earlier) is where to settle after retirement. To someone who has lived in one country for many years and effectively made a home there, it may be obvious that that is where they will stay (local residence laws permitting). For those whose career has been more varied it may be less obvious, with a choice between 'staying away' or 'going home'. The more far-sighted may have invested in property in the home country or elsewhere, with a view to settling there on retirement. Others may not have that choice, with increases in property prices since they left ruling out that possibility. The lack of an adequate pension plan throughout their career, since paying into such a plan is not as automatic for international school teachers as it would be for teachers in many national systems, may also be an issue.

Whether returning 'home' mid-career or on retirement, 'reverse culture shock' can be as hard-hitting as it is unexpected for those who are not prepared – and even, perhaps, for some who are. Storti discusses at length a range of issues affecting returners, including the various re-entry stages that it is argued are experienced, and summarises the feelings of those in this position:

> Upon re-entry ... you are something of a cultural hybrid, viewing and responding to the world around you from the perspective of two different

> realities, partaking of each but not fully belonging to either. … You have become … a marginal person, functioning more – and better – at the edges of your society rather than at the center, more likely to be an observer of, rather than a participant in, the scene around you. (Storti, 2003: 54)

Intuitively, it would seem that the longer one has been away, the more difficult the re-entry might be; the more likely it is that the society the traveller thought he/she knew has changed, the less likely it is that he/she can have confidence in knowing 'how things are done'. Those who return on retirement, however, while potentially facing many challenges, will not have to face the additional difficulties confronted by those returning to teach 'back home', possibly having children who need to be re-settled in new schools and a spouse who may also have to find new work. Such a situation is not helped by the reverse culture shock being experienced in different ways by different family members, exacerbated possibly by resentment from some younger family members at the decision to relocate to somewhere their parents refer to as 'home' but where they may never have lived and thus to which they may not feel any particular allegiance.

Professionally, the returning teacher will face challenges. They may share the experiences cited by Storti of returners feeling that their new colleagues do not value or capitalise upon their international experience (they may even be suspicious of it), of loss of status ('when you were our man in Riyadh ... some very important people passed through your life. Now ...'), or of having to catch up as they are 'behind the times professionally' (2003: 68). A study undertaken in England by Black and Scott of returning teachers and heads responsible for making appointments highlighted just how real an issue this can be. One teacher respondent referred to encountering a 'complete indifference to any experience gained abroad', while another suggested that prospective employers seemed to 'think that you have spent your time sitting on a desert island' (Black and Scott, 1997: 48–9). Returning teachers will not usually face other challenges referred to by Storti in the business context of returners moving back to the 'home' office of a company that placed them temporarily overseas, since in most cases teachers will be returning to a different school than any in which they had previously taught. There will, however, be the whole process of forming new professional relationships to contend with.

Any lack of value apparently placed on the returning teacher's international experience (which will vary, of course, depending on the location, curriculum, student and teacher population, and 'ethos' of the new school), could well have been exacerbated by the difficulty of finding an appropriate teaching post to return to in the first place. Those with skills in shortage subject areas may find it easier than others, but even they can face difficulties. Black and Scott's study was based on questionnaires completed by 51 teachers (25 male, 26 female and all British, with a British degree and/or British teaching qualification, and at least one year's experience of teaching in both a UK and an international school) who had, successfully or unsuccessfully, sought UK teaching posts after teaching abroad. In addition, interviews were conducted with six such teachers and with three heads.

Their findings suggested that, in general, teachers' international experience was seen at best as irrelevant and at worst in more negative terms. A number of possible reasons were suggested for such perceptions on the part of the heads, including the relative expense of employing more experienced teachers (especially since the introduction of local management of schools), a lack of up to date knowledge of the English education system (where the national curriculum was then less than ten years old), and a certain suspicion of any career that had not followed a 'normal' path (with a parallel being drawn by the authors with the difficulties sometimes experienced by women who take career breaks while their children are young). At least one respondent perceived his/her interviewers to have 'felt that I should not be able to come back into teaching because I had not "suffered" as the UK teachers had suffered with all the recent changes' (Black and Scott, 1997: 48). Clearly the findings of this study may have been affected by sensitivities at that time to the recently introduced national curriculum requirements and to the delegation of financial management to schools; the study was also a small one. Anecdotal evidence would suggest, however, that the situation might not be so different ten years on.

CONCLUSION

This chapter has highlighted a number of issues relating to the community of teachers in international schools. With different reasons for embarking upon teaching in such a context, with different personal situations, skills and interests, it would be impossible to generalise about how these issues affect each teacher. What *is* clear, however, is that there is more to embarking upon teaching in an international school than simply moving to a school in a new location: awareness in advance of some of the differences and challenges may help to ensure that the international school teaching experience is a positive one for all concerned.

CHAPTER 7

Administrators

The international schools context provides ample evidence of the old adage of two (or in this case many) nations being divided by a common language, and in no respect is it more applicable than in relation to organisation and administration. The word administration itself is a case in point: in many international schools an administrator is someone who has reached a level of what might be described as senior management: a deputy head or principal, for instance. To others an administrator is quite different and some, from say a British background, would be more familiar with terms such as 'manager' (or the more recently popularised 'leader'). The term 'administrator', however, has become so prevalent in international schools as to be almost commonplace, and it is in this sense that it will be used in this chapter.

Not that the potential for confusion ends here. Other examples of inconsistent terminology include the title of principal; in some cases used to describe the most senior administrator, in others to describe the second tier of high school principal or elementary school principal reporting to the school's head. Even the ascription of headship has its variations. The titles headmaster and headmistress have largely disappeared from international (and other) schools in favour of the gender-neutral head of school. Other titles not uncommon in the international school world include chief executive officer (CEO), superintendent, director or even (as in the case of a large school such as the multi-site International School of Geneva) director general. The seemingly growing trend of appointing CEOs, who may or may not have a teaching background, raises interesting issues with respect to the relationship between that person and the academic leader (whatever their title) within a school. Such differences in terminology can be confusing for both parents and prospective teachers. For the purposes of this chapter, while 'administrator' will be used in the generic sense outlined above, unless there is good reason to use an alternative, the term 'head' will be used to describe the most senior academic administrator: 'the person who leads and supervises the daily operations of the school, ensuring that the policies of the Governing Body are put into practice' (CIS, 2003: 5).

INTERNATIONAL SCHOOL ADMINISTRATORS: WHO ARE THEY?

It has already been noted (Chapter 6) that teachers take up posts in international schools for many reasons, and Hardman's (2000) study helpfully suggested a number of categories into which international school teachers can be grouped. It comes as no surprise, therefore, to know that there are also variations among those who become international school administrators. Although to some extent Hardman's categorisations still apply (including career professionals with or without children, mavericks, senior career professionals and senior mavericks), administrators are, by dint of the experience required for such a position, less likely to be 'bright young things' setting off to see the world for a few years before returning home to settle down.

One notable issue relating to administrators, assuming their previous career has been in teaching, is that of whether the classroom teaching experience gained was in international schools or in a national system. This is a particularly interesting point in relation to senior administrators, many of whom will have taken on such a role after experience in international school teaching or in what might be described as 'middle management' (Blandford, 2001: 136–52). But this is not always the case, and heads are sometimes appointed on the basis of no previous international experience at all. Schoppert refers to the 'fresh thinking' that may come from such individuals, while noting that many schools would not give them strong consideration (2001a: 121).

In some cases, however, perhaps where an international school has a particular national affiliation, a board may perceive prestige in the recent and relevant national experience of such an appointee, especially if that person has headship experience in that context. Indeed a nationally experienced head may welcome the challenge of a new context for the application of his/her already developed skills. And a challenge it undoubtedly will be: if headship in a national setting is demanding, how much more potential is there for different cultural practices, assumptions and expectations to lead to unanticipated challenges within an international school? That is not to say that such a transition cannot be successful, and there are some notable examples of heads who have skilfully negotiated the national/international divide, but it may require a special sort of person (probably one who is adaptable, flexible in thought and open to new working practices) to respond effectively to the many and varied challenges they will face, some of which will be considered below.

Administrators: Managers and Leaders

There is no shortage of literature relating to the importance of the role of school head. Arising from a good deal of work conducted in the linked areas of school effectiveness and school improvement, Sammons et al identified eleven factors contributing to the existence of an effective school, including shared vision, environment conducive to learning and high expectations, with professional leadership the key factor (1997). How the head provides such leadership is another issue: as Bossert et al point out, 'No simple style of management seems appropriate for all schools ... (Heads) must use the style and structures most suited to their own local situation' (1982).

The difference between the concepts of what, in some situations, would traditionally have been called management and the more topical leadership can be difficult to pin down precisely, but a helpful distinction is made by Louis and Miles, who say that 'Leaders set the course for the organisation; managers make sure the course is followed. Leaders make strategic plans; managers design operational systems for carrying out the plans. Leaders stimulate and inspire; managers use their interpersonal influence and authority to translate that energy into productive work' (1990: 19–20). That said, it is more often than not implicit in the role of anyone who is a manager (or administrator in the international school context) that they will demonstrate some leadership skills. Middle managers in international schools, Blandford points out, are 'player-managers', participating in the daily tasks of teaching while fulfilling their role of team leaders/managers. 'Their role', she argues, 'is to teach, lead teams and be a team member' (2001: 140–42). Within the context of this chapter, it will be assumed that the roles of all international school administrators – at whatever level in the school hierarchy – will include elements of leadership, management and administration, the balance depending upon the particular responsibilities of the post in question (and the terminology depending on the school).

Gender Issues

The administrator gender balance is more even in international schools than in some national systems, though only 20 per cent of international school directors/heads were women in the survey conducted in 1997 by

ECIS (Thearle, 2000: 113). Thearle (an experienced international schools administrator herself) argues that this matters partly because a lack of women in the most senior administrative position discourages capable female administrators from aspiring to such roles, and thus deprives the profession of potentially effective heads.

More importantly perhaps, she argues that international educators have a responsibility to provide positive role models of both sexes for all students. 'What price the explicit spoken and written commitment to equality of opportunity for men and women espoused in the majority of international schools worldwide', she asks, 'if the "hidden curriculum" operating within the school perpetuates a perception that such equality of opportunity is a phenomenon that applies only to middle-management level?' (2000: 120). Thearle's work in this area served to highlight how complex a set of issues are at play, as did the study of issues relating to women in international schools in Africa undertaken by Bridglal (2002). Superimposed on issues affecting women's career progress in national systems (Randell, 1991) are those associated with the difficulty of two partners coordinating globally mobile careers. For international schools not to promote equality of opportunity, however, as Thearle has pointed out, could well be inconsistent with the ethos and mission of the international school itself. It would seem that such an issue is in fact part of a much bigger picture, and symptomatic of the more general tension already highlighted between the pragmatic and ideological dimensions of the international school context.

PARTICULAR CHALLENGES

Only relatively recently has literature begun to emerge that highlights the particular challenges faced by managers/leaders (referred to in this chapter as 'administrators') when working in multicultural contexts. Dimmock and Walker, in a collection focusing on educational leadership and cultural diversity, explain that 'the emergence of culture as a conceptual framework for ... the analysis of practice in educational leadership and management is a recent phenomenon' (Hallinger, 2005: xi). They make three main propositions:

- leadership is a culturally and contextually bounded process inextricably intertwined with its larger environment (organisational, local community and larger environment);
- cultural influence on leadership is multi-dimensional, 'often difficult to discern, subtle and easy to overlook – to the point that it is underplayed by many, and even dismissed and ignored by some';

- recognising the nexus between leadership on the one hand, and cultural and contextual influences on the other, can lead to improvement in its practice. (Dimmock and Walker, 2005: 3–4)

Effective international school administrators will, of course, be aware of the importance of the relationship between leadership and the cultural context, even if they have absorbed their awareness over time in quite subtle ways and without articulation. As Dimmock and Walker go on to point out,

> Given the multi-ethnic nature of schools around the world, leaders nowadays shoulder responsibility for shaping their organisations in ways that value and integrate heterogeneous groups into successful learning communities for all. The successful leadership of such communities calls for very specific knowledge and skills attuned to ethnicity and multiculturalism. (2005: 4)

Are international schools, one might ask, any different in this respect from the multi-ethnic schools appearing in national systems worldwide to which Dimmock and Walker refer? Maybe not: certainly there are major similarities which make much of what these two authors have to say of potential interest to any international school administrator. Shaw, for instance, discusses some of the challenges associated with managing mixed-culture teams in international schools. She points out that 'the potential for dissonance through misunderstanding exists in every school, but in an international school this potential is increased when people of different culture have differing expectations of each other' before going on to describe a number of difficult situations in international schools which, as she says, 'arose by people not understanding, or not conforming to, what was expected of them in those circumstances' (2001: 157).

One such illustration is that of an international school in Asia, where an appraisal system introduced by its Western managers with the prime function of improving staff development required that heads of department 'provide frank feedback to their staff, discussing areas for improvement as well as recognising and praising achievement' (2001: 158). Even though training was provided, many host-country heads of department seemed unable to do this. Another of Shaw's examples focused on an 'international school in Asia' with increasing numbers of local students whose parents the head found difficult to engage in school life. He called a meeting at which parents agreed with his suggestions, but he received feedback via the community that they resented what he was trying to do. And thirdly, an illustration is given of an international school head returning from a leadership course and setting up a less centralised structure with greater delegation to her mixed-culture middle management colleagues. Despite all new roles and responsibilities being set out in a new handbook, some staff appeared unwilling or unable to make the decisions that they were now entitled to make, 'constantly referring back up to her' (Shaw, 2001: 157–8).

What are the solutions to such situations? How does a well-intentioned administrator overcome difficulties of this type? Shaw goes on to make some suggestions, which are not included here. The examples above are included merely as illustrations of the skill levels required of administrators when working in an international school, over and above the leadership, management and administration skills that may be developed in less multicultural contexts. Add to the multicultural complexities the different structural arrangements that many novice international school heads might be familiar with, and a truly challenging environment is indeed in evidence. Such differences might be apparent in some or all of the following situations, a number of which are clearly overlapping.

Relationship with Non-academic Administrators

Garton highlights the role in an international school of business manager or financial manager as one providing the opportunity for employment of a host-country national in a senior decision-making capacity or, alternatively, the potential for the undermining of what he describes as 'a truly international ethos' when such an opportunity presents itself but is not taken (2002: 152). In many international schools such host-country appointments are indeed made, and can prove invaluable in terms of the understanding they bring to the most effective ways of interacting with the host context. Indeed, with increasing international concerns about security (for example kidnap attempts, terrorist threats) and health scares (such as SARS or Avian flu), such a person can play a critical role in drawing up and revising contingency plans, and implementing them if required. The relationship between this person and the head is crucial in terms of where each stands in the administrative hierarchy and where responsibility and authority rest.

In some countries the question of whether a senior host-country administrator is in post is non-negotiable in legal terms. The laws of Thailand, for instance, require that a Thai 'licensee' be in place for each international school, and Thai labour law requires that a certain number of Thais are appointed in both high and lower level positions:

> In general, international schools (in Thailand) are run by associations, foundations and as businesses for profit. Ostensibly, all the governing committees of substance must have a majority of Thais on them and their chief executives must be Thai nationals. In school businesses for profit, the

> licensee is often the owner, or appoints an investor as his nominee. (Sharples and De'Ath, 1997: 23)

Again, the experience and support provided by such a person can be invaluable to a head responsible for running the academic dimension of an international school – provided relationships are good and both understand and accept from the outset exactly where the boundaries of their decision-making responsibilities lie.

Relationship with the Board

Likewise, and sometimes related to the above scenario, the overlap between responsibilities of the head and those of the board can be a grey area and a somewhat blurred addition to the Venn diagram of international school administration. A head familiar with such a relationship in a national context, and with demarcation lines between the two sets of responsibilities, may make a set of assumptions on appointment that turn out to be ill-founded in practice. For a head prepared to adapt to the new situation, such differences may be taken in his/her stride and treated as a learning experience.

Others for whom such differences are unpalatable or completely unacceptable may find their term of office short-lived. Is the fact, for instance, that a head is informed by the board chair on the last day of the school year that his high school principal and business manager have both been dismissed a resigning issue, or simply an indication of different ways of doing things? Should a head who returns after the long holiday to find a brand new purpose-built sports hall (about which he knew nothing when last in school) be delighted or infuriated? Responses to these (genuine) situations, and to others like them, will undoubtedly determine the extent to which – in some contexts – a head and the board will work well together. Further such issues are discussed in Chapter 8.

Top of Which Tree?

Due in part to the ambiguities of terminology noted earlier, and in part to differences in organisational structures, it may be that those appointed as head may not enjoy so much autonomy as they may have expected (and not only in relationships with the board). Who, for instance, is the ultimate decision maker in a school with an overall head, but with principsals of high school, middle school and elementary school? Does the answer to this question vary according to whether the school has a total enrolment of 600 or 3,000? What exactly is the nature of the relationship between the person appointed head of the international school which is effectively an international stream within a national school, and the head of that national school? How does the head, if he/she is the senior administrator responsible for the academic dimension of the school, relate to the owner in a situation where the school is privately owned and has no board? The answers to such questions may not always turn out to be as envisaged by the new recruit to international school headship, and need to be ascertained at the time of interview before commitments are made on both sides.

Responsibility for What?

The illustrations above relate, by and large, to situations where a head may have less responsibility or autonomy than might have been expected based on their own previous experience. But the reverse may also be true: the head may find that he/she becomes involved in taking on responsibility for aspects of school life that he/she would never have dreamed previously would be part of a head's brief. Take the head, for instance, who finds that there is an expectation that she will continue her predecessor's established practice of driving to the airport to meet each newly-arriving expatriate teacher and ensuring that the new recruits are happily settled into their school-provided accommodation. Or perhaps the head lives in such accommodation as a neighbour of teaching colleagues and is expected to participate in social activities with his/her family.

The international school very often provides services to its community over and above anything that might be expected elsewhere: a parents' room for non-working spouses, for instance (see Chapter 3), or a manual for expatriate families including information on local support services in addition to that relating to the school itself (Langford et al., 2002: 9). What is the head's role in all of this? How does the head, who may be suffering from culture shock personally, help to ensure that new teaching colleagues are supported through their own transitional experiences? Rader and Sittig provide a helpful set of guidelines for working with mobile families, parents and children which, while aimed at classroom teachers, could equally apply to senior international school administrators (2003: 9–12).

Familiarity with a whole raft of issues relating to the globally mobile child will clearly be an expectation of any such senior personnel; while they may be expected to act as role models for more junior colleagues in this respect, if their own international experience is relatively limited this may prove challenging. Indeed, given the stronger community element often taken on by an international school then would be the case for a national counterpart, the head may be perceived as more of a community leader than heads would be in schools elsewhere. It is also the case that the 'normal' responsibilities of administrators may be more complex in international schools than they might be otherwise. The question of finding suitable substitute teachers to cover staff illness, for instance, can be a particular headache in a situation where language and curriculum differences mean local options are limited.

Long-Term Planning

Terminology is imprecise in the area of planning, as elsewhere, and a number of expressions such as 'long-term planning', 'strategic planning', 'long-range planning' and 'development planning' tend to be used in both national and international contexts as though interchangeable. Though a number of authors highlight differences between the various concepts, what is certain is that the relatively high turnover of senior international school administrators – including the head – can militate against planning for anything other than the relatively short term, particularly if there is also a fairly high turnover of board members.

Nelson, himself an international school head of considerable experience, highlights the importance, notwithstanding (or perhaps because of) high turnover of personnel, of developing an institutional strategic plan and the central role of the head in that process, as well as in its implementation and regular review. As he points out,

> Certainly, strategic planning is demanding of time, but so too is the alternative – not planning! Being in a constantly reactive mode is time-consuming, wasteful of resources and ultimately debilitating to students, staff and parents alike. A well-crafted, flexible, strategic plan can be a powerful way of saying 'no' to whimsical, ill-conceived, or politically motivated ideas, from whatever quarter they may emanate. (Nelson, 2000: 171)

Powell similarly notes that

> In the clutter of day-to-day events and problems, the *urgent* can easily become confused with the *important* and such planning can be neglected with the school suffering as a consequence. Mature schools will have long range planning built into the annual cycle of governance activities so that it doesn't become lost in the swirl of daily 'urgencies' (2001: 14 original emphasis).

Much has been written about such issues within national systems. Within international schools Blaney, another experienced head, highlighted the responses often heard during school visits when someone asks to see a copy of the school's long-term plan, including 'We do not have a long-term plan but ... we've made it a priority to do one' and 'It's tough enough to plan for next year, never mind for the "long term"'. As an alternative, he says, the visitor may be handed a copy of a plan 'probably prepared for the school's last accreditation, handsomely bound and looking very much as though it has not been touched by human hands since its publication' (2000: 159).

Leggate and Thompson report a study undertaken in international schools which investigated the extent to which development planning then existed in international schools, and the expectations of heads with respect to who should be involved in the development planning process. Responses from heads of 40 international schools worldwide indicated overwhelming awareness of the importance of long-term planning, even though not all respondents had managed to generate such a plan. While the majority rejected the notion that high mobility among staff and students was a reason for not creating effective long-term plans, hindrances to the process of long-term planning were noted as including 'the variety of cultural expectations of such an exercise, linguistic and legal complexities, the impact of transiency on financial planning particularly, limited input from alumni and uncertainties generated by external forces, political or climatic' (Leggate and Thompson, 1997: 272). A sample five-year plan in Hodgson and Chuck (2004) is intended to help international school administrators to overcome some such difficulties.

RECRUITMENT OF ADMINISTRATORS

A number of issues relating to recruitment of teachers in international schools are discussed in Chapter 6 and many of these would equally apply to the recruitment of administrators. All teachers play a pivotal role in any school. Given everything that recent research has highlighted, however, about the crucial role played by the head as leader, it is understandable that Mattern should refer to the appointment of a head in an international school as 'The Most Important Decision' (1994). The role of head is a challenging one: 'They have to deal with governors, teachers, parents, pupils, accountants, and journalists' (TES, 2005). In a national system they may have to respond to government initiatives and liaise with local authority officials; in an international school they need to keep abreast of a range of initiatives relating to international schools and quite possibly, depending on the nature of the school, keep on top of developments in at least one national system.

So how does an international school decide who its next head should be? If the process is complex in a national context, how much more complicated is it in an international school? Does the school prefer to appoint an experienced head from a national system, or an administrator from an international school with no headship experience? Is a particular nationality of head sought? How should suitable potential recruits be identified? Who might be interested in applying? An individual wishing to pursue a career in international schools may well find it necessary to move between countries if promotion is to be gained, since there are limited opportunities available worldwide. The source of potential administrators is therefore global.

Stories from some national situations make for rather gloomy reading at present. In the UK for instance, a 2005 annual report on the appointment of heads observed that the situation was in 'crisis': 'of 2,125 primary headships advertised, 37 per cent had to be re-advertised for lack of a suitable applicant – sometimes for lack of any applicant at all. ... Of the 418 headships advertised in the secondary sector, 27 per cent had to be re-advertised'. In each case, the equivalent figure from ten years previously was 15 per cent (TES, 2005: 11). Is such a situation, (projected to get worse rather than better) reflected in the recruitment of heads to international schools? Or could a national system's loss be the international schools' gain, as potential heads look to wider horizons for future career prospects? As there are no equivalent data currently publicly available relating to the recruitment of heads in international schools, such comparisons are impossible. What would seem to be similar, however, is the use of headhunting as a means of identifying suitable applicants, as well as word of mouth. Also adopted in some schools is what is known as 'succession planning' – identifying younger members of staff with leadership potential and giving them early opportunities to develop that potential, ideally then appointing them to more senior positions within the same school, An additional complication in international schools, of course, is the globally mobile nature of many members of staff: though some 'Penelopes' (as Hardman, 2001, described them) remain faithful to one school for many years, others are likely to move on before the school would see a return on its investment.

As might be expected in the diverse world of international schools, there is huge variation in the efficiency and form of the head recruitment process. As Mattern explains, some schools

> have done it well – gracefully, efficiently, with high percipience and to the enormous benefit of their schools; others have done it awkwardly, with unnecessary expense of time and energy and money, and have finished with an insensitive or inappropriate choice, to the detriment of their schools – and have had the job to do all over again in a year or two (if they were lucky)! (1994: (i)

Indeed Mattern's very useful booklet has as its major focus the provision of advice about good practice in the recruitment of heads for international schools: from the formation of a search committee through to the decision itself, including a mine of detailed suggestions drawing from many years of experience. As Mattern himself says,

> It might seem logical to assume that, with so much coming and going, with so many good examples to emulate and so many less happy ones whose mistakes (in retrospect) should be avoided, some fund of experience on the subject would have been accumulated to guide Boards ... and it is quite true that the fund exists. The problem is that, in many instances, it is not on deposit with a particular Board at the particular time an institution needs to deal with the whole complex business of conducting a search and making a new appointment. (1994: (i))

In addition to advertising in the press, international schools now have the opportunity to seek assistance in the recruitment of administrators through organisations such as Search Associates (2006), the Council of International Schools (CIS, 2006) and International Schools Services (ISS, 2006).

Contractual Issues

Such is the nature of some international schools that not only may there be an absence of sufficient learning from previous mistakes (even at the same school if, for instance, board turnover has been high), in some cases the basis of the head's appointment may be relatively informal. Difficult to imagine, perhaps, for someone moving from employment in a national context, but the foreword to the CIS sample contract for heads of international schools makes clear at least some of the reasons why a contract should always exist between the head of a school and its board (with a clear implication that this is not always the case). Of the six reasons given, three in particular conjure up images of difficult situations with which at least some readers may be able to identify:

- because the euphoria of a board finding just the right head and the head finding just the right school goes on, like all honeymoons, to other states of mind;
- because the unexpected does happen to people, including those who have an unwritten understanding with each other – which may not be understood in quite the same way by those who have not been privy to the original agreement; and
- because in international schools, the composition of boards can change both like and with the seasons, and a very temperate climate can in short order become a very chilly one. (CIS/ECIS, 1993: 2)

Underpinning each of the reasons given is the suggestion that change is commonplace within such a context, and it is undoubtedly the case that turnover in both international school boards and heads can be high.

Turnover

No doubt some readers, when reflecting on international schools they have known, will be able to conjure up images of unpleasant scenarios they have either experienced first hand, observed, or heard of second hand, where a head's tenure has been unexpectedly fore-shortened. Indeed a lack of any expectation of long-term security, job-wise, would seem to be one of the characteristics of the international school head. Not everyone would aspire to emulate the legendary Frank Boyden, who served as head of Deerfield Academy, Massachusetts for sixty-six years (1902–1968) (Deerfield Academy, 2006), but a little more long-term security than is commonplace in many international schools would often be considered desirable. Difficult to envisage perhaps for a teacher or administrator more used to a higher level of long-term professional security, the tenure of an international school head can sometimes be surprisingly short.

The reasons for such high turnover are complex but, while every case is unique, there are undoubtedly some common factors that appear with unwelcome frequency. Turnover of teaching staff in some international schools is high, for a variety of reasons (which can itself lead to larger amounts of time being spent by administrators on teacher recruitment than would be common in national schools). Though relatively little research has been undertaken about high turnover of international school administrators, Hawley conducted a (1994) study which considered the employment history between 1980 and 1990 of heads (336 in total) in 251 international schools accredited by US accrediting agencies (not including schools within the USA or those associated with the US Department of Defense). In just one school year, 1985–86, almost a third of heads left their positions, and Hawley's research concluded at that time that 'the average length of time a school Head remains on the job' was 2.8 years. In concluding some of the reasons for this relatively short duration (and indeed for the fact that 15 per cent of heads left after one year; odd, as Hawley points out, when most heads are offered two or three year contracts), Hawley suggests that:

- 'in schools where members of the Board do not have children enrolled in the schools, school Heads tend, on average, to remain longer', with an implication of longer-term interest and commitment, and greater objectivity, when the interests of board members were not 'defined and driven by the needs of their children currently enrolled in the school';
- heads stay longer when school board policy exists in written form, and where the head's performance is evaluated (or 'appraised' – a word used elsewhere in this chapter) by the board;
- the more multinational the board, the shorter the duration of the headship; the higher the turnover of board membership, the shorter the head's time in office;

- those with previous teaching experience in international schools last longer than those without, though experience as an administrator in international schools seemed not to be predictive of duration;
- international school heads stay longer in some parts of the world than in others (in Europe notably longer than in Africa, for instance) and they also tend to stay longer in larger schools than in smaller schools (possibly linked to the fact that heads tend to move from small to larger international schools as they become more experienced);
- they stay longer when the percentage of faculty employed full-time is higher, in schools where the IB Diploma programme is offered, in 'prestigious' schools, and in countries where no 'Travel Advisories or warnings' have been issued by the US Department of State (in other words, in countries that are relatively stable). (1994: 13–14)

Hawley is careful to point out that a causal relationship between any of these factors and headship duration has not been proven by his research; the findings do, nevertheless, suggest a number of factors which could well be relevant in determining whether an international school head's time in office is a successful one.

LANGUAGE ISSUES

An expatriate teacher in an English-medium international school may be able to operate effectively without managing to learn to speak the host-country language. For an administrator there may be a greater necessity to converse with those external agencies with which the school has to interact: the Ministry of Education, the Ministry of Labour (in relation, perhaps, to work permits) and so on. The board may also conduct its meetings in the host-country language, as in the case of the newly-arrived head who turned up to his first board meeting to find, without any warning, that it was to be conducted in the host-country language which he had not yet mastered.

It may not be unreasonable to expect international school teachers and administrators to attempt to learn the local language, but whether it is practical – given the relatively short duration of many administrators' tenures – to expect them to become sufficiently fluent to participate in high level meetings in every country in which they work is another issue. Where they are not able to do so, not only may frustration ensue for the administrator, they may also become more dependent than they would wish upon whoever it is (secretary, business manager for instance) they rely on to act as translator/interpreter.

SUPPORT FOR SENIOR ADMINISTRATORS

If it is true that relatively little has been written about teachers in international schools, then it is certainly the case that there is a dearth of material to be found about administrators, including the heads of such schools. So far as support is concerned, while the need is arguably at least as great for heads as it is for their more junior colleagues, it may be less in evidence. Some forms that such support might take are as follows.

Training/Preparation for Headship

There are at least two major aspects of preparation for headship of an international school: how one prepares to be a head in general terms, and how one prepares particularly for the international school situation. For some new heads of international schools the first issue may not arise, in that they have already gained what might be referred to as 'generic' headship experience in another, national, situation. The challenge for these heads may be in not making too many assumptions about the transferability of their earlier experiences to the new context, and in identifying which of those experiences are and are not directly relevant. Even for the head transferring from headship at another international school there may well be areas where a new set of skills is required arising from cultural and other differences. Those who come from a post as senior administrator in another international school may be in a similar position, with the additional challenge of not being quite certain what the role of head entails. Some may have been fortunate enough to work previously with a head who delegated certain responsibilities to them, either on an ongoing basis or from time to time during the head's absence from school. Others may have had little or no first-hand experience of 'being a head', even on a temporary basis.

Fortunately for the new international school head, the importance of preparation for the role has become increasingly recognised. Aside from some national contexts where any newly-appointed head must have successfully completed headship training, a number of organisations are now offering preparation for those who aspire to international school headship. The Academy for International School Heads, for instance, established in 1999 with a mission to 'provide professional and personal development opportunities, support and assistance for current and former international school Heads' (AISH, 2006) offers a three day 'Institute for Aspiring International School Heads' for 'educational leaders who are seeking their first international school Head position'. Aimed particularly at those aspiring to headship in American-style international schools, the institute incorporates a review of what skills and competencies will be required as well as issues relating to preparation for the application and recruitment process. And the longer-established (1989) Principals Training Center for International School Leadership (PTC) was founded to 'meet the professional development needs of leaders in international schools', offering an 'Essential Skills Programme' leading to the Certificate of International School Leadership, as well as the possibility of working towards an Advanced Leadership Certificate (PTC, 2006).

Induction

Culture shock may well affect senior administrators, including the head, in just the same way as it does any other expatriate new recruit. In essence perhaps the only difference might be in the potential sensitivity of a relationship between a new head, say, and a colleague who takes on the supportive role of mentor or buddy notwithstanding their relative lack of seniority. More importantly, perhaps, is the question of who provides the professional induction (or orientation) for a new head in terms of his/her role. Is it the chair of the board or other board members? Or senior administrator colleagues? Littleford points out that 'New Heads are cautioned to lay low in the weeds', observe, and make no sudden or controversial moves in their first year' (1999b: 1). This, he argues, is good advice. But they do need support in adjusting to their new role, particularly if the new context is quite different from that of their previous experience.

A head appointed to a school owned by one of the large commercial organisations increasingly operating internationally, for instance, may take time to adjust to a commercial culture with the attendant pressure to keep costs low and return on investment high, and with relative isolation from the ultimate decision-making authority. Within the school, it may not always be clear whence such support will come. As Matthews points out: 'Heads are usually the only person in a school with any experience of headship. Rarely will there be anybody else on the faculty or on the Board who can directly relate to the complexities and pressures of the Head's role' (2001b: 7). In some cases arrangements are made for the incoming and outgoing heads to overlap so that there can be an element of 'handover', though this may not always be possible to arrange. From outside the school, many of the regional associations of international schools provide peer support and opportunities for mentoring new heads, as do organisations such as CIS.

Appraisal

Once the head has settled in to their new role, it is to be hoped that he/she will be effective; indeed each group of stakeholders will have their views on the head's effectiveness. Bowley suggests that 'School Heads are constantly being evaluated. Most of the evaluation is informal: it takes place in the teachers' lounge, the playground and at dinner parties. (It) may be informal and misinformed but, for better or for worse, it can carry weight' (2001a: 128). If the head is not simply to be left to his or her own devices, however, some form of more systematic judgement – whether referred to as 'evaluation' or 'appraisal' – is necessary. As Bowley points out, in such a situation 'Boards must regard the evaluation process as much as a means for motivating, developing and retaining the effective Head as a means for terminating the ineffective one' (2001a: 128), and indeed CIS now publish a set of guidelines for use by boards in evaluating the head.

Bowley goes on to suggest a number of points to be borne in mind when the board is undertaking a head's evaluation, stressing just how helpful such a process can be to all concerned. Matthews, likewise, stresses the importance of what he terms 'appraisal' and, as Bowley has also done, highlights the importance of such a process not being used solely as a contributor to decisions about contract renewal. As Matthews argues, 'If appraisal is seen as part of the contract process, it will not be in the interest of the Head to collaborate openly in discussing areas of strength and weakness' (2001b: 5). Matthews goes on to propose a model of appraisal similar to that which he proposed for teachers (see Chapter 6) in being based on the notion of accreditation, including self-appraisal by the head as well as input from other stakeholders (possibly including board members, administration, teachers, students and parents). Synthesis should then follow, Matthews suggests, by 'a credible external moderator, perhaps a small team of judiciously selected representatives' who will act as an 'Appraisal Team'. Ideally this team would include a visiting head from another international school as 'peer appraiser'. Following a meeting and discussion between the head and appraisal team a report, including recommendations with respect to professional development and goals, would be written.

While arguing strongly for the merits of such a process, Matthews recognises the burdensome nature of what is proposed and admits that every three years might be a realistic frequency, supplemented by an annual 'interim appraisal' with the board chair in which progress in pursuing the recommendations is reviewed. Involvement in the head's appraisal, or evaluation, of not only board members is also recommended by Hodgson, who argues that members of the senior administration team should be asked to complete a questionnaire, responses to which will be fed back to the board chair for consideration in discussions with the head during the evaluation process (Hodgson, 2005b: 47).

Professional Development

Much of what has been written about Professional Development, or Continuing Professional Development, refers more to classroom teachers than to senior administrators, and some of the points raised in Chapter 6 in relation to teachers will also have relevance here. Undoubtedly the same principle applies to administrators as to teachers: that it is not sufficient to develop a set of skills at the outset which then remain unmodified for the remainder of one's career. Again, organisations such as AISH, CIS and PTC offer programmes of support in which administrators may participate on an ongoing basis, as do many of the agencies and regional associations of international schools discussed in more detail in Chapter 10. And there are courses offered by representatives of national educational developments which may be of relevance, though the type of professional development where outside experts visit an international school (as discussed in, inter alia, Powell, 2000) is less likely to be found in relation to administrators, and particularly senior administrators, than in relation to classroom teachers.

Perhaps it is not so likely that in relation to senior administrators there are, as Richards suggests in the context of international school teachers, 'courses to suit every school's pocket and needs, as well as courses to cure every malaise known to education, including a number not yet identified by the researchers ... In the frontier territory of international education, purveyors of snake oil abound' (2002: 99). It is not altogether clear whether universities would be considered purveyors of snake oil in Richards' definition, but it is certainly the case that one area of growing interest among international school administrators in recent years has been that of postgraduate qualifications.

In many international schools today it would be considered essential for anyone with headship aspirations to possess a masters degree. Indeed, as increasing numbers have masters degrees, the number of administrators embarking on doctorate programmes has increased: another example perhaps of the 'credentialism' referred to by Lowe in relation to assessment in international schools 'when examination results are used to select for scarce and desirable opportunities in education and employment' (2000: 20). As Lowe points out, 'one consequence of credentialism is that educational outcomes improve, in the sense that more students gain higher levels of qualifications' (2000: 24). While the push for increasing numbers of administrators obtaining postgraduate qualifications may be essentially pragmatic, one outcome may be a better-informed administrator workforce (with the hope that being better informed will feed into the improvement of practice).

Relationship with the Board

The role of head vis-à-vis the board may vary. In some international schools the head is a voting board member (on all issues but their own position and salary); in others they are not. Aspects of the role of the international school board are discussed in more depth in Chapter 8, but the role of senior administrators cannot be considered without at least passing reference to the importance of the crucial relationship between the head and the board and, indeed, the head and the board chair. As Bowley points out, 'A strong relationship between the Board Chair and the school Head may not alone guarantee the smooth running of a school, but the converse is certainly true; a stormy Chair/Head relationship inevitably causes disruption to the school community' (2001b: 110).

Differences in understanding about the roles of head and board are almost certainly at the heart of many of the difficulties that lead to some heads leaving employment prematurely (as noted earlier) in an atmosphere of suspicion, mistrust and ill-feeling not only between head and board, but also within the school and its communities more widely. As Bowley argues, 'an effective Chair/Head partnership is based on trust and mutual understanding ... [and] ... on the mutual acceptance of each other's good intentions ... Trust is a necessary pre-condition for a successful partnership. It has nothing to do with agreeing to like each other. It has everything to do with an assumption of each other's integrity' (2001b: 110). So widely recognised is the crucial nature of the head/board chair relationship that support is provided for it through, for instance, CIS (2006) which runs what are referred to as Partnership Development Program Workshops designed 'for that crucial partnership: the Head of School and the Board Chair' (CIS, 2006) and offered only to those who participate as the two-person team of board chair and school head. Interestingly, in again stressing the importance of the head/chair relationship, Littleford emphasises that it is not only mistrust and distance that have to be avoided, but also a situation where the two become too close:

> 'as when the Chair can become too staunch a defender and confidant of the Head at times. This may look like a healthy relationship, but that kind of partnership can create resentment and apathy among other Board members who feel their role diminished. ... In addition to being the Head's public and private supporter, the Chair (needs to be) one of his or her most important private critics. (2005d: 2).

Clearly this particular tightrope balancing act is not an easy one to complete successfully.

CONCLUSION

This chapter has only begun to scratch the surface of a number of issues concerning administrators as one of the communities to be found in international schools: each could have been explored in a great deal more depth, and undoubtedly other issues have gone unmentioned which would equally have merited discussion. The head, and other administrators, in an international school have a delicate course to steer in sustaining effective relationships with the many different stakeholder groups with whom they interact, and in balancing the pragmatic and ideological demands placed upon them. The next chapter will discuss in more detail issues relating to one such stakeholder group: the board.

CHAPTER 8

The Board

Chapter 7 began with an observation that the terminology used in relation to international school administrators can be confusing. The potential for confusion arises in equal measure in the context of governance. As Mattern points out, some international schools 'have Governors, while others have Directors – or Trustees or Advisors or Overseers or simply Board members' (1994: iii). Such differences are more than cosmetic, says Malpass. In particular, he argues, use of the term 'director' is misleading in suggesting that board members are expected to 'direct' when in fact they are not: 'trustee' would be his preferred word to describe the responsibilities involved (1994: 24). Differences in terminology arise in part from the different national origins of the schools in question – as Mattern explains, international schools do not generally share an agreed terminology (1994: iii) – and in part from the very varied bases on which schools have been established.

A recent Council of International Schools (CIS) survey of 119 international schools highlighted just how many different names are used to describe the body with formal responsibility for governance: most (27 per cent and 20 per cent respectively) had a board of directors or board of governors, while 18 per cent had a board of trustees. The remaining 35 per cent had various names, with no one title being more common than the 6 per cent referred to simply as the school board (CIS, 2005a: 1). The same CIS publication goes on, helpfully, to explain how at least some of these differences are likely to have arisen: while in US private schools the term generally used would be 'board of trustees', for instance, UK schools would usually have a 'board of governors'.

'The governance and management of [international] schools might be determined', say Blandford and Shaw, 'by the school, the owner, the Board, the senior management team or Head of school or a managing agency' (2001a: 2). From the school owned and run as a business by one individual, through parents' cooperative and proprietary company to state maintained school, the governance of an international school may vary from being much as one would recognise in a large commercial organisation through to that where the same person wears the hats of owner, head and chair of the board (as illustrated by the comment of one head, in Blandford and Shaw, who explained that 'I am the Chair, and the rest of the Board consists of my daughter and my son-in-law' (2001b: 23). Whatever its constitution, the Board is 'the employer, the maker of the policies to be administered, the arbiter of performance. It must be satisfied that the leadership the Head is providing is suitable for the school' (Mattern, 1994: 4). In this chapter, the term 'board' will be used to describe the body which has that responsibility within an international school, and the term 'board member' will be used as a generic description of those who, in reality, might have one of a number of other titles.

BOARD MEMBERS: WHO ARE THEY?

The nature of the membership of an international school board will depend on a range of factors relating to, inter alia, the origins of the school and the community it serves. The governance of various forms of proprietary schools, for instance, can vary enormously: some have no board, some (as in the example above) are family-run, with the same person in the roles of head and chair of the board, some employ a head to whom the owner makes regular 'suggestions' – and there are doubtless other variations on this theme.

Many international schools, however (as noted in Chapter 2), had their origins in what might be described as 'parent cooperatives': the initiative of a small group of expatriate parents who felt the need to provide a form of education for their offspring that was not otherwise available. It is not surprising, therefore, if international schools with such origins will allow only parents to be voting board members. Neither is it surprising if a school established under the auspices of the United Nations is required to have a number of UN representatives as board members, or if the board of a school established principally to provide education for the children of employees of a large multinational organisation has as members a number of senior managers of that organisation.

As Blandford and Shaw point out, the board of an international school may have as members 'the founder/owner, parents, interested members of the community, specialists from local business, headteacher, teacher representatives and others' (2001b: 23). Littleford in fact suggests that boards to be found in international schools can be categorised as follows:

- self-perpetuating, where current board members select the new members;
- elected, where an annual general meeting of the parent body elects the board (with no control by the board and the possibility of 'wild card' candidates or those with personal agendas being elected);
- elected, where the board screens and recruits potential parent members prior to the election 'to try to ensure endorsement of the board's slate of candidates' (less stable than the first type, but more stable than the second type);
- appointed by outsider groups, where embassy or 'key supporting corporations' have the right to appoint a certain number of board members 'from their own ranks'.

As well as various combinations of these four types, Littleford suggests that there exists one other: the 'shadow' board of between two and five individuals (or embassies or corporations) who hold the real power by retaining certain key rights while most policy decisions are made by the entire board (2002a: 1–2).

Interestingly, Littleford argues in favour of the self-perpetuating board as usually the most stable and leading to the best long-term decisions, a view seemingly shared by CIS in lamenting the transformation of many boards that were once appointed or self-perpetuating into elected or partially elected boards (2005a: 2). CIS cites for support in this view the findings of Pearl, in the context of American public schools, who writes that 'the politicising of many public school Board elections, along with the tendency of single-issue or ambitious zealots rather than wise moderates to seek office, has severely damaged many public school districts' (CIS, 2005a).

The different types of board found in international schools are described by Hodgson as including the proprietor/for profit schools which 'often have Boards that are made up of the shareholders, or the shareholders plus appointed members' (2005a: 9–10). Such boards, she writes, risk their decisions being overly influenced by the profit motive (rather than student need) and do not always have enough checks and balances 'to safeguard against poor judgement and self-interest'. Other types of board include those existing in the context of business partnership schools, where board members may be recruited from the company and their nominees. Many of the newer international schools (as in, for example, Asia and the Middle East) are, Hodgson points out, proprietary or business partnership schools. In such cases, she argues, it is essential that the roles and responsibilities of the board are clear 'from day one' so that investors and everyone else concerned are certain where they stand.

In terms of the make up of the board, Tangye argues in favour of it being neither wholly appointed (running the risk, he suggests, 'of being divorced from the community and being perceived as a self-perpetuated oligarchy') nor wholly elected (running the risk 'of abrupt changes in policy to the inevitable detriment of the school and the prevalence of personal agendas') (2005: 12). Wariness about personal agendas on the part of board members is in fact a point raised by many authors in the context of international school governance, whether on the part of representatives of organisations or of parents. 'Nothing but nothing', says Tangye, 'is more destructive of Board effectiveness than a member pursuing his or her personal agenda without consideration for the views of others or the good of the school' (2005: 15).

Littleford, for instance, cites the case of an international school where the host-country parents who make up half the board want stability, process and happy faculty, and are committed to long-term building plans, while expatriate parents tend to 'want change now, progress now, and they want that new innovation in place NOW. ... They tend to be less concerned about process and future building needs. They will not be there for those new buildings in any case' (2002a: 2). As Littleford states elsewhere, parent board members 'are often the most enthusiastic and committed, but can also be among the most conflicted', citing as an example a situation where a pattern had been established in a school whereby, whenever teachers were dissatisfied with any aspect of the head's actions, they 'went to the parents, who went to the Board, who undercut the Head' – a common pattern, according to Littleford, in many schools (2005b: 2).

The role of parents on the board also emerged as an issue in Hawley's research into the longevity of international school heads, where one conclusion reached was that heads tend to remain longer in international schools when board members are largely 'disinterested' in the sense that they do not have children enrolled in the school: this finding was supported by the interviews Hawley conducted which indicated that heads strongly preferred such members, whose interest in the school tended to be longer term and more objective than that of those whose interests were 'defined and driven by the needs of their children currently enrolled in the school' (1994: 13–14). Hawley also recommended that boards should include 'long-term members of the community where the school is located' (1995: 35).

Being a parent on a school board is never an easy task, suggests Littleford, while pointing out the importance of such a board member learning 'to remove his or her "parent hat" when in the Board room' (2003: 5). Parent board members, Littleford states elsewhere, 'must be very careful not to jump channels or cross boundaries, to try to engage staff, other parents, or other (Board members) in personal agendas that center around their own child (or) family interests' (2005c: 3). Essential though parents are as board members, says Walker, 'the fewer there are of them, the more likely they are to research the general parental will to match against their own parental prejudice' (2004a: 11), a sentiment shared by Vinge in remarking that in his forty years of working with boards in one capacity or another, 'the least effective model were totally elected untrained parent Boards. Even with training, many parent Board members have difficulty in separating the needs of their family from those of the school' (2005: 30).

Parents are not, of course, the only board members potentially to have a personal agenda, though the extent of their representation on many international school boards may lead to any conflict of interest that does arise being fairly high profile. Littleford recounts the case of a building fire in a school whose board chair was an insurance agent for the company representing the school, and where the insurance policy did not cover the full replacement value of the building. The extremely acrimonious situation that followed is used to support Littleford's contention that in general 'those who receive income from the school in almost any capacity should not serve on the Board' (2003: 3). Other situations where conflicts of interest have the potential to arise include those where the spouse or child of a board member is a member of staff at the school, and where the board member himself/herself is a member of staff. Littleford suggests that many schools do not have faculty representatives or indeed other 'representatives' on the board for the same reasons as those highlighted in relation to 'interested' parents: the worry 'that an individual will not rise to the larger purpose of the Board, to serve the mission of the school' but will rather 'focus on the narrower (purpose) of representing the interests of the group that elected them' – even though it should have been made clear to such individuals that they have not actually been 'elected' to represent that group's particular interests (2005c: 5). Indeed Littleford goes so far as to argue that there is no reason for the interests of faculty to be represented on the board by anyone other than the head (2000: 4), though this view would not necessarily be widely shared.

Some of the particular characteristics associated with different categories of board members in Schoppert's experience tend to relate to their background and interests:

> Business people may try to 'run the school like a business'. The school is, of course, a business, but the bottom line is more than dollars and cents. Parents tend to have a short-term view, and want things to change immediately to serve their own children's needs. Diplomats may be trying to keep the school more 'American' or more 'British', or indeed more 'international', rather than focusing on the population which the school serves. Non-working spouses may be looking for a fruitful way to spend their time, and while time is a valuable commodity for Board members, it can also produce micro-managing situations. (2001b: 164–5)

In offering advice to board members, Carver and Carver point out that

> You will understand and personally identify with one or more constituencies more than others. That provincial streak is natural in everyone, but your ...

> obligation is to rise above it. If you are a teacher, you are not on the Board to represent teachers. If you are a private businessperson, you are not there to represent that interest. You are a Board member for the broad ownership ... Think of yourself as being from a constituency, but not representing it. (1996: 12–13)

These are clearly not easy issues to deal with in practice, and where a board member has indeed been elected – or believes him/herself to have been elected – because they have particular expertise or links to a certain constituency, the contradiction with a 'leave personal issues outside the boardroom door' stance is evident. In many international schools whose board functions smoothly and effectively, however, it may well be that the notion of conflict of interest never really arises as an issue. In order to encourage such a situation, and avoid difficulties arising, it helps if all involved are clear about what exactly the role of the board and its members is intended to be.

THE ROLE OF THE BOARD AND ITS MEMBERS

The Role of the Board

'Schools with healthy Boards do not have crises' writes Littleford, 'They have solutions. Schools with unhealthy Boards make small incidents into crises and respond with hysteria rather than wisdom' (2002b: 2–3).

Key to many of the issues which arise with respect to the effectiveness of the board would seem to be the question of what exactly is its role and, perhaps as important, what that role is perceived to be by individual board members. Littleford argues that the members of the board are the trustees of the mission of the school. While interpretation of their role will not be precisely the same in every international school, certain key factors are likely to be found in all cases. CIS now includes in its standards for accreditation of international schools a number of standards relating specifically to the role of the 'governing body' or board, which provide detailed guidance as to what is perceived to be good practice in this context (2003).

It is clearly important to bear in mind that not only do international schools have a lot to learn from good practice established in national systems worldwide, they also have to take into account what it is that makes them different as international schools. As stated by Wilkinson,

> There must be a recognition by individual [international] school boards that, although they have a principal responsibility for the well-being of their own schools, they have, by calling themselves 'international', taken upon themselves a commitment to a wider concept that makes of them both practical and philosophical demands. These will need to address practical

concerns such as the high mobility of the student body and their teachers, the lack of initial training of teachers, the cultural impact of the host city or country, and the local market forces operating on the school. (2002: 191)

Malpass argues that in general an international school board should:

- assume responsibility for the legal and financial probity of the school;
- concern itself with the formation, revision and monitoring of general school policies;
- support the school in all its aspects;
- approve the budget and set school fees;
- appoint, supervise and evaluate the head; develop and monitor short-, medium- and long-term plans;
- seek to build up financial reserves. (1994: 25)

Tangye, meanwhile, believes that an effective board is one in which the members:

- work together by consensus, while not being afraid to debate contentious issues;
- leave any personal agendas outside the boardroom door;
- are responsive to the views of others, and voice any disagreement only within the confines of the meeting;
- leave the management of the school to those entrusted with this task;
- retain the strict confidentiality of all discussions;
- maintain both a sense of proportion and a sense of humour;
- set objectives for the board and evaluate themselves against those objectives;
- retain clear focus on their objective to improve the learning environment for students. (2005: 13)

Those issues which relate to governance – the legitimate domain of the board – are, as pointed out by Powell, matters of policy, long-range planning or significant financial impact. A board 'should be future oriented, focusing its attention on what the school should look like in five or ten years and what resources will be needed to carry it in that direction' (2001: 13). Powell goes on to summarise the 'commonly accepted governance responsibilities of a Board' as including:

- *Personnel*: hiring, developing, motivating, evaluating and retaining (or dismissing) the head (but not other members of staff, a role normally delegated to the head and/or other administrators).
- *Finance*: developing (with the head and business manager) and approving the annual budget and a multi-year financial development

plan, as well as (usually) setting tuition fees and determining teachers' salaries and benefits.

- *Planning*: as the 'architect of the school's future', the board 'needs to devote a significant portion of its time and focus to strategic planning'.
- *Policy formulation and adoption*: often involving a great deal of input from the head and other administrators, some policies would always be board responsibilities (for example, school mission and philosophy, admissions criteria and financial policies such as who holds spending authority) while others might or might not be, depending upon the school (for example, annual calendar, policy on consumption of alcohol on campus).
- *Curriculum and Instruction*: not generally for issues such as routine curriculum revision or teacher appraisal but for 'large and far reaching curricular changes' such as the adoption of the International Baccalaureate or making host-country language study compulsory; also for 'the broad ... area of quality assurance' including, for example, benchmark comparison, analysis of examination results and/or participation in accreditation self-studies. (Powell, 2001: 14–15)

Carver and Carver, though not writing specifically in the context of international schools, regret the fact that

> almost all published definitions of the Board's job are statements of activities or methods: approve budgets, make policy, oversee finances, participate in discussion, hire the CEO, read monitoring reports, listen to input, review plans, read the mailings, learn to read financial statements, become better communicators, attend meetings, keep minutes, call on donors, and so on *ad infinitum.* (1996: 4)

Their regret arises not because they feel there is anything wrong per se with such activities, but rather because fulfilling them does not necessarily lead to the board fulfilling its role. In providing a helpful distinction between what they term board 'responsibility' (direct responsibility for its own work) and board 'accountability' (bottom-up accumulation of responsibility for others' work together with its own), Carver and Carver point out that if the board's responsibility (its job description) is carefully defined and carried out appropriately, its accountability will be fulfilled (1996: 5–7).

In a nutshell, as Carver and Carver argue, only three products (as they describe them) cannot be delegated by the board, 'an irreducible trio applicable to all governing bodies' (which) if accomplished, as direct job responsibilities will 'ensure the Board's overall accountability as well'. The trio are the organisation's linkage to the 'ownership', explicit governing policies, and assurance of executive performance (in this case ensuring that the head is effectively implementing the board's policies). (1996: 6). Carver and Carver's point is perhaps not a million miles from the succinct summary provided by an experienced head of a number of international schools cited in Blandford and Shaw, who suggested that 'governors should hire the Head, set the long-term goals for the school, maintain overall budget control – then get out and let the professionals get on with it' (2001b: 23).

The Role of Board Members

Understanding the role of the board is one thing, but it must be remembered that the board is likely to be made up of individual members bringing with them different experiences and expectations, who also have individual responsibilities which need to be met if the board is to function effectively. Malpass argues that these responsibilities within an international school are for the board member to:

- understand the school;
- act as a link between the school and the community;
- support the school at all times;
- seek information and partake in important decision making;
- listen to the head and staff;
- defuse playground gossip;
- devote time and attention to board meetings. (1994: 6)

If these are the responsibilities of each individual board member, then what of the person who is expected to ensure that this group of individuals together perform effectively as a board: the chair? While writing in the context of independent schools generally, the points Littleford raises would have applicability to many international schools. Chairs, he says, are not usually paid for their role but are expected to give of their time and to support both fellow board members and the head. 'Assuming the role of Chair', says Littleford, 'is a feather in the cap professionally and personally to many chairs. To some ... it is a role by which they serve and support the school attended by their children or even grandchildren' (2005a: 2). Hodgson believes that 'the role of the Board Chair is to lead and direct the Board so as to ensure the long-term viability and future of the school' (2005b: 46). In order to do so, she argues, the board chair must:

- be passionate about the school's vision and mission and inspire others;
- be committed and have the ability to attract commitment;
- listen and hear.

Four major skills required by the board chair, Hodgson goes on to say, are the abilities to:

- facilitate and develop a group process;
- develop and manage relationships;

- plan and evaluate;
- communicate. (2005b: 46)

ISSUES AND CHALLENGES

'Sadly', writes Hodgson, 'international schools frequently lurch from Boards that micro-manage, to those that purely rubber stamp senior administrators' recommendations', before going on to quote Carver's suggestion that 'Boards tend to be ... incompetent groups of competent people' (2005a: 7). Or, as Vinge puts it: 'Board members ... usually include a collection of "successful" individuals who may not perform well as a group' [but who do nevertheless] 'sincerely desire to be effective Board members' (2005: 30–1). It is important to remember, however, in focusing on issues relating to boards and governance that, as in other walks of life, the stories that tend to travel best are those that relate to situations where problems have arisen and relationships have broken down. Stories about what is going well and boards that function smoothly and effectively do not tend to make the news. The purpose of discussion in this section is to focus on those situations where difficulties can occur, but do not necessarily lead to insurmountable problems if there is an awareness of and sensitivity to the potential issue in more general terms before it arises.

Multicultural Membership

One respect in which international school boards may differ from school boards found in many national contexts is in the multicultural nature of the membership. Aside from issues relating to the role of board members in general are those relating to the different ways in which those roles may be interpreted as a result of different previous experiences and expectations. While the school philosophy and mission may be something with which all can agree, the perception of how policy arising from it should be interpreted may be quite different. Student behaviour and school discipline, for instance, are just one area where it could be envisaged that those from different cultural backgrounds might take a variety of stances, thus leading to challenges which would be less likely to arise in a more monocultural context. When there are cultural differences between the head and board members, and/or between the head and board chair, such challenges may be exacerbated.

Relationship with the Head

Not unique by any means to the international schools network is the issue of the importance of the relationship between the board and its chief executive officer: in this case the head of the school. Ideally, says Vinge, the board and the head will have a partnership based on mutual support and trust. The head,

> engaged full-time in the school, is viewed as being experienced in governance and as an expert in education. This mutual dependence is a unique relationship in which the Board and Head rely on each other to exchange information and support that enables them to perform their respective roles more effectively (Blau, 1986). This assumption requires that the Head and Board members can function as critics, friends, counsellors and confidants. (Vinge, 2005: 31)

The relationship between head and board chair is particularly important. Littleford posits that

> Heads need Chairs who are kind, thoughtful, nurturing, supportive and wear 'iron pants' when the Head or school is challenged. They need Chairs who will critique them privately while supporting them publicly and who will guard against inappropriate [Board member] 'boundary crossing' and micro management [while ensuring that Board members] focus on the key strategic, policy and governance questions that can sometimes be the defining moments of leadership of great Chairs and great Boards. (2005a: 2).

Vinge quotes De Kuyper's (1998) analogies of a three-legged race, a tennis doubles partnership and baseball's catcher-pitcher relationship to describe how harmoniously the two need to work together for the good of the school (2005: 34).

Given the number of horror story anecdotes that abound on the international school circuit, it would be tempting to infer that there cannot be too strong or too close a relationship between head and board chair. Not so, according to Littleford, who suggests that a close relationship between head and chair can lead to other board members feeling that the chair is perhaps too likely to 'defend the head at every turn' and can lead to those board members distancing themselves from both, thus undermining, as Littleford writes, 'the one safety mechanism the Head has: the respect the Chair commands to deflect excessive or inappropriate attacks on the Head' (1999a: 29).

For many international school heads, and ex-heads, the idea of being perceived as too close to the board chair may seem less of a likely problem than that which by all accounts is more frequently encountered, when the relationship between head and board and/or board chair becomes dysfunctional to the point, in some cases, of being entirely unworkable. It has already been noted (see Chapter 7) that international school heads have a notoriously high turnover rate, and it is undoubtedly the case that a large proportion of heads leaving international schools do so because of difficulties in their relationship with the board. Hawley's research, for instance, indicated that a total of 61 out of 83 international school heads surveyed had left for a reason associated with the board: the two most frequently cited situations being a change in board membership (proving the most frequent and discussed later in this chapter) and board involvement in running the school (1995: 24).

Micro-management

The issue of board involvement in running the school will strike a chord with many readers who have experienced, or heard stories of, what might be summarised as 'micro-management' by the board. In an ideal world the head and the board would work together as noted above: essentially by the board determining policy and the head ensuring implementation of the same. In stressing the importance of a board and its administration discussing and determining 'what constitutes policy that is destined for Board approval and what is in the arena of administrative regulation', Powell suggests that 'In most cases, "policy" will address the questions of what, why and how much. Administrative regulations will answer the questions how, by whom and when' (2001: 11).

Walker, however, cautions against being too precise in attempting to draw a line between the roles of management and governance. A myth exists, he says, that

> in most effective organisations, a clear distinction will be drawn between management and governance; the Head manages and the Board governs. But in reality that never happens. The Head will want to use her professional knowledge and experience to influence policy; otherwise, why was she ever appointed? And the Board will need to know enough about the way the school works to be able to develop realistic policies ... So let us forget the myth of total separation and recognize that most of the interesting action takes place in that difficult-to-negotiate no-man's-land where governance and management overlap. (2004a: 10)

Striking a happy and realistic balance is clearly not an easy thing to do, and some board members seemingly cannot resist becoming involved to an extent that some heads consider as constituting interference. As one head in Hawley's study observed; 'Would you accept as a surgeon that the hospital administrator tells you how to operate?' (1995: 26). While a blurring of the distinction between the roles of board and head may be either positive (as noted by Walker) or problematic, less clear perhaps is why problems arise when they do. Malpass suggests that they often occur because of lack of understanding of the two distinct roles, or in some cases because of misleading terminology (where, for example, as noted earlier, the board is described as a 'board of directors', which suggests an expectation of board members 'directing' more closely than might actually be the case) (1994: 24).

CIS cite an article by Jazzar (2005) that gives six reasons why boards tend to micro-manage:

- lack of clarity of board members' roles and responsibilities, leading to them doing 'what they think they should be doing';
- board members not having a clear set of policies that define their own specific (as opposed to staff) decisions;
- the day-to-day experience of many board members of managing rather than policy making: in the absence of clear definitions of their role, they 'continue to do what comes naturally';
- many members are invited to join the board as a result of having certain expertise, leading to them being invited to perform particular tasks rather than to share in policy making;
- boards sometimes begin to micro-manage in the event of a crisis, 'to make sure the institution survives', but then continue in the same pattern after the crisis has passed;
- board members are sometimes afraid that if they don't do it, 'no-one else will or no-one will do it as well'. (2005b: 1–2).

In short, 'Oftentimes, schools get into difficulties when a Board attempts to step into an operational or management role. Such micro-management, however well meaning, almost inevitably leads to role confusion and potential conflict' (Powell 2001: 13).

It is how such conflict is managed, according to Stout, that determines the outcomes of potentially difficult situations. Conflict, he points out,

> is a natural concomitant of social interaction and has been so since the day of Eve and her apple ... Social groups require a certain degree of dissonance in order to achieve progress. ... Conflict can have positive as well as negative effects, but which state predominates largely depends upon the way in which it is managed. (2005a: 16)

In referring specifically to the conflict that can arise in international schools between heads and boards, Stout focuses on how such conflict can be either avoided or, failing that, managed. 'In many cases', he says, 'the initial cause of governance/management conflict begins with a tiny issue. This escalates into a personal agenda, and then all too often becomes a cause célèbre for a Board member' (2005a: 16). Suggestions for dealing with such situations will be discussed later in this chapter.

Changes in Board Membership

Hawley suggests that board member turnover is highly predictive of the duration of international school heads: in other words, the higher the turnover of board membership, the greater the likelihood that the head will not last very long (1994: 15). Such a pattern is not difficult to understand, given the expectation there might be of loyalty towards a head on the part of those board members by whom he/she was appointed, compared with the lower level of commitment that might be shown by those without such a vested interest. As Littleford notes, 'Only the original Board and Search Committee remembers why the Head was hired in the first place and the vision that the new Head articulated so well' (2000: 1).

Clearly the departure of a board member – or indeed chair – may not always be within the control of the board if, for instance, an employee of a multinational organisation is relocated at relatively short notice, or board membership requires individuals to be the parents of a child at the school and that child has now left. But in some cases it seems that turnover is higher than might be desirable because of regulations requiring board members to step down after a fixed, relatively short, period of time. Schoppert suggests that such 'term limits' should probably be eschewed in order to help to ensure board stability (2001b: 163). Hawley recommends that the very minimum period served by a board member should be two years (1995: 35), while Littleford suggests that, in order to preserve institutional memory, 'THREE terms of either three or four years each, or rolling three year terms with NO limits' are appropriate – with the proviso that such a policy will work so long as an effective board member evaluation system is in place (2003: 5).

If turnover of board members is an issue, what then of the optimum term of office of the board chair, whose relationship with the head and whose role in developing the board into a cohesive unit, acting together as a team on strategic issues facing the school, is so crucial to the effective running of the school (Daignault, 1999, in Nelson, 2000: 172)? Indeed, how is the chair identified in the first place? Littleford argues strongly that the process of chair selection should NOT be democratic, and stresses the importance of consulting the head about who the next chair should be, with 'significant weight' being given to the head's first choice: such consultation could best be done, he argues, by a very small group of 'wise men and women' who consult in confidence with the head and the existing chair 'to ensure the proper choice of a new Chair is made' (2000: 3). Stout goes so far as to argue that 'it is vital that the Board allows the Head to nominate the new Chair either from within the Board or without', suggesting that 'Chairs who are not parents, but who may have been associated in the past as parents, often make the best Chairs' (2005a: 19).

In criticising many boards for neither planning far enough in advance for chair turnover nor ensuring that effective chairs serve for longer periods, Littleford proposes that chairs should serve at least three to five years, and should be encouraged to stay longer if the board supports the chair's leadership, the chair has a good working relationship with the head, and the chair's 'personal and professional life is not adversely affected by continued service' (2000: 3). Littleford also suggests that the outgoing chair, assuming that person was reasonably effective and respected by the board, should remain a member of the board for at least two years after stepping down (challenging though that may be for the new chair), so that the board does not lose that person's accumulated wisdom and experience (1999b: 5).

SUPPORT FOR GOOD PRACTICE

Clearly, micro-management and high board turnover can be real issues for an international school; other causes of difficulty can also arise and may lead to major problems. At least one of the underpinning reasons for such difficulties would seem to be genuine misunderstanding – perhaps, as suggested by Hawley, exacerbated by cultural differences within the board and between the board and the head – about the respective roles of the board and the person appointed to be their chief executive officer (1995: 27). Not surprisingly, this highlights the question of if and how boards are trained for their role.

Board Training

Training for newly-elected board members and for those already serving is essential, argues Wilkinson, 'even when Board members have some educational experience. It cannot be assumed that experience and understanding in a national context is sufficient for a (board member) to make an effective contribution in an international context' (2002: 193). Similarly, Vinge highlights the importance of the head (or head and chair) accepting 'the ongoing obligation of regular Board development and training. ... The need for training is particularly important in international schools where there tends to be a high turnover of both Heads and Board members' (2005: 31).

In acknowledging that 'many school Boards start the year with a disparate group of experienced and novice members' and that 'the potential for discord and lack of direction is therefore great', Bowley argues that some form of board training in international schools is 'essential' (2001a: 23–4). Littleford concurs, suggesting that a board can learn in two ways: by 'baptism of fire' or by being taught 'actively and proactively' (2005c: 6). CIS also argues that board training 'on site and off site can be of great benefit and must be done on an annual basis' (2005b: 3). Orientation for a new board member, according to Bowley, should include a thorough introduction to their new responsibilities 'through the provision of a detailed information package detailing all aspects of the school, a tour of the school and briefing meetings with the Head, Business Manager and Board office holders'. It may also include, he notes, new members participating in 'Board training institutes' (2001a: 24–5).

As noted by both Bowley and Littleford, boards are increasingly building into their planning the notion of a 'board retreat', whose chief aim is to 'forge a team whose members pursue a common purpose and abide by a common code of practice, while respecting each other's different backgrounds and points of view'. Ideally led by an external, impartial facilitator and held at the beginning of the school year, such retreats would be annual events: 'not a one time occurrence' for new board members to learn the rules, as Littleford points out, since 'the rules are learned over time through repetition and application to new circumstances and issues' (2005c: 4). Indeed, Littleford argues that training is required not only by board members but also specifically by board chairs (2005a: 2).

Board Evaluation

It has already been emphasised that an effective board, working well with the head, is central to the running of an effective international school. How then does a board know whether it is effective? CIS now includes the expectation that boards will have a 'clear evaluation system in place' within their Standards for Accreditation of international schools (2003: 45). The board should, says Hodgson:

- evaluate itself;
- invite the head and the administration to evaluate the board;
- evaluate the board chair;
- incorporate the findings into the governance section of the annual review of the strategic plan.

Judgements should be made 'against a clear and detailed statement of expectations' (Hodgson, 2005b: 45).

Bowley similarly stresses the importance of the board monitoring its own performance as objectively as possible, notwithstanding the difficulties of self-evaluation and of evaluating the performance of a team. 'If it fails to do this', he suggests, 'it may discover that parents and other members of the school community will find other means of passing judgment on the Board's performance. Many an Extraordinary General Meeting has been convened for this reason' (2001b: 130). The board's self-evaluation, Bowley argues, should be annual and against specific pre-established criteria. It should assess its performance in terms of progress towards achieving not only the school's philosophy and goals, but also any goals determined by external accrediting agencies and the school's strategic plan, as well as the board's goals for the year as determined in the previous evaluation cycle. Bowley goes on to advise that the evaluation should be in written form, signed by the board chair and secretary, and should incorporate a written evaluation from the head and any other frequent observers of board meetings (2001b: 130).

Indeed Hodgson adds that the opinions of all senior administrators should be sought (2005a: 8). The board may, says Bowley, undertake a separate evaluation of the board chair, the crucial point being that whether or not such an evaluation is undertaken should be a matter of policy and not based on ad hoc decisions (2001b). Evaluation of the board chair by the board, both Hodgson (2005a: 8) and Littleford (2005a: 2) suggest, should be annual. Littleford actually goes one step further than other authors, in arguing that each individual board member should be required to undertake an annual self-evaluation based on the completion of a standard questionnaire. At least part of one board meeting a year should then be devoted to reviewing the outcomes of the board self-evaluation, he says, providing an opportunity for board members to reflect upon their own contributions (2002b: 1–2).

Conflict Resolution

Earlier reference was made to the challenge of conflict arising, particularly, within the board/head relationship, and the disastrous consequences that may follow if such conflict is not managed appropriately. Stout recommends that board policy and heads' contracts should 'make provision for the implementation of conflict resolution intervention' (2005b: 43). He also points out that while international schools will generally have disciplinary and grievance procedures in place, these are either ineffective or inappropriate for handling board/head conflict for which relevant procedures rarely exist. It is thus vital, he argues, that both parties recognise the early signs, admit that conflict exists and declare formally a conflict situation:

> This in itself signifies the mutual recognition of the problem, sees a cessation of 'hostilities', prevents further escalation of the conflict and allows for a cooling off period during which time the parties can negotiate in-house, preferably chaired by a neutral third party acting as a mediator. (Stout, 2005a: 19–20).

If such in-house negotiations fail to resolve the problem, it is argued, the chair and head should jointly inform their 'professional membership organisation' of the situation and seek advice as to the way forward. Such organisations, Stout says, do not currently have formal procedures in place for dealing with such situations (though informal support has been provided in the past) and should consider introducing them in the current climate of all-too-frequently-occurring board/head conflict which, more often than not, is 'resolved' by the premature departure of the head.

The Role of Accreditation

As might be expected, those agencies which accredit international schools have a view on various aspects of school governance, some of which have been noted in earlier references in this chapter to the role of CIS. Some, such as Stout (in relation to conflict resolution), would like to see that role extended. Issues relating to accreditation will be discussed in further detail in Chapter 10.

CONCLUSION

Much that has been written in this chapter could equally apply to non-international schools in national systems around the world. Good governance, it could be argued, is good governance wherever it is to be found. What arguably makes the international school context different, however, is the relative transience of some board members (where short-term commercial contracts are involved) and the multicultural mix of board members linked, perhaps, to varied previous experiences and expectations based on other cultural contexts. Taken together with the cultural differences often to be found between the head and board members, the complex set of requirements and regulations that may affect the school, unpredictable enrolment and many other challenges faced on a daily basis, it is not surprising that tensions should surface occasionally. The many international schools that run smoothly and effectively are likely to be those where such tensions are anticipated and suitable systems are in place to deal with them when they arise.

There is, however, another argument advanced from time to time which focuses on the wider horizon and challenges the very notions of good governance that have been advanced in this chapter. Hodgson summarises such a view in arguing 'that the world is rapidly changing and the challenges facing international schools, the size of their budgets and their responsibilities as an employer, have outgrown the most frequently used governance model taken from nineteenth and twentieth century philanthropy'. 'When one reflects on the evolution of school administration in the last 100 years', she writes, 'the lack of a similar change in the approach to governance is remarkable' (2005a: 7). Perhaps, given the difficulties and challenges faced not infrequently in this context, it is indeed time to reflect on the relevance of the existing governance model to international schools of the twenty first-century.

CHAPTER 9

The Curriculum

Previous chapters have focused on issues relating to a number of different communities central to the functioning of an international school. No less central to the functioning of such a school is the curriculum, the means by which expectations of the various communities may be realised and to which they all relate in some way, whether by determining policy as to its nature, delivering it, experiencing it as a learner or taking it into account as a deciding factor in the choice of school.

If we accept Lawton's assertion that the curriculum is a selection from the culture of a society, leading to a list of cultural priorities for schools in best maintaining and developing that culture (1989), it quickly becomes apparent how complex is the question of curriculum in international schools. From which society's culture(s) is an international school to select? What sort of society or culture is the school aiming to promote? And what does the term 'curriculum' mean anyway? Widely used in some cases to mean what might elsewhere be described as 'the syllabus' (the statement of content to be taught in lessons), it can also be used in a much broader sense to encompass every dimension of the student's school experience. That is the sense in which it will be used in this chapter, which will also incorporate consideration of assessment as a subset of the broader curriculum context.

One helpful categorisation of different dimensions of the curriculum is that based on the notion that distinctions can be made between what is planned by the school and what is actually experienced by the student. Kelly refers to the 'official curriculum and the actual curriculum' or the 'planned curriculum and the received curriculum', explaining that 'By the official or planned curriculum is meant what is laid down in syllabuses, prospectuses and so on; the actual or received curriculum is the reality of the pupils' experience' (2004: 6). Robitaille referred to three different components of curriculum: the designed or intended; the taught or implemented; and the learned or attained (1993). In other words this inserts an additional category between Kelly's planned and received curriculum, where the taught or implemented curriculum 'is the set of activities, learning experiences and pedagogic strategies which teachers use in order to enact the intended curriculum' (Nampota, 2005: 84). In an ideal world, all three dimensions would be the same and such a distinction would be redundant. In the less than ideal world of reality, however, there can be inconsistencies between the three. The categorisation of what will be described here as the intended, implemented and learned curriculum will be used in this chapter as the basis for discussion of a number of issues of particular relevance to international schools.

THE INTENDED CURRICULUM

The intended dimension of the curriculum can helpfully be broken down into what Bulman and Jenkins describe as three main (and overlapping) aspects:

- the academic curriculum: what is formally 'taught' in schools;
- the pastoral curriculum: including social skills, study skills, counselling for careers and occupations; and
- the hidden curriculum: 'those practices and outcomes of schooling which, while not explicit in curriculum guides or school policy, nevertheless seem to be a regular and effective part of the school experience ... covert, unintended, implicit, or simply unacknowledged ... educational practices treated as part of the hidden curriculum include ability grouping, teacher-pupil relationships, classroom rules and procedures, implicit textbook content, sex-role differentiation of pupils, and classroom reward structures' (Vallance, 1991: 40). (Bulman and Jenkins, 1988)

The intended curriculum will be considered here firstly in relation to these three aspects in international schools, to be followed by discussion of a number of issues that may arise particularly in that context.

The Academic Curriculum

Deciding which academic programmes to offer can be a major challenge for some international schools. Those with a national affiliation may have little flexibility: a British international school, for instance, may be expected by all concerned to offer the national curriculum from 'back home' up to the age of 16 – or a modified version of it – while an American international school will undoubtedly be expected to offer a curriculum that is recognisable to parents and teachers with American connections and experience. The intended academic curriculum may thus be that intended by the school that devised it for its own use, or that intended by an external organisation that develops programmes for use by international, and possibly other, schools.

As the number and diversity of international schools have grown over the years, so too has the number of programmes developed for their potential use. Thompson produced a four-way categorisation of attempts to devise curricula for use internationally, summarised as follows:

- *Exportation*: the marketing abroad of existing national curricula and examinations, with little if any adjustment to take account of the different context, and a value system 'unapologetically that of the country from which it is exported'.
- *Adaptation*: where existing national curricula and examinations are adapted for the national context, with the 'inherent value system' not likely to change at all and the risk of, as Thompson puts it, an 'unwitting process of educational imperialism'.
- *Integration*: where 'best practices' from a range of 'successful' curricula are brought together into one curriculum for operation across a number of systems or countries (with attendant challenges potentially to be faced from the different values and ideological positions in question).
- *Creation*: the development of a programme 'from first principles'. (1998: 278–80).

Some of the curriculum programmes developed for use in international schools can be considered under these categories, as follows.

Exported

There are numerous examples of exported programmes in international schools around the world including French, German, Japanese and, frequently in English-medium international schools, British and American.

Adapted

Among the national programmes adapted for the international school context, a number of widely offered programmes have a high profile including the following:

- *The Advanced Placement (AP) International Diploma*: adapted from the AP program established in 1955 by the College Board in the USA to provide high school students with college-level academic courses 'accepted for credit, advanced placement, or both, by most American colleges and universities' (College Board, 2004: 2), the AP International Diploma (APID) was introduced in 1995 as 'a globally recognized certificate for students with an international outlook. The English-medium APID is available to students attending secondary schools outside the

United States and for US resident students applying to universities outside the country' (DiYanni, 2006).

- *The International GCSE* (IGCSE): an adaptation of the General Certificate of Secondary Education (GCSE) introduced in the mid-1980s, the English-medium IGCSE was first examined in 1988 by the University of Cambridge Local Examinations Syndicate to be consistent with the GCSE but to be more relevant outside the UK context (Cambridge International Examinations, 2006). While certificates are awarded in individual subjects, a group award, the International Certificate of Education (ICE), reflects success in a wide range of subjects (Beedle et al., 2006). Interestingly, a more recent development has been the introduction of a second IGCSE, this time offered by a different English Awarding Body, Edexcel. Again an adaptation of the national GCSE (Edexcel, 2006), this IGCSE is a smaller scale operation than its Cambridge namesake.
- *The Advanced International Certificate of Education* (AICE): again developed by Cambridge International Examinations, the English-medium AICE is designed for an international market and requires successful completion of six credits, where an AS level is equivalent to one credit and an A level is equivalent to two credits. At least one of the courses selected must be from each of three curriculum areas: Mathematics and Science, Languages, and Arts and Humanities.
- *French Baccalauréat Option Internationale*: offered only by international schools recognised by the French Ministry of Education, the option internationale has two programmes: British and American, supervised by the Cambridge Local Examinations Syndicate and College Board respectively, in conjunction with the Inspection Générale d'Anglais et d'Histoire de l'Education Nationale (scol@gora, 2006).

Integrated

- *The European Baccalaureate*: taught in the final two years of secondary education of the European Schools (DfE, 1994: 7) and first awarded as a qualification in 1959, the European Baccalaureate is consistent with the overall emphasis on language competence within the European Schools: 'On the one hand, they attempt to guarantee the development of the child's first language and cultural identity, while on the other they strive to promote a European identity through instruction for all pupils in at least two languages, compulsory learning of a third as a subject, and options regarding a fourth language' (Baetens Beardsmore, 1993: 122). Syllabuses for the European Baccalaureate are 'harmonised' in the sense that they are designed to meet the requirements of all European Union member countries (Gray, 2003: 329–30).
- *The International Baccalaureate Diploma Programme* (IBDP): the oldest of the international programmes offered within international schools (other than the small group of European Schools), the pre-university

IBDP's development and early days have been well documented in, inter alia, Peterson (1987 and 2003) and a series of articles by Hill (2006b). The IBDP model, based on a requirement that all students complete a compulsory Theory of Knowledge (TOK) course, Extended Essay and Creativity, Action, Service (CAS) programme as well as choosing six subjects from different subject groups, is often represented as a hexagon (Thompson, 1988, in Fox, 1998: 69) and has much in common with other baccalaureate models (Thompson et al., 2003). It is offered in both international and national schools worldwide, in three working languages (English, French and Spanish) in which all materials are produced and all assessment/examinations may be undertaken. Thompson suggests that integration characterised the early days of the IB Diploma in the sense that input from experts from many different parts of the world brought together examples of good practice from a number of systems (1998: 279). Arguably, some dimensions such as the compulsory Theory of Knowledge course could be considered to fit more neatly into Thompson's 'creation' category, suggesting that the categories are not entirely discrete.

Created

Although the following programmes frequently found in international schools would seem to fit most clearly into the 'created' category, it could be argued that no programme can ever be considered to have been created entirely *de novo*, since any educationists involved in its development are bound to have been informed and influenced by their previous experiences of other educational programmes.

- *The IB Middle Years Programme* (IBMYP): initially the creation of the International Schools Association, the International Schools Association Curriculum (ISAC) as it was first known, was taken over by the IBO in 1992 (Ellwood, 1999: 35) and is designed for the 11–16 age range. With the emphasis heavily on teacher assessment, the possibility of external moderation exists for those schools/students who require external certification (IBO, 2006).
- *The IB Primary Years Programme* (IBPYP): created initially as the International Schools Curriculum Project (ISCP) which was the first international programme to be developed for the primary age range (3–12), the IBO took over its administration in 1997. A set of student learning outcomes provides the aims for the curriculum, which centres around five 'essential elements': concepts, knowledge, skills, attitudes and action (Bartlett, 1998: 83).
- *The International Primary Curriculum* (IPC): developed by Fieldwork Education, the IPC is offered within both international schools and

national systems (IPC, 2006). More explicitly structured than the IBPYP, the IPC 'main programme' provides detailed documentation relating to units offered across three different stages (or mileposts) for ages 6–7, 8–9 and 10–12. The more recently developed Early Years IPC is designed for the 4–5 age range (IPC, 2006).

- *The Cambridge International Primary Programme*: as the newest of the programmes described here, this is designed specifically with international schools in mind. Including the core subjects of English, mathematics and science, the programme is organised into six stages, covering the 5–11 age range (CIE, 2006).

The Pastoral Curriculum

The term 'pastoral curriculum' may not be widely used within international schools, but is nevertheless useful as a means of describing those parts of the formal curriculum that are

> concerned with promoting pupils' personal and social development and fostering positive attitudes: through the nature of relationships amongst pupils, teachers and adults other than teachers; through arrangements for monitoring pupils' overall progress, academic, personal and social; through specific pastoral structures and support systems; and through extra-curricular activities and the school ethos. (DES, 1989)

Drake argues that such concepts are just as essential in international schools as elsewhere:

> The development of a pastoral care programme within an international school ... is of very real importance. It should certainly receive as much attention as it does in any national system, perhaps more so, since many of the students in an international school are not only facing the normal challenges of adolescence but also have to deal with cultural and other forms of dislocation, often in the absence of extended family and friendship support networks. (1998: 153–4)

In fact many international schools, whether or not they use this terminology, include a 'pastoral' dimension in the students' school experience, though different emphases are placed in respect of some dimensions such as value systems and social competence, where different cultural contexts require different sets of skills (Drake, 1998: 154).

Indeed, it could be argued that many international schools are already providing at least as strong a pastoral dimension as many national schools when the range of support provided for globally mobile students and their families is taken into account. In a case study of the implementation of a pastoral programme at one international school, Drake highlighted a number of challenges likely to arise in formally devising such a programme, including how it is staffed (if teachers perceive their primary role as to teach and not to take on other responsibilities), the challenges of cross-cultural counselling (when some students and tutors would feel more comfortable discussing some 'life skills' with others of the same sex and cultural background), and values (the need for clarity with respect to what values the international school should promote, and how these are decided). Arguably such issues are to be found in any international school, though perhaps under the surface in some cases rather than being made explicit. The formal development of a pastoral programme seems likely to bring such issues to the surface, which may be both beneficial and challenging to all concerned.

The Hidden Curriculum

The potential for the hidden curriculum to have both negative and positive effects is at least as high within international schools as it would be within a national system, given the emphasis often placed on values and cultural sensitivity within such a context. Individual teachers and administrators, for instance, may unwittingly either reinforce or undermine through their own behaviour the school's mission (of, for example promoting respect for all, regardless of cultural or linguistic background), and the choice of teaching materials may convey unintended messages to students as to who or what is valued by those making such choices. This dimension of the curriculum has clear overlaps with the implemented and learned curriculum, and a number of issues particularly relevant to international schools will be discussed under that heading later in this chapter.

Issues in the Intended Curriculum

Even within national contexts, there may be much soul-searching as to what is appropriate curriculum content for young people who need to develop skills for their adulthood which are not currently predictable. How much more complex, then, is the question of curriculum content for the many children attending international schools whose future country of residence, let alone the skills they are likely to require, is virtually impossible to predict?

Breadth vs Specialisation

One fundamental question that arises in devising a formal curriculum is just how much it is reasonable to include at every stage of a child's schooling. Considerations of national programmes suggest that differences tend to become more marked as the age level increases, with quite clear distinctions between the perceived benefit of continuing breadth of study for as long as possible, as opposed to the increasing specialisation to be found in, for example, the A-level system of England where, notwithstanding the groundswell of support for the broadening proposals of the ill-fated Tomlinson Committee (DfES, 2004b), a very narrow specialisation is still possible from the age of 16, if not earlier.

The case of the IB Diploma programme is interesting in highlighting such differences. Influenced by the work of, inter alia, Phenix (1964) in the USA and Hirst and Peters (1970) in the UK, the requirement to study six subjects plus the TOK course, CAS activities and Extended Essay is variously seen as very broad in, for example, England (and viewed either positively or negatively on that basis) or quite narrow in, say, some countries of continental Europe where students in the national system would follow a much wider range of courses through to the end of compulsory schooling. The IBDP also provides an interesting illustration of pragmatism in this context, where the ideal intended of the breadth for all students including study of subjects from six different areas has been modified to allow the sixth subject to be selected – rather than from one of the Arts subjects – as a second choice from one of the other groups. The ideal in terms of balance has thus been tempered by recognition of the need for a certain amount of pragmatism in allowing students the opportunity for some specialisation if they are not to be disadvantaged in applying for university-level study.

Pragmatism vs Ideology in the Curriculum

The mission statements of many international schools suggest that they see as part of their role not only the development in students of what might be described as pragmatic skills for international adult life, but also the more ideologically-focused skills which will enable them to be good international citizens, promoting global understanding, respecting their fellow citizens and having a tolerant and open attitude to others. Such a philosophy is also to be found in the programmes developed for use within this context: some quite overtly and others less so. The IBO, for instance, and the IPC, claim that the study of their programmes will contribute to the student's developing international understanding, which for some international schools will be important in supporting their own mission. In this sense the curriculum can be seen to fit into Thompson's 'A, B, C' model of a learning environment for international education (see Figure 9.1), where administrative style, a balanced curriculum and cultural diversity all play crucial roles in contributing to an environment in which international education may flourish (1998: 288).

Quite what the balance should be between the emphasis on pragmatism and ideology is clearly a matter for the school to decide, not only in relation to the programmes it chooses to offer but also in relation to how it implements them. It may well be the case that the balance across the age range will vary as the prospect of leaving school, moving on to university/college

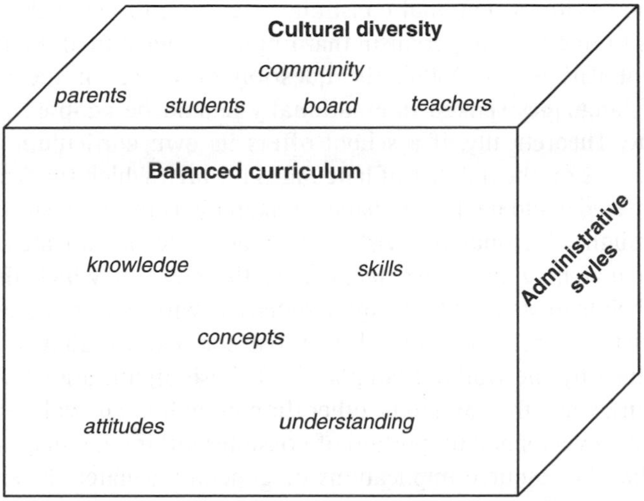

Figure 9.1 Model of a learning environment for international education (Thompson, 1998)

entrance and possibly of completing external examinations impinges upon the older students in such a way as to give the more pragmatic dimensions a higher profile.

Languages: the medium of instruction

Aside from the issue of what content should be included in the curriculum is that of the medium of instruction to be adopted. No longer a simple question in many increasingly multicultural national systems (for example, the London comprehensive school teaching some parts of the curriculum in Turkish since 400 of its 1100 students are native Turkish speakers: see Hayes, 2006), the question of which languages of instruction should be used in an international school is complex.

At one end of the spectrum is the argument that English, as the predominant world language (Grimshaw, 2006), is the obvious choice of medium of instruction for international schools. Indeed, English-medium instruction is the main reason cited by many parents for choosing an international school education for their child (see Chapter 3). Certainly the majority of such schools offer only English-medium teaching, although there are those that place a heavy emphasis on bilingualism. Others operating within a clearly defined multilingual context require students to study through the medium of several different languages, the European Schools being one of the most obvious illustrations, though even they are facing challenges as the European Union, and the number of its associated native languages, continue to expand (Gray, 2003).

To a school with no national constraints, wishing to avoid the potential for charges of linguistic imperialism that might be levied in an English-only environment (Grimshaw, 2006), the question of which of the enormous number of languages spoken internationally should be adopted is a challenging one. Theoretically, if a school offers its own curriculum, then the only constraints on the number of languages through which that curriculum might be offered could be the languages spoken by its teaching staff, the languages through which parents wish their children to be educated, and the logistics of matching these two factors. At the point at which the school wishes to heighten its credibility by association with externally developed and administered programmes (such as those summarised above), they will be constrained by the working languages of those organisations. And such organisations, when they aim to be other than monolingual, will clearly need to select only a very small proportion of possible working languages because of, inter alia, the resource implications of generating materials, employing staff, offering professional development and (where appropriate) examinations, including translating examination papers and appointing suitable examiners who are fluent in those languages.

Given the number of cultural and linguistic backgrounds represented by students in many international schools (upwards of 30 being not uncommon) the fact that not all languages can be included is self-evident. The question of which small number of languages should be selected over others is altogether more contentious. English would seem to be the prime contender for first place in such a choice, though which form of English is not necessarily a straightforward question. Which other languages should be included is less clear. The IBO, the only one of the organisations noted above to offer its programmes in other than English (with the exception of the French Baccalauréat Option Internationale and the possibility of the IPC being offered in Dutch as well as English), opted originally for English and French as its working languages, which were joined later by Spanish when the introduction of a southern hemisphere November examination session brought in a number of schools from Latin America. To this day the three working languages of the IB Diploma programme remain English, French and Spanish. The IB Middle Years and Primary Years programmes, without the constraints of external examinations, can be more flexible in terms of languages and in fact Chinese is also a working language in the MYP, with the possibility of both the MYP and PYP being taught in yet other languages (IBO, 2006).

The question of working languages has taxed the IBO as the cultural contexts of the increasing numbers of schools offering its programmes have become more diverse. Accusations of 'Eurocentricity' are not uncommon: fuelled by the choice of working languages, but also relating to the nature of the curriculum (and assessment, in the case of the Diploma programme's external examinations), there has been much debate within the IBO as to what selection of working languages, if any, might be more appropriate and viable in resource terms. What, then, is the solution to such a challenge? Should the current working languages be changed? In purely pragmatic terms, on the basis of student numbers there is now little justification for one of the working languages being French – but to drop French as a working language would be to raise a major political, not purely pragmatic, issue. And is the issue of working language relatively cosmetic compared with the deeper issues of cultural dimensions of the programmes offered?

Those who devise the curriculum and assess the examinations may be from a wide range of cultural and linguistic backgrounds, but the basic premise of IB programmes is culturally based. Heyward argues that, notwithstanding the addition into the IBDP curriculum of subjects such as the History and Culture of the Islamic World, 'the degree to which the curriculum either is genuinely international or remains eurocentric and western-biased is a matter of ongoing debate within IB circles' (2002: 24). And Drake points out that

> All IB programmes actively cultivate critical thinking skills. At age appropriate levels students are encouraged to challenge received wisdom, including that imparted by the teacher. However, in societies where there are high power-distance relationships, such as many African nations, China and Japan, open criticism of elders ... remains culturally unacceptable. Moreover, a Chinese or Japanese child successfully adapted to the skill of independent enquiry would find it difficult to distinguish appropriate critical analysis at school from an inappropriate lack of respect at home, producing an inevitable cultural dissonance. (2004: 195)

Acknowledging points such as these, Walker, then Director General of the IBO, wrote

> When I hear the oft-repeated criticism that the IBO is too 'westernised', I ask myself exactly what that comment means. That the headquarters is in Geneva instead of Jakarta? That IBCA [the IB Curriculum and Assessment Centre] is in Cardiff instead of Cairo? That the three official languages of the IBO are European in origin? None of that matters unless they are symptoms of a deeper problem, namely that the educational philosophy of the IBO is largely monocultural. The IBO mission statement, for example, refers to 'individual talents', 'responsible citizenship', 'critical thinkers' and 'informed participants', all key phrases from the handbook of humanist education. For the moment I do not know how this issue can be addressed beyond saying that [one of my objectives] of international education is to encourage its students to appreciate the diversity of modes of learning, of which western humanism is one. (2004b: 51)

It should be stressed that the points above are not made here as criticism of the IBO, and apply also in differing degrees to the other programmes discussed. They are included in order to highlight the challenges faced by any organisation that aims to be truly international rather than simply a nationally-based programme exported abroad. As the largest and most well-established curriculum organisation in this context, and the only one claiming to be multilingual in its programmes and assessment, the IBO is at the forefront of facing a number of difficult challenges to which there are no ready answers.

Language as a 'subject' for study

In addition to the issue of which language of instruction should be used within international schools is that of which foreign or additional languages should be studied. In practice, the languages that can be offered for study are constrained by the teaching staff available, the numbers of students needed to make the resourcing of a particular language viable, and the school's view as to the desirability – perhaps related to perceived 'usefulness' – of particular languages to their students. No doubt influenced by such perceptions, and by the wishes of the parent body, one respect in which international schools vary is in their attitude towards the study of the host-country language. An English-medium international school located in a Spanish-speaking country, for instance, might be more inclined to offer host-language study, or indeed to make it compulsory, than might an international school in an African country whose languages are expected to have limited usefulness outside of that local or national context.

For an organisation offering programmes of study in international schools, such as the IB or IGCSE, the question of which languages should be offered for study is equally difficult. The IB Diploma programme, for instance, offers its Language B (second language) group of subjects to students with 'some previous experience of learning the language' (Carder, 2006: 122), with the possibility of self-study by students when a school is not able to offer formal teaching of that language. Language A1, the student's 'first' language, is offered in the IBDP 'as part of the IBO policy of encouraging students to maintain strong ties to their cultures' (Carder, 2006: 122), again with the possibility of self-study where the student's choice of language is not offered by the school. But with an international school student population, the issue of language is never straightforward, and the IBDP has evolved its language offerings to try to accommodate the vast range of language capabilities and aspirations of the students who follow its programmes. In addition, therefore, to Language A1 and Language B are now offered languages described as Language A2, for students with 'an already high level of competence' in the language, and *Ab Initio*, for those with 'no previous experience in the language' (Carder, 2006: 122).

In the Advanced Placement International Diploma successful students must, amongst other requirements, have successfully completed two different AP examinations from the English and World Languages areas of the programme, which includes French, Spanish, German, Italian and (from 2006) Chinese. A list of languages which might have been perceived as Western-centred is thus clearly being tempered by an element of pragmatism in expanding into non-European languages, consistent with the increasing globalisation of curricula which DiYanni describes as also being reflected in the development of courses in, for instance, World History to replace those in Western Civilization (2006).

Moves are thus being made towards increasing internationalisation of such programmes in relation to language, as they are in national systems where more varied offerings of non-traditionally studied languages are becoming commonplace. In the face of what is to some the unpalatable and increasing dominance of English as the international language, and given the need to place some limit on the numbers of languages available for study, decisions about which languages are offered to students seem likely to continue to be based on a mixture of the ideological and pragmatic, with the pragmatic being hampered by the absence of a crystal ball to allow us to predict the future world in which the children of today will live as adults.

Assessment

As with respect to the nature of the intended curriculum, the question of how that curriculum should be assessed is complex. Controversial sometimes even within national education systems, for international schools responding to the needs of students often from a wide range of national, cultural and linguistic backgrounds such questions can be even more challenging. Some classic differences in approach arise between, for example, internal assessment by teachers and external assessment by outside examiners, as exemplified by the essentially teacher-assessed IBMYP (using criteria established by the IBO) and the externally-assessed IGCSE, with the clientele for these two programmes overlapping in grades 9 and 10 (ages 15–16).

Based on quite different philosophies (holistic, reflective and constructivist in the case of the MYP, and more compartmentalised, prescriptive and skills-based in the case of IGCSE: Ellwood, 1999), the MYP assessment structure is likely to be more familiar to those with a background in countries of, for example, continental Europe while their British counterparts, for instance, are likely to identify more strongly with the external examinations and certification of the IGCSE. Ellwood argues that, notwithstanding the different philosophies and assessment structures of the two programmes, 'The philosophical mind-set of the holistic MYP could be of considerable value in the delivery of the IGCSE and the well-defined structures, skills development and assessment criteria of the IGCSE could be a useful model to assist the MYP' (Ellwood 1999: 43), concluding that there is no reason why a hybrid, whereby a school offers both programmes, should not be successful. Indeed a similar conclusion was reached by the heads of the American British Academy Oman and Munich International School in working with colleagues to develop an integrated IBMYP and IGCSE curriculum which 'offers the best of both worlds' (Nashman-Smith and Taylor, 2004: 19).

Any debate about the differences between such international programmes, however, has to be recognised as a debate between programmes which all share an essentially Western liberal provenance and assessment structure – whether internal or external, coursework or external examination based. Brown's discussion of the different value systems and associated cultural values to be found in different national contexts highlights the challenges to be encounted in offering a formal curriculum, and associated assessment system, which can be 'truly reflective of the values of all cultural groups' (2002: 76). Brown goes on to argue that perhaps the most appropriate international assessment system will include a range of different internally and externally assessed components which will 'provide flexibility for the matching of cultures and assessment', encouraging students, teachers and other members of the school community to use forms of assessment from cultures other than their own:

> Such assessments will not only incorporate subject-based assessment but will also value non-traditional areas of the curriculum by recognising students' performance in these areas. Broadening the forms of assessment allows for cultural diversity, encompassing the broader perspective of internationalism; in other words it provides students, within the assessment regime and through the inevitable backwash effect of assessment, the opportunity to experience the cultural values found in groups that are different from their own. (2002: 76)

One might ask, however (and Brown goes on to acknowledge this point to some extent in highlighting the importance of recognising the requirements of the 'users' of such assessments, such as further and higher education institutions and employers), to what extent such flexibility and breadth of assessment are likely only to arise within the Western liberal framework to which many of the students of international schools either belong or aspire.

Issues in the Implemented and Learned Curriculum

If there is potential for discrepancies and mismatches between the intended, implemented and learned curriculum in schools in general, then the potential for such differences is at least as great within an international school. Indeed it is arguably the case that, in those situations where the intended curriculum is developed externally to the school, there are two subsets of the implemented curriculum: what might be described as the school-implemented curriculum and the teacher-implemented curriculum.

Take, for instance, the case of the IB Diploma Programme where, theoretically, students are allowed to select (in the intended curriculum) from a range of subjects at two different levels (Higher and Standard) in six groups, and to choose a subject area in which to base their Extended Essay, in addition to completing the compulsory Theory of Knowledge and CAS programmes. The school-implemented version of the IBDP in reality varies according to a range of factors including, inter alia, the size of the student population, and the teaching staff available; it is therefore possible that a student in a particular school might have no choice at all and be required by the school, if enrolling for the IBDP, to study a compulsory combination such as English A1 HL, French B SL, Spanish B HL, History SL, Biology HL and Mathematical Methods SL, with their Extended Essay in Biology.

Or there may be an international school in Africa that chooses to teach the British rather than African History option to its (mostly African) students, because that is what the (African) teacher himself studied at university and therefore feels most comfortable teaching. Or a school's decision to recruit teachers from a part of the world where particular pedagogical practices are likely to lead to certain types of emphasis being placed on the curriculum might have led to different emphases had teachers been recruited from elsewhere.

Such are examples of the school-implemented curriculum, which may be different from the curriculum intended by the planners, or that implemented by the teachers. Differences may be conscious or unconscious and, even assuming no conscious or deliberate attempt on the part of teachers to implement the curriculum other than in the way it was intended by either the original planners or the school, different cultural influences among teachers, the way in which individuals have themselves studied the material to be taught, and the varying levels of enthusiasm likely to arise in any group of teachers with respect to particular topic areas, are bound to mean that the curriculum implemented, even by teachers of the same subject and age range within the same school, will vary.

At the level of the learned curriculum – what is actually experienced by the student – there is again enormous scope for each student's experience to be quite different, even within a class for all of whom the curriculum is apparently implemented in the same way. Perhaps the non-native English speaking students find the speed at which the teacher addresses them makes her difficult to follow at times; perhaps some of the native English speakers find it difficult to comprehend her strong accent; perhaps the girl from a strict Muslim family finds the teacher's tee-shirts and bare legs difficult to reconcile with the notion of an authority figure to whom respect must be shown; perhaps the Thai student usually knows the answers but is so concerned about the possibility of losing face if an answer is wrong that he would never volunteer the answer to a question asked by the teacher, leading to the possibility of a situation such as described by Ginsberg and Wlodkowski whereby 'students who reserve judgment out of respect could conceivably be misjudged as linguistically or cognitively limited ... lacking in initiative ... or arrogant' (2000: 9, in Deveney, 2005: 165) – resulting in the teacher's expectations of the student being lower than would otherwise be the case.

If the learned curriculum is indeed different for different children, then a logical sequitur would seem to be 'How do we know what each child is learning?', which leads to the areas of assessment and evaluation – minefields not only in terms of how we plan to assess, but also whether in practice the basis of our assessment and evaluation is the same for every child. Language differences may be the most obvious area where misinterpretation between intended and learned can arise: can we be sure that the clarity of the questions in an external examination is such that all students understand in exactly the same way what is being asked? Can we be confident that we are using 'culture fair testing' (Foreman, 1982: 71–82)? These are big enough issues even within relatively monolingual contexts, let alone in terms of whether non-native speakers (or, indeed, native speakers of a different form of the language) interpret meanings in the same way as intended by those setting the examination or test. Where the same examination is set in more than one language, for instance, can we be certain that the nuances of the question's phrasing in Spanish are exactly the same as they are in the English version?

Less obvious perhaps, but no less important, are the differences which might lead to students responding differently to the same question as a result of their cultural backgrounds and previous experiences. Is a mathematics question that assumes an understanding of the game of cricket, or familiarity with a particular currency, less valid for some groups of students than for others? Fan (1999) suggests that a question on lotteries in the USA would not be suitable in China, where lotteries 'were once regarded as a particular part of capitalist culture and strictly prohibited' (in Brown, 2002: 72) and there are many such examples that could be quoted. Much work has been undertaken in recent years within formal assessment systems, both internationally and in increasingly multicultural national contexts, to ensure that the possibilities of different interpretations arising as a result of linguistic and/or cultural differences are minimised. It would be rash, however, to claim that either in the formal external assessment context or within the context of internal assessment undertaken by the student's own teacher(s), where relatively high teacher turnover means that internationally inexperienced teachers are joining international schools all the time, the question of equal validity of experience for all students is not an ongoing issue.

CONCLUSION

This chapter has highlighted a number of issues relating to the curriculum in international schools. Some of these issues are particularly thorny and no easy solutions are proposed: what is clearly important is that those involved are aware of them, as indeed many are, and that they continue to debate the means by which the curriculum can be made as valid as possible for all of those studying in the international school context.

CHAPTER 10

External Influences

The extent to which international schools identify themselves as part of a cluster of like-minded institutions or, alternatively, plough a lone furrow, varies enormously. Factors external to such schools which may impinge upon them to differing degrees are many and varied. A number will be discussed in this chapter, categorised in relation to:

- the local community;
- the global community; and
- quality assurance.

THE LOCAL COMMUNITY

In an age of Internet connections, efficient international travel and regular global mobility, the notion of what is meant by 'local community' for international schools is not at all clear. Bunnell highlights the lack of an explicit definition of the term 'local community', illustrating his point with reference to an American-oriented school in London which might conceivably perceive the state of Texas, the 'home' of most of its prospective students, as its local community (2005: 45). For the purposes of discussion in this chapter, 'local' will be interpreted in geographical terms, to mean the host-country community situated geographically close to the school's environs. Some international schools, including those with some host-country funding, may feel very much a part of that local community; for others, the link is more tenuous or practically non-existent. Particularly in less developed countries, they may be 'private islands of plenty in contrast to an impoverished local public education system' (Cambridge, 1998: 205) and in some cases the economic differential between those within the school and those outside its walls can lead to the need for the sort of security (including on occasion barbed wire and armed security guards) which is unusual around schools in the more developed world. This may be true where students are principally host nationals from the country's socio-economic elite, where in some cases even the architecture, by mimicking that of particular schools in other countries, can deliberately proclaim the notion of 'foreignness' and thus 'promote the idea of difference rather than communality' (Allen, 2000: 125). When the students are largely expatriate, the schools may provide a 'cultural bubble' (Pearce, 1994) 'by isolating their children's educational environment from exposure to local culture' (Cambridge and Thompson, 2004: 165).

Such isolation may more likely be found where there is perceived to be a 'culture clash' between school and local community, 'which poses a paradox in that the students can be in close contact with communities thousands of miles away yet be isolated from the community to which they are geographically close' (Bunnell, 2005: 49). This is not necessarily the case for all international schools of course, and McKenzie describes the case of Maru a Pula School Botswana (with about half its students from Botswana and the other half from around 40 different countries), whose facilities are used in the evenings and at weekends by many sporting, educational and cultural groups and include what is effectively the national theatre of Botswana, run as a community partnership project (1998: 251). Likewise the situation at Machabeng College (The International School of Lesotho) as described by Wilkinson, whereby in addition to catering for children from the expatriate community, attendance by a much broader cross-section of Lesotho society is encouraged through the provision of scholarship funding awarded on merit to Basotho (Lesotho national) students (1998: 229–30).

It needs also to be borne in mind that lack of contact with the local community is not peculiar to international schools, and would also be true of many schools in national systems: collaboration with the local community was found to be minimal, for instance, in a study of 63 per cent of all schools in Scotland (Thornton, 1999). And some international schools, such as the New International School of Thailand, have community links as a central theme in their philosophy (Allen, 2000: 127). As ever, there is wide diversity within international schools; in this case, with respect to the extent to which they wish, or are indeed able, to integrate or form links with the local community. A number of issues arising in this respect are discussed under the following headings.

Language

One factor relevant to potential links with the local community is the main language of the host country, vis-à-vis the language of instruction in the international school. Where the school is English-medium (as is often the case in international schools) and the host-country mother tongue is English, or English is widely spoken as a second or official language, then one less hurdle in the formation of links will be presented. Where the host-country language is not English, an issue may be how the local language is perceived in terms of its 'status' internationally. An English-speaking teacher or student, for instance, who anticipates being based for only a relatively short period of time in the host country, may be more motivated to learn the local language if it is, say, Spanish than if it is a local language perceived to have little transferability beyond the borders of the host country.

Some international schools include the study of the local language on the curriculum. Schwindt, for instance, describes the mandatory study of German by all students to tenth grade at one Germany-located international school (2003: 77), a policy by no means unique among international schools. The attitude of teachers and administrators to the local language will certainly be one of the hidden, if not overt, messages received by students about attitudes to the host culture. The absence of effort on the part of, for example, the head to learn the local language may also negatively affect relationships with host-country national staff, whether teachers, administrators or support staff. On the other hand, a school policy that requires all staff to study the local language and, indeed, to be examined in it (as in the case of Italian at the United World College of the Adriatic, Trieste), or that provides (non-compulsory) lessons for staff, is likely to convey a positive message both to students and to the local community about the value placed by the school on the culture of the local environment.

Staff

Host-country teachers, administrators and support staff may (as noted in Chapter 6) provide a potentially valuable resource in relation to links with the local community upon which some international schools capitalise. Allen argues that 'local' teachers are likely to be more stable than expatriates in terms of the length of time they will spend at the school, and also to be 'well attuned to the nuances of the local community'. In his experience, such colleagues have been of outstanding value: within the classroom, in the wider school community and, most particularly, in the development and sustenance of 'community links'. 'If you want an inclusive school', he says, 'include local teachers' (2000: 137). If, however, local staff – and more particularly local support staff – are virtually ignored or even looked down upon by students and teaching/administrative staff, then links with the local community will be tainted by the hidden, or not so hidden, messages being conveyed to students (quite possibly in conflict with the explicit claims of the school's mission statement) about the superiority of those within the confines of the international school 'bubble'.

The place of local teaching staff within an international school is also interesting, and the wide variation in contracts and salaries that can be found in some contexts, with its potential to lead to difficulties and resentments, is discussed in Chapter 6. Some international schools choose to appoint host-country nationals only where they really need to – to teach the host-country language. Where such teachers have not had international experience, and where there are many of them (as in a school where study of the host-country language is compulsory), they may be seen by others within the school as having a limiting effect on the promotion of international-mindedness, particularly if they do not embrace participation in cross-school activities beyond their own immediate area of responsibility (Schwindt, 2003: 77).

The attitudes of expatriate staff to the local context will vary according to a range of factors such as previous experience, transferable hobbies and interests – and the individual personalities involved. What is it, for instance, that causes one expatriate teacher to embark upon and persist with study of the Japanese language as soon as he arrives in the country, while another can still not communicate in Japanese at even a very basic level after ten years of living there? Accommodation, too, can be an issue. A teacher required to live in housing on an expatriate compound is likely, with the best will in the world, to find it more difficult to make personal links with the local community than is one who lives in accommodation within that community; an issue related in part to whether the school is located within a city or is a long way out of town, local security concerns and so on. The expatriate lifestyle offered by clubs, sports facilities and social networks, together with ease of communication where language is an issue, may also be attractive. There are those who reject such a lifestyle in favour of an 'authentic' local cultural experience, but that rejection in itself may cause resentment from members of the expatriate community locally. The very nature of the short-term contract experience of many expatriate international school teachers, where there is an expectation of moving on every two to four years or so, may also militate against making any effort to forge local community, rather than fellow expatriate, links.

Students

As with some of their globally-mobile teachers, expatriate students within international schools may have a tendency to anticipate moving on in the not-too-distant future and thus, as noted in Chapters 4 and 5, avoid the forming of strong ties and links that cannot easily be broken. The attitudes and experiences of their parents are also likely to be crucial in determining the extent to which, outside school, they view integrating with the local community as desirable; again, if the family lives on a compound such integration may be less likely than if they live within the local community. It must also be borne in mind that it is not helpful to think of expatriates as a single group, since there will be variation in relation not only to individual nationality and cultural background but also to how long they have lived in the country and their cross-cultural skills (Allen, 2000: 128).

Whether or not during the school day, or evening/weekend in the case of residential schools, students have any interaction with the local community will depend on the relationship between the school and that community: is the community perceived as a rich resource to be drawn upon for the students' benefit, or is it almost an irrelevance to the way in which the community school operates? The stance taken may well relate to the extent to which the school's philosophy could be described as 'inclusive' ('open to all constituencies') or 'encapsulated' ('encouraging cultural separatism') (Sylvester, 1998), as well as to the extent to which the community is perceived to be welcoming, hostile or indifferent.

The fact that few schools, including international schools, 'have any genuine or sustained contact with their ambient society' (McKenzie, 1998: 250) may explain the response of over 3,500 international school students (in three groups aged approximately 16, 17 and 18) who, in a survey seeking their views about perceived importance of various factors as important components of the experience of international education, all ranked exposure to others of different culture outside school and links with the local community lowest in importance, while a similar survey of international school teachers placed the same factor next to last in their ranking (Thompson, 1998: 285).

Encouragement of student links with the local community is provided in some cases through formal programmes such as those of the International Baccalaureate Organization, whose Diploma programme, for instance, requires the completion of a number of Creativity, Action, Service (CAS) activities if the Diploma is to be awarded (IBO, 2006). Service activities in particular can involve the local community, leading to the learning intended for the student (Linden, 1995) and clearly valued by many of them (Kulundu and Hayden, 2002: 31). Particularly where the socio-economic gap between international school and local community is high, however, such links need to be carefully handled by the school if they are not simply to reinforce a notion of 'us and them' and to be perceived by students and/or 'recipients' as essentially paternalistic in nature (Garton, 2002: 155).

A more evenly-balanced interaction described by Jackson involves students from the International School of Maastricht in the Netherlands taking part in an annual excursion to Switzerland with students from the Dutch parent (non-international) school to work together on a series of outward bound activities. Students who have had no previous interaction frequently, says Jackson, 'express surprise that the members of the other group are in fact "normal", just like them and not the alien creatures they had imagined them to be' (2005: 202); if the school builds on this new awareness by helping to maintain contact between students on their return it can, she says, lead to a much deeper understanding of the host culture on the part of the international school students rather than the stereotypical image that can result from more superficial local contact.

Summary

Clearly, the issue of contact with the local community can be complex. In some cases an international school's raison d'être may include 'minimiz[ing] the discomfort and perceived educational disadvantage that accompany engagement with host cultures' (Heyward, 2002: 27), and contact with the host culture is seen as undesirable. Likewise some host communities may be resistant to the presence of the international school, 'fearing that their own culture might be contaminated by the Anglo-American culture which the school is perceived to bring with it' (Jackson, 2005: 207). Brown's comment, in referring to American-oriented international schools, that 'Our overseas schools are light-house beacons in often hostile environments to call others to the benefits of democratic thought, theory and reality' (2002: 9) may help to explain such a perception on the part of some local communities.

Indeed the local political situation in some countries may be such that security concerns dictate the extent to which students can safely interact with the local community: one of a number of issues discussed by Garton (2002) with respect to what he describes as the 'location factor'. Where more interaction would be possible, Bunnell argues for links with the local community to be managed in such a way that they are seen to involve more than a small number of individuals or the one 'Public Relations practitioner' as he describes them, whose responsibility (in those schools that employ someone in such a role, full-time or part-time) is to promote local awareness of the school (2005: 59).

Allen imagines international schools as atolls in a coral sea, often significantly different from the local community within which they operate:

> The people of the atoll can adopt a significantly 'monocultural' system (with a few exotic details) or work towards a multicultural approach. If they succeed in following the difficult path towards *strong* multiculturalism, they may find that interactions with the sea of cultures outside fits neatly into this system, with the local communities merely representing an additional handful of equally valid cultures. On the other hand, if they follow the easier monocultural path, they have to choose the 'flavour' of monoculture. Emphasis on either the 'Western' or 'global' paths is more likely to lead to 'culture clash' with the community than adapting the school culture to some key values found within the local community. (2002: 134)

THE GLOBAL COMMUNITY

The fact that some international schools can be in much closer contact with communities thousands of miles away than they are with the local community has already been noted; with increasing ease of communications and travel such international contacts are not difficult to sustain.

Expatriate children will have their own international networks linked to families and previous friendships, but the school itself will also have links of some sort with the wider global community. An international school essentially catering for host-national children is likely to have links with, for instance, the international organisations whose curriculum programmes they offer and/or from whom they seek accreditation (see below). An international school catering either in part or exclusively for expatriates is likely to have those contacts and more.

Some are part of a network (such as the European Schools, or United World Colleges: see Chapter 2). Others are more individual in terms of their origins but may have, to a greater or lesser extent, linkages with networks of schools sharing a similar philosophy or value system. The Association of American Schools in Central America (AASCA, 2006), for instance, the Federation of British International Schools in South and East Asia (FOBISSEA, 2006), the Swiss Group of International Schools (SGIS, 2006) and the Association of International Schools in Africa (AISA, 2006) are just some examples of organisations which provide membership and support for international schools that are in some way like-minded as a result of national affiliations, geographical location and/or ideology. Such organisations, to varying degrees, provide informal support networks for heads, administrators and teachers, as well as providing more formal support through professional development opportunities (workshops and conferences) offered on a regular basis, and a range of inter-school sports events, exchanges and other student-focused activities.

Professional development opportunities are also provided by organisations such as the European Council of International Schools (ECIS, 2006) and the Association for the Advancement of International Education (AAIE, 2006) which organise conferences for teachers and administrators. The Academy for International School Heads (AISH, 2006) likewise provides opportunities for the sharing of common concerns and experiences. Organisations providing training for first-time teachers in international schools, such as Fast Train (2006), and for those aspiring to administrative responsibility such as the Principals Training Center (PTC, 2006), again offer external support to those working in this context.

Such gatherings do not only provide the formal professional development intended: the informal networking that takes place can also be, as suggested by anecdotal evidence, hugely beneficial in providing support for teachers and administrators who can sometimes feel relatively isolated in their international school setting, and are motivated by the opportunity to interact with others in similar situations to themselves. It has been noted in Chapter 6 that many international school teachers and administrators choose to engage in professional development leading to postgraduate qualifications including masters and doctoral degrees, and those institutions that offer such programmes, such as the University of Bath, also provide a link to a global community of participants connected through participation in, for example, summer school courses and on-line interaction (University of Bath, 2006).

The nature of the formal curriculum offered can also provide a global community for international schools. Those authorised to offer one or more of the three International Baccalaureate programmes, for instance, become part of a community with links to staff in regional offices as well as the central Curriculum and Assessment Centre; they receive materials, newsletters and other communications on a regular basis, and have access to professional development including workshops led by experienced teachers, examiners and IBO staff. Similar networks exist for other programmes including, inter alia, the International Primary Curriculum and Cambridge International Examinations. The agency by which an international school is accredited (if it has chosen to opt for this form of recognition: see below) will also form part of the global network to which the school belongs.

A range of other links and partnerships can be supportive too in terms of obtaining materials, participating in joint activities and so on. The relatively recently formed Alliance for International Education (AIE, 2006) provides a global network for those promoting international education, whether schools (national or international), other organisations, or individuals, and the opportunity to come together at a bi-annual conference to discuss issues of common interest. Subject-focused networks such as the IB Diploma Programme science project's encouragement for gathering data across different schools (IBO, 2006), and the International Schools Theatre Association (ISTA, 2006), as well as links with non-international schools such as those organised through the Schools to Schools project (Kenny, 2005: 22–3), or through the Model United Nations programme (MUN, 2006), all provide the opportunity for international schools' students and teachers alike to feel part of the wider global community.

QUALITY ASSURANCE

However independent it may aspire to be, no international school can float completely free of all external influences, some of which have been discussed above. Since none has an entirely captive audience of students and parents, and most are privately funded, they will need to have due regard to the perceptions of those who might be described as their 'customers' (in the case of fee-paying institutions, whether run for profit or not-for-profit), their 'sponsors' (in the case of, for example, United World Colleges whose students are largely funded through scholarships) or, in the case of government-funded schools (such as the European Schools, or the group of international schools in the Netherlands that are effectively international streams of Dutch 'parent' national schools: see Jackson, 2005: 201–2) their Ministries of Education or other branches of local and/or national government. Any such school is likely to have a limited life span if it is not seen as successful and effective (however such terms are defined) by its various stakeholders. Indeed most international schools have an interest not only in being seen by those outside the school to be performing an effective role, but also in knowing themselves (teachers, administrators, boards and students) that the quality of the educational experience provided is high.

What benchmarks then do such schools use, when they are not constrained by the requirements of a national system, to judge the quality of that experience? One means of demonstrating to their stakeholders, and indeed to themselves, the quality of the educational experience provided is through external indicators such as examination results (for those schools that offer, for example, SATs or IGCSE examinations). Another benchmark might be through self-evaluation, as in the case of the scheme used by the United World Colleges, or through using an instrument for the review of international values such as that currently being trialled in a number of schools by the International Schools Association (ISA) (Cambridge and Carthew, 2006). Yet another is through aligning themselves with already well-respected organisations which have international credibility, on the basis that recognition of a school by such an organisation will act as an indicator of success. Three variations on this notion of what could be described as 'recognition by association' are accreditation, authorisation and membership.

Accreditation

As the number of teachers and administrators employed by international schools continues to grow, it is becoming increasingly the case that individuals with relevant experience and expertise are seeking ways of having such skills recognised. Aside from postgraduate qualifications, to which reference has already been made, two recent developments which could loosely be considered under the heading of accreditation for individuals are the International Teacher Certificate launched by ECIS (ECIS, 2006) and the Teacher Awards developed by the IBO (IBO, 2006). The context in which the term accreditation is more commonly used, however, is that of the international school as an organisation. Murphy suggests that 'It is a commonplace that schools – and the community from which they draw their students – benefit from some outside evaluation by fellow professionals: every country has its system of inspection' (1998: 213). Those international schools that are linked in some way with a national system may be subject to just such a system of national inspection, or accreditation. Even those that are independent of local or national government funding may be subject to local 'inspection', depending on the requirements of the particular host country (Garton, 2002: 151). Since no international school is *required* to be accredited by any external international organisation, however, there will be an element of choice in the form of accreditation a school feels is most appropriate for its own circumstances.

Those with a strong 'home country' affiliation may invite individuals experienced in that national inspection system to undertake an inspection or audit: the National Association of British Schools in Spain is one example of a group of schools where such a system operates (NABSS, 2006). Indeed some national inspection systems have moved into inspecting or accrediting schools based outside their national borders. Murphy points out, for instance, that the US-based Middle States Association of Colleges and Schools, Western Association of Schools and Colleges, Southern Association of Colleges and Schools, and New England Association of Schools and Colleges all began in the 1970s and 1980s to offer accreditation to 'overseas schools', with a number of American-type international schools continuing to be part of one of these programmes (1998: 213).

For those schools wishing to be externally accredited through a non-nationally linked route, one option is the accreditation service developed in 1970 by the European Council of International Schools (ECIS) and today operated by its sister organisation, the Council of International Schools (CIS). Whereas 'the first ECIS accreditation instrument was very much based on existing American accreditation practice, adapted to take into account the varying and different circumstances of schools abroad' (Murphy, 1998: 213), the very detailed CIS Guide to School Evaluation and Accreditation is now, in its seventh edition, less nationally-focused with, for instance, the inclusion of standards concerning the provision of international/intercultural experiences for students (CIS, 2003: 3). As is pointed out in the CIS guide, a school under consideration for CIS accreditation is evaluated against two benchmarks: the school's own philosophy and objectives (how successful it is in meeting its own stated purposes) and the CIS Standards for Accreditation: 'developed and endorsed by educational peers ... [and] designed to reflect the characteristics of a high quality educational experience' (CIS, 2003: 6).

The five-stage process of accreditation outlined includes a preliminary visit by one or two visitors to clarify the requirements of the accreditation process; a self-study lasting one or two years which involves the whole school community (including the board, students and parents, as well as teachers, administrators and other staff) and covers all aspects of the school; and a visit lasting approximately one week by a team of teachers and administrators from other schools (with the numbers varying according to the size and complexity of the school), leading to a CIS decision on accreditation based on the visiting team's recommendation. The fifth stage consists of follow-up after one year, when the school produces a report responding to any recommendations contained in the visiting team's report, and a five year report written by the school, again following up any recommendations and including action plans for the future. A visit by two or more people then follows. For accreditation to continue, the process has to be repeated on a ten year cycle (CIS, 2003: 7–9).

So what are the issues associated with accreditation of international schools? Clearly the process is complex and time-consuming, in recognition of which CIS and other accrediting organisations are now prepared to undertake collaborative accreditations, involving one self-study report and one team visit, with independent decisions on accreditation by their respective organisations. For those who are successful, there are a number of advantages, some of which are highlighted in three interesting case studies described by Murphy (1998: 217–22). Anecdotally, there would seem to be additional benefits relating to the self-study process in particular. CIS points out that

> Schools earning accreditation status tend to agree that introspection has been the most valuable aspect of the entire process. Also of significant benefit is the opportunity for school staff to meet collaboratively, often across disciplines and divisions of the school, to discuss issues, to identify concerns, and to propose improvements. (2003: 9)

It needs to be recognised, of course, that the very concept of goal-setting, self-reflection and action planning arises from a particular cultural paradigm, as does that of peer review (Ratté, 1987). Dimmock and Walker (2005: 154–5) discuss the difficulties that may be encountered in the context of teacher appraisal if individuals from some cultural backgrounds interpret the exposing of problems as a sign of weakness, or the admission of potential areas for improvement as leading to individuals potentially losing face. Similar arguments could be made with respect to the notion of self-study in the context of accreditation, where clearly there is a need for cross-cultural sensitivity and recognition that such an approach may not sit as comfortably with some as it does with others operating in the international context.

Authorisation

To those more familiar with the concept of a compulsory national curriculum, or an examination system for which any school can pay to register students, the notion of a school having to be authorised to offer a particular curriculum may seem strange. Such is the case for some programmes offered in international schools, including the three programmes of the International Baccalaureate Organization. In each case three stages have to be successfully completed before a school can be authorised: a feasibility study which includes teaching and administrative staff undertaking IBO-approved professional development; a trial implementation period of at least a year during which a representative from the IBO regional office will visit and support the school; and an authorisation visit during which the school's preparedness to offer the programme is evaluated (IBO, 2006).

Such authorisation, whether for the IBO or for any other programme with a similar requirement, can be considered a form of quality assurance in the sense that the fact that the school is allowed to offer the programme (regardless of the eventual outcomes) is an indicator of a certain level of quality as adjudged by an internationally respected external organisation.

Membership

Last but not least of the three forms of 'recognition by association' considered here is that of membership. Membership of an organisation for any individual, be it professional or social, says something about them to others, and this is no less the case for an international school. Not only may the organisations with which (aside from issues of accreditation and authorisation already noted) they choose to be associated offer opportunities for teacher/administrator professional development and student inter-school activities, the fact that they are accepted as a member of a particular 'club' (be that a grouping of American international schools or of international schools based in a particular location) is likely to be interpreted by stakeholders as an indicator of the school's acceptance by others, and also as an indicator of its particular values, ethos and aspirations. For parents newly relocated from another part of the world such indicators, whether relating to membership, accreditation and/or authorisation, may be crucial in convincing them that this is the right school for their child.

CONCLUSION

While external influences may be considered more important by some international schools than by others (and it is true that some schools face more challenges from such influences than do others), no school can ignore them completely. As the international school sector increases in size, growing emphasis on aspects of quality assurance such as authorisation and accreditation – of the school itself and of its teachers and administrators – seem likely to help to ensure that the students who attend such schools, and their parents, are assured of the quality of the educational experience upon which they are embarking. The quality of that experience is also likely to be enhanced where links can be forged with local and global communities to positive effect. The challenge, no doubt, lies in developing such links to the benefit of all.

CHAPTER 11

Future Roles for International Schools

To attempt to write about what will happen in the future is ambitious, if not foolhardy. While some may believe in Nostrodamus-like powers or use of a literal or metaphorical crystal ball as the basis of predicting future events, it is not given to most of us to do other than consider past and current trends, observe changes and plans, and attempt to extrapolate into the relatively near future on the basis of such evidence. And even then we may not have much confidence in the accuracy of our predictions. There are, however, certain factors and current areas of development that would seem likely to impinge upon international schools in the near future at least, and these will be considered in this chapter. While no attempt will be made to predict what will happen in any precise sense, a range of issues will be raised which seem likely to determine in some way how international schools might develop. The first such set of issues, against the backdrop of which all others will be discussed, are those relating to the changing nature of the global environment.

GLOBALISATION

While it has become something of a cliché to refer to our shrinking world, it is certainly true that for those in the developed world, at least, sophisticated technology and increased ease of travel have led to a steadily increasing awareness of what is happening beyond our own national boundaries and of the interdependence of human beings across those boundaries.

Much has been written in recent years about globalisation, though with different interpretations of that well-used term. Held et al. (1998) refer to three different interpretations of globalisation. The *hyperglobalist* view is that globalisation relates to transnational networks of, for instance, trade, finance and production with the associated denationalisation of national economies and an application of the same standards internationally. The *sceptical* interpretation of globalisation, meanwhile, is that while regional, national and international markets may be converging, the task of regulating and facilitating international trade still falls to national governments and, if anything, identification with national and regional cultures is becoming heightened rather than lessened. The third, *transformationalist,* interpretation 'brings together the global with the local' such that 'distribution of cultural difference may depend less on geographical dispersion and more on the distribution of wealth and resources' (Cambridge, 2000: 181), with members of a country's socio-economic elite likely to have more in common with those of similar status in other countries than with their less privileged compatriots, with whom they will nevertheless still share certain cultural values.

International schools, as Cambridge (2000: 180–1) points out, can be viewed as relating to each of these interpretations in different ways. They fit the hyperglobalist interpretation as one example of cultural homogenisation, when international schools promote a form of education that 'may be compared with other globally marketed goods and services such as soft drinks and hamburgers; a reliable product conforming to consistent quality standards throughout the world' (Cambridge, 2002a: 231). In this interpretation, it is not difficult to see why international schools should be attractive to globally mobile expatriates. International schools can also be seen to fit the transformationalist interpretation in those contexts where host-country nationals are permitted by law to attend them, and members of the socio-economic elite see the international school as a route to advancement for their children. 'As more people gain local educational qualifications' says Lowe, 'those who can afford to do so seek a new competitive edge by taking qualifications that they hope will give them a local advantage .... [and that will give them] access to a labour market that is becoming increasingly globalized' (2000: 24–5). In the sceptical approach to globalisation, international schools are responding to the needs of expatriates who seek a non-national education for their child which may well be in a school such as those Sylvester (1998) described as 'encapsulated' – relatively isolated from the local environment.

These perspectives on the place of international schools, however, relate only to what Cambridge describes as the 'globalizing current' of international education, which is 'influenced by and contributes to the global diffusion of the values of free-market capitalism ... expressed ... in terms of quality assurance, through the application of international accreditation procedures, the spread of global quality standards and the global certification of educational qualifications' (2002a: 228). They do not relate to the other competing 'internationalist' perspective (2002a: 228) which is identified with promoting peace, international understanding and cooperation, and an internationally-minded outlook: what has been referred to elsewhere as the 'ideological' as opposed to 'pragmatic' dimension of international schools (Hayden, 2001). Arguably the United World Colleges are the only schools whose main raison d'être is the promotion of such values. As Cambridge points out, however, the internationalist and globalising approaches are rarely seen in their pure forms and most international schools offer a reconciliation of the two, so that international schools 'appear to be heterogeneous because each reconciliation is unique to the historical, geographical and economic circumstances of the institution' (2002a: 228–9).

The globalising approaches referred to here are invariably linked to the values of capitalism in one or more forms, itself becoming increasingly internationalised with the spread of multinational organisations and their products. Fuel outlets of international companies and advertising hoardings for Coca Cola are found in even remote parts of less developed countries, and so-called 'knowledge workers' operate call centres in India (for example) with assumed Western names and accents in order to sell their products to customers in the more developed world. As noted by Greider

> A great shift of productive wealth is under way, reflected in the extraordinary growth rates of some developing nations. Korea and Taiwan follow Japan up the ladder, then attention shifts to Indonesia, Chile, Malaysia, Thailand or Turkey. Who's next? Maybe Vietnam and Mayanmar, maybe Bangladesh. As multinationals survey the world, China, India and Brazil are seen as the main contenders racing to become the world's next major manufacturing economy. (1997: 32)

Three Eras of Globalisation

Friedman argues that we are now in the third great era of globalisation, the first having lasted from when Columbus set sail in 1492, opening up trade between the Old and New Worlds, until around 1800. During that era, the key agent of change was the creative deployment of muscle or power (horse power, steam power, wind power). The period from 1800 until around 2000 was the second great era of globalisation (with interruptions during the Great Depression and the two World Wars). While the first era shrank the world from large to medium size, Friedman argues, during the second era it shrank from medium to small size, with the key agent of change being the multinational companies. In the first half of the era, the Industrial Revolution, the railroad and the steam engine led to falling transportation costs, while decreasing telecommunication costs ('thanks to the diffusion of the telegraph, telephone, the PC, satellites, fibre-optic cable, and the early versions of the World Wide Web') led to the beginnings and development of a global economy (2005: 9–11).

The period from around 2000 is described by Friedman as era 3, in which the world is shrinking from small to tiny in size; while the dynamic force in era 1 was countries globalising and in era 2 was companies globalising, he argues, in era 3 it is the 'newfound power for *individuals* to collaborate and compete globally' (2005: 10, emphasis in original), facilitated not by horsepower or hardware but by software, in conjunction with a global fibre-optic network. This shrinking, says Friedman, is different from that of eras 1 and 2 in that it will be driven not primarily by Europeans and Americans, but by a much more diverse group of individuals from every part of the world. In doing so, it is levelling the playing field for countries and individuals who have not previously competed for global knowledge work but are now able to do so; as Friedman puts it, 'the world is flat'.

Rischard (2002: 3–4) refers to such aspects of globalisation as the 'New World Economy', one of two big forces he believes will change the world as we know it by around 2020. The other big force, he asserts, is the 'demographic explosion' which will take us from an already over-stretched planet of 5 billion people in 1990 and 6 billion in 2002 to about 8 billion by 2020–2025 (2002: 5). Rischard argues that these two forces will lead to unprecedented changes in our world, characterised by what he lists as the twenty global issues that need to be solved, categorised as follows:

- sharing our planet (issues such as global warming, fisheries depletion, deforestation and water deficits);
- sharing our humanity (issues such as peacekeeping and conflict prevention, education for all and the fight against poverty);
- sharing our rule book (issues such as trade, investment and competition rules, illegal drugs and intellectual property rights).

It is how we respond to these issues in the near future (the twenty years from when he wrote in 2002), he argues, that will determine how well the planet will fare over the next generations: the response from China and India alone, for instance, with their total populations together accounting for half the population of the developing world, will matter enormously (2002: 203).

Against this overarching global backdrop, a number of related factors seem likely to be relevant to the future role of international schools, some of which are discussed below.

ENGLISH-MEDIUM EDUCATION

The increasing pre-eminence of English as the world language has already been noted in this book. While not spoken by most people as their first language (Chinese is the most widely spoken in this respect, followed by Hindi and Urdu taken together: Gray, 2006), in 2005 there were estimated to be approximately 1.5 billion users of English worldwide, divided roughly equally between native speakers, English as a Second Language (ESL) and English as a Foreign Language (EFL) users. It is estimated that by 2015 half the world's population (approximately 3.5 billion) will be speaking or learning English, before the numbers drop by 2050 to about 500 million as English is replaced to some extent by Hindi/Urdu, Spanish and possibly Arabic as widely spoken international languages (Gray, 2006).

Thus, in the short term at least, it seems likely that bilinguality (mother tongue plus English), currently the norm for educated elites worldwide, will become the norm for many more, if not for all (Thomas, 2006). English being increasingly perceived as the international language brings with it many challenges and issues; whose English is it, for instance (that of the UK, USA or other native English speaking countries)? Jenkins, in discussing English as an International Language (EIL), argues that 'We are not justified in regarding English language contact involving native speakers as natural and acceptable, but that involving non-native speakers as in some way contaminated' (2004: 2). And Phillipson (1992), cited in Allen (2000: 130), argues that the growing emphasis on teaching and learning of English causes cultural, social and psychological damage: 'Fallaciously identified with modernity, progress, freedom, civilization and reason, English commands monumental financial, official and popular backing in parts of the globe where its role is dubious'.

Such concerns aside, and unpalatable as this may be to some, estimates suggest that the demand for English language teaching, and by extrapolation English-medium education, is likely to continue to increase in the short term at least. If, as suggested by research discussed in Chapter 3, a major factor in determining parents' choice of an international school for their child is the English-medium education provided (or the 'proxy language school' nature of many international schools: see Deveney, 2000: 36), then it seems likely that the demand for international school education will continue to increase, if for that reason alone.

HOST COUNTRY DEMAND FOR INTERNATIONAL SCHOOLS

Rischard suggests that of the 2 billion by which the earth's population is predicted to increase by around 2025, 95 per cent will be living in developing countries; most will continue to flock to the cities, leading to there being some 60 cities with more than 5 million inhabitants - almost double the number there was in 1990 (2002: 6). In such a scenario, it is not difficult to imagine a situation in developing countries where those who are economically able to do so, and are allowed to do so by law, increasingly look to an international school education for their child as a means of providing the competitive edge referred to by Lowe (2000: 24–5) and/or because they lack confidence in their home country's educational system (Cambridge, 2000: 181). There may well continue to be countries that 'tolerate rather than encourage expatriate educational institutions in their territories, and legislate to prevent the participation of their own citizens in them' (Cambridge, 2000: 181), fearing that participation by host nationals in international schools will negatively affect the host culture; in Singapore, for instance, Singaporeans may not attend such schools (Allen, 2000: 130–1).

In countries which do not prevent host nationals from attending international schools, however, it might be imagined that the number of such schools could increase substantially. Thailand, for instance, since relaxing restrictions on its nationals attending international schools, has experienced a steady increase in the numbers of such schools to around 100 in 2006 (Macdonald, 2006). Some international schools cater almost exclusively for Thai nationals, while others effectively operate a quota system by capping numbers in order to ensure a more balanced population with the expatriate children from many national, cultural and linguistic backgrounds who also attend the school. Taken with the likely increasing desire for an English-medium education already noted, it would be surprising if the demand for international schools in such contexts were not to continue to increase within the foreseeable future.

NATIONAL SYSTEMS OF EDUCATION

The growing awareness within many national systems of the desirability of an international focus within the education programmes devised for mainstream schooling has already been noted. Nineteenth century peace movements in Britain, USA and continental Europe led to the creation of School Peace Leagues in the USA, Britain and the Netherlands (Heater, 2002) and more recently the UNESCO 1974 Recommendation on Education for International Understanding (UNESCO, 1974) influenced developments in national systems that in some contexts are described as global education. The welcome address from the 2002 Europe-wide Global Congress leading to the European Strategy Framework for improving and increasing Global Education in Europe to the Year 2015 contains the following extract:

> For some years now, the concept of global education – that is, education for greater justice, democracy and human rights, with a global perspective – has been gaining credence and momentum. However, the ideas and actions behind the concept are certainly not new. Many in Europe and elsewhere have been engaged in those constituent types of education that go together to make up global education – development education, human rights education, intercultural learning, education for peace and conflict resolution, environmental education and education for sustainability. What is relatively new, however, is the notion that these types of education might be brought together internationally through the umbrella term of global education. (Rugus, 2002: 1, in Marshall, 2006)

However described, it is clear that an international perspective is being adopted within growing numbers of national systems, which in the developed world are themselves becoming increasingly multicultural in population and more acutely aware of the need for their students to develop broader perspectives than those limited by national boundaries. The International Education week founded in UK mainstream schools in November 2003, following the similar USA model launched in 2000, are just two examples of initiatives designed to respond to the growing recognition that students without an understanding of how the world works, and an appreciation of other cultures and countries, are likely to get left behind in an increasingly global marketplace (Hastings, 2003: 3 and DfES, 2004a). The growth in numbers of schools in national systems worldwide offering programmes such as the International Baccalaureate Diploma (IBO, 2006) could also be interpreted as an indication of growing awareness of the importance of an international perspective in education, although care has to be taken to acknowledge other attractions of the IB Diploma such as its relative breadth (compared to, say, the English A level system) and its high academic standards (cited by Spahn, 2001, as an attraction in the many US high schools now offering the IBDP) (Hayden, 2006).

In any event, where once international schools might have been unusual compared with national schools in incorporating an international dimension to the curriculum and, indeed, in having a multicultural student body, such differences are being reduced as national systems themselves become increasingly international in diverse ways. Such differences seem likely to continue to diminish in the future, with the prospect of international schools perhaps becoming less distinctive in some respects than has so far been the case.

INTERNATIONAL CURRICULUM PROGRAMMES

The first international curriculum programme developed was by common agreement the IB Diploma (Peterson, 1987) which since its inception in the 1960s has been joined by a number of other programmes aimed at an international market (see Chapter 9). The fact that such programmes are being seen as attractive within national systems as well as by international schools suggests that they are likely to continue to grow and expand with an eye quite possibly on both markets. Notably, however, with the exception of the French Baccalauréat Option Internationale, and the IB programmes' Spanish, French and Chinese working languages, these programmes are all being offered through the medium of English only. Given the predicted increase in demand for English language education, it seems likely that the market for such programmes will continue to be largely in the English-medium context – in the short term at least.

FUTURE POSSIBILITIES

The twin concepts of pragmatism and ideology have been referred to throughout this book, acknowledging that the balance between the two in any one school will depend, as Cambridge pointed out in describing the related twin concepts of globalising and internationalising perspectives, on the particular circumstances prevalent there (2002a: 228–9). Some, such as the United World Colleges, are almost entirely ideologically driven in their mission of promoting international understanding and global awareness (UWC, 2006): they do not respond to the needs of a local market, and pragmatic dimensions are relevant only really in so far as they need to ensure that sufficient funds are raised by national committees to provide for student scholarships. Ongoing work to develop what would be the newest UWC in Bosnia and Herzegovina highlights the ideological nature of their mission: to be based within the prestigious Mostar Gymnasium, the UWC will have ethnically integrated classes unlike other parts of the Gymnasium where, since the war which ended with the 1995 Dayton Agreement, students are taught in different streams according to ethnicity (IBO, 2005: 2).

The UWC are unusual in that most international schools have a market-driven pragmatic dimension: they would not survive should their local market disappear. For some international schools the pragmatic dimension is all, and very little of the ideological focus of promoting international understanding infuses the student experience. For many, however, the experience is mixed: while the pragmatic dimensions provide the reasons for the school's existence, the experience offered to the students attempts to capitalise on their situation: often a culturally mixed population with experience of, and contacts in, different parts of the world, having expectations of further international mobility and taught by staff with international experience and interests.

Parental motivations for the selection of international schools would seem to be largely pragmatic, including the demand for English-medium education and internationally recognised curriculum and examinations. In that sense, the more ideologically-focused dimensions could be seen by parents either as irrelevant or as a 'bonus' – believed to be important by the school in educating the young internationally mobile adult of the twenty-first century, but not necessarily a high priority for host national families or for those families who in sending their children to international schools 'move freely around the world, educating their children "on the hoof" (often a well-heeled hoof), not only safeguarding but actually enhancing their prospects for university entry, and equipping them to become self-confident members of today's international community' (Sutcliffe, 2006: 80).

Given the predictions made so far in this chapter, it is difficult to avoid the conclusion that the number of international schools geared towards host country nationals will continue to grow, quite possibly at a rapid pace, as the population increase in less developed countries leads to those who can afford to do so seeking the means of establishing a competitive advantage for their children. The determining factor likely to govern the extent and scope of this growth would seem to be the extent to which national governments see international schools either as beneficial to their citizens, or as a threat to local culture and national identity. Where governments of less developed countries allow their citizens to attend such schools, particularly if the national education system is not well-regarded, the potential for expansion could be immense.

So far as the globally mobile expatriate population is concerned, it is possible to envisage two different routes to the development of international schools in the foreseeable future. One route anticipates that the developing global economy will lead to increased numbers of multi-national organisations and associated increased numbers of (largely professional) employees moving round the world with their families and seeking a non-local, largely English-medium, education for their children (whether or not they are English speakers themselves). In this scenario, numbers of international schools catering principally for the children of expatriates seem set to continue increasing, and it may be that the balance of different types of international school – some entirely expatriate, some entirely host-country nationals, some a mixture of the two – may remain similar to the status quo.

The alternative route anticipates that, instead of continuing to expand geographically, those organisations operating on a multinational basis (and there seems little doubt that the numbers of multinational organisations, or national organisations with multinational connections, will continue to grow) will change their style of operating by making greater use of increasingly sophisticated technology. It is possible to imagine a scenario in which the frantic flying around the world of professional employees of multinational organisations that characterised the latter years of the twentieth century will, for reasons including concerns about increasing fuel costs and security, be replaced by communication based around the Internet, video conferencing and telephone contact. Even the nature of the diplomatic service is changing with increased accessibility and improved communications: 'What about ... diplomacy?', says Binyon, referring to changes in the UK Foreign and Commonwealth Office, 'Is that still needed? Or can it now be done by email?' (2006: 19). If such were the scenario, then the numbers of international schools whose principal market is expatriate globally mobile families might either remain reasonably static or even decrease.

But what of the other, ideological, dimension of education in international schools? The dimension that sees as the main purpose of education the preparation of internationally-minded young people for life in a world with enormous problems that their parents' generation has failed to address adequately, in the hope that they may contribute to solving at least some of those problems for the sake of future generations? While it seems likely on current evidence that the UWC movement will continue to expand and to promote its ideological mission, it seems likely too that – notwithstanding the fact that other ideologically-driven organisations may be created – they will be swamped in number by the international schools whose mission is more pragmatically driven, some of which may have no particular interest in more ideological dimensions of education.

Many international schools will no doubt continue to see as part of their mission, albeit in a context where parents' primary motivation may be an English-medium internationally recognised education for their child, the promotion of such internationally-minded values. It seems likely, however, that many national school systems will also move to incorporate such a dimension into their mainstream programmes, with some opting to take on international programmes such as the IB, IGCSE and IPC. 'The future depends on humanity's ability to transcend the limits of individual cultures' says Edward T. Hall (1989: 2). A major challenge for international schools in the twenty-first century will be in balancing the many pragmatic and ideological demands placed upon them, in order best to prepare future generations of adults for life in a complex world.

References

Association for the Advancement of International Education (AAIE) (2006) www.aaie.org, accessed 18 March.

Association of American Schools in Central America (AASCA) (2006) www.aasca.net, accessed 18 March.

Alliance for International Education (AIE) (2006) www.intedalliance.org, accessed 18 March.

Association of International School in Africa (AISA) (2006) www.aisa.or.ke, accessed 18 March.

Academy for International School Heads (AISH) (2006) www.academyish.org, accessed 18 January.

Adler, M. (1997) 'Looking Backwards to the Future: parental choice and education policy', *British Educational Research Journal*, 23(3) 297–313.

Akram, C. (1995) 'Change and Adaptation: children and curriculum in international schools', *International Schools Journal*, XV(1): 39–53.

Alice Smith School (1996) *The Alice Smith School, Kuala Lumpur: A Celebration of 50 Years, 1946–1996*. Kuala Lumpur: The Alice Smith School.

Allan, M. (2002) 'Cultural Borderlands: a case study of cultural dissonance in an international school', *Journal of Research in International Education*, 1(1): 63–90.

Allan, M. (2003) 'Frontier Crossings: cultural dissonance, intercultural learning and the multicultural personality', *Journal of Research in International Education*, 2(1): 83–110.

Allemann-Ghionda, C. (2003) 'The Yellow Streetcar: Shaping a Polyphonic Identity', in T. Tokuhama-Espinosa (ed.), *The Multilingual Mind: Issues Discussed by, for, and about People Living with Many Languages*. Praeger: Westport, CT. pp 171–88.

Allen, K. (2000) 'The International School and its Community: Think Globally, Interact Locally', in M. C. Hayden and J. J. Thompson (eds), *International Schools and International Education: Improving Teaching, Management and Quality*. London: Kogan Page. pp 124–39.

Allen, K. (2002) 'Atolls, Seas of Culture and Global Nets', in M. C. Hayden, J. J. Thompson and G. R. Walker (eds), *International Education in Practice: Dimensions for National and International Schools*. London: Kogan Page. pp 129–44.

Arabsheibani, G. (1988) 'Educational Choice and Achievement: the case of secondary schools in the Arab republic of Egypt', *Higher Education*, 17, 637–46.

Baetens Beardsmore, H. (1993) 'The European School Model', in H. Baetens Beardsmore (ed.), *European Models of Bilingual Education*. Clevedon: Multilingual Matters. pp 121–54.

Baker, C. (2001) *Foundations of Bilingual Education and Bilingualism* (3rd edition). Clevedon: Multilingual Matters.

Bartlett, K. (1998) 'International Curricula: More or Less Important at the Primary Level?', in M. C. Hayden and J. J. Thompson (eds), *International Education: Principles and Practice.* London: Kogan Page. pp 77–91.

Bauman, Z. (1996) 'From Pilgrim to Tourist – or a Short History of Identity', in S. Hall and P. du Gay (eds), *Questions of Cultural Identity*, London: Sage.

Beedle, P., Eason, T. and Maughan, S. (2006) 'From Natural Economy to Environmental Management and Beyond: A Case Study in Curriculum Development', in M. C. Hayden, J. Levy and J. J. Thompson (eds), *Handbook of Research in International Education*, London: Sage.

Bell, L. (1997) *Hidden Immigrants: Legacies of Growing Up Abroad.* Notre Dame, IN: Cross Cultural Publications.

Benn, C. (1989) 'Preface', in H. DeLyon and F. Widdowson Migniuolo (eds), *Women Teachers: Issues and Experiences.* Milton Keynes: Open University. p xix.

Bereday, G. Z. F. and Lauwerys, J. A. (eds) (1964) *The Yearbook of Education 1964: Education and International Life.* London: Evans Brothers.

Berry, J. W., Poortinga, Y. H., Segall, M. H. and Dasen, P. R. (1992) *Cross-cultural Psychology: Research and Applications.* Cambridge: Cambridge University Press.

Bibby, C. (1959) *T H Huxley: Scientist, Humanist and Educator.* New York: Horizon Press.

Binyon, M. (2006) 'Diplomatic Baggage That Has To Go', *The Times*, 29 March, p 19.

Black, D. R. and Scott, W. A. H. (1997) 'Factors Affecting the Employment of Teachers Returning to the United Kingdom after Teaching Abroad', *Educational Research*, 39(1): 37–63.

Blandford, S. (2001) 'Middle Management in International Schools', in S. Blandford and M. Shaw (eds), *Managing International Schools.* London: RoutledgeFalmer. pp 136–52.

Blandford, S. and Shaw, M. (eds) (2001a) *Managing International Schools.* London: RoutledgeFalmer.

Blandford, S. and Shaw, M. (2001b) 'Introduction', in S. Blandford and M. Shaw (eds), *Managing International Schools.* London: RoutledgeFalmer. pp 1–8.

Blandford, S. and Shaw, M. (2001c) 'The Nature of International School Leadership', in S. Blandford and M. Shaw (eds), *Managing International Schools*, London: RoutledgeFalmer. pp 9–28.

Blaney, J. (1991) 'The International School System', in P. L. Jonietz and D. Harris (eds), *World Yearbook of Education 1991: International Schools and International Education.* London: Kogan Page. pp 199–205.

Blaney, J. J. (2000) 'Long-term Planning in International Schools', in M. C. Hayden and J. J. Thompson (eds), *International Schools and International Education: Improving Teaching, Management and Quality.* London: Kogan Page. pp 158–68.

Blau, P. M. (1986) *Exchange and Power in Social Life.* New Brunswick, NJ: Transaction.

Bossert, S. T., Dwyer, D. C., Rowan, B. and Lee, G. (1982) 'The Instructional Management Role of the Principal', *Educational Administration Quarterly*, 18, 34–64.

Bowers, J. M. (1998) 'Making Informed Decisions', in J. M. Bowers (ed.), *Raising Resilient MKs: Resources for Caregivers, Parents, and Teachers.* Colorado Springs: Association of Christian Schools International. pp 263–70.

Bowlby, J. (1969) *Attachment and Loss: Attachment*, London: Hogarth Press.

Bowley, N. (2001a) 'New Board Members: Recruitment and Orientation', in W. Powell, N. Bowley and G. Schoppert (eds), *School Board Governance Training: A Sourcebook of Case Studies.* Great Glemham, Suffolk: John Catt. pp 22–32.

Bowley, N. (2001b) 'Evaluating the Head and the Board', in W. Powell, N. Bowley and G. Schoppert (eds), *School Board Governance Training: A Sourcebook of Case Studies.* Great Glemham, Suffolk: John Catt. pp 128–42.

Bradley, G. (2000) 'Inclusive Education in International Schools: a case study from Singapore', in M. C. Hayden and J. J. Thompson (eds), *International Schools and International Education: Improving Teaching, Management and Quality*, London: Kogan Page. pp 29–41.

Bray, M. and Yamato, Y. (2003) 'Comparative Education in a Microcosm: Methodological Insights from the International Schools Sector in Hong Kong', *International Review of Education*, 49 (1–2): 51–73.

Bray, M. and Yamato, Y. (2006) 'Economic Development and the Market Place for Education: Dynamics of the International Schools Sector in Shanghai, China', *Journal of Research in International Education*, 5(1): 71–96.

Brein, M. and David, K. (1971) 'Intercultural Communication and the Adjustment of the Sojourner', *Psychological Bulletin*, 76(3): 215–30.

Brickman, W. W. (1950) 'International Education', in W. S. Monroe (ed.), *Encyclopedia of Educational Research*. New York: Macmillan.

Brickman, W. W. (1962) 'International Relations in Higher Education, 1862–1962', in W. W. Brickman and S. Lehrer (eds), *A Century of Higher Education: Classical Citadel to Collegiate Colossus*, New York: Society for the Advancement of Education.

Bridglal, K. (2002) *A Study of the Under-representation of Women Teachers in Senior Management Positions in International Schools*. Unpublished dissertation for the MA in Education (Educational Management), University of Bath.

Brown, G. (2002) 'School Mission Should Include Transmitting and Preserving Democracy', *The International Educator*, October, p 9.

Brown, P. and Lauder, H. (2001) *Capitalism and Social Progress: the Future of Society in a Global Economy*. New York and Basingstoke: Palgrave.

Brown, R. (2002) 'Cultural Dimensions of National and International Educational Assessment', in M. C. Hayden, J. J. Thompson and G. R. Walker (eds), *International Education in Practice: Dimensions for National and International Schools*. London: Kogan Page. pp 66–79.

Bruner, J. S. (1985) 'Vygotsky: A historical and conceptual perspective', in J. V. Wertsch (ed.), *Culture, Communication and Coginition: Vygotskyan Perspectives*, Cambridge: Cambridge University Press. pp 21–34.

Bryceson, D. F. and Vuorela, U. (2002) 'Transnational Families in the Twenty-first Century', in D. Bryceson and U. Vuorela (eds), *The Transnational Family: New European Frontiers and Global Networks*. New York and Oxford: Berg. pp 3–30.

Bulman, L. and Jenkins, D. (1988) *The Pastoral Curriculum*. Oxford: Blackwell.

Bunnell, T. (2005) 'Perspectives on International Schools and the Nature and Extent of Local Community Contact', *Journal of Research in International Education*, 4(1): 43–63.

Cambridge International Examinations (CIE) (2006) www.cie.org.uk, accessed 18 March.

Cambridge, J. C. (1998) 'Investigating National and Organizational Cultures in the Context of the International School', in M. C. Hayden and J. J. Thompson (eds), *International Education: Principles and Practice*, London: Kogan Page. pp 197–211.

Cambridge, J. C. (2000) 'International Schools, Globalization and the Seven Cultures of Capitalism', in M. C. Hayden and J. J. Thompson (eds), *International Schools and International Education: Improving Teaching, Management and Quality*. London: Kogan Page. pp 179–90.

Cambridge, J. C. (2002a) 'Global Product Branding and International Education', *Journal of Research in International Education*, 1(2): 227–43.

Cambridge, J. C. (2002b) 'Recruitment and Deployment of Staff: a Dimension of International School Organization', in M. C. Hayden, J. J. Thompson and G. R. Walker

(eds), *International Education in Practice: Dimensions for National and International Schools*. London: Kogan Page. pp 158–69.
Cambridge, J. C. and Carthew, C. (2006) 'Schools Self-evaluating their International Values: a Case Study', in M. C. Hayden, J. Levy and J. J. Thompson (eds), *Handbook of Research in International Education*. London: Sage.
Cambridge, J. C. and Thompson, J. J. (2004) 'Internationalism and Globalisation as Contexts for International Education', *Compare*, 34(2): 161–75.
Canterford, G. (2003) 'Segmented Labour Markets in International Schools', *Journal of Research in International Education*, 2(1): 47–65.
Carber, S. and Reis, S. (2004) 'Commonalities in IB Practice and the Schoolwide Enrichment Model', *Journal of Research in International Education*, 3(3): 339–59.
Carder, M. (1993) 'Are We Creating Biliterate Bilinguals?', *International Schools Journal*, 26, 19–27.
Carder, M. (2006) 'Bilingualism in International Baccalaureate Programmes, with Particular Reference to International Schools', *Journal of Research in International Education*, 5(1): 119–36.
Carver, J. and Mayhew Carver, M. (1996) *Your Roles and Responsibilities as a Board Member*. San Francisco, CA: John Wiley, Inc.
Casey, K. (1990) 'Teacher as Mother: Curriculum Theorizing in the Life Histories of Contemporary Women Teachers', *Cambridge Journal of Education*, 20(3): 301–20.
Chesworth, N. and Dawe, A. (2000) *The Executive's Guide to International Schools*. London: Kogan Page.
Church, A. I. (1982) 'Sojourner Adjustment', *Psychological Bulletin*, 91(3): 540–71.
Clarke, V. (2004) 'Students' Global Awareness and Attitudes to Internationalism in a World of Cultural Convergence', *Journal of Research in International Education*, 3(1): 51–70.
Coldron, J. and Boulton, P. (1991) 'Happiness as a Criterion of Parents' Choice of School', *Journal of Education Policy*, 6(2): 169–78.
College Board (2004) *IB & AP*, accessed via www.collegeboard.com 30 March.
College Board (2006) www.collegeboard.com.
Collier, V. and Thomas, W. (2002) *A National Study of School Effectiveness for Language Minority Students' Long-term Academic Achievement*. Santa Cruz, CA: Center for Research on Education, Diversity and Excellence (CREDE). Available via CREDE website at www.crede.ucsc.edu/research/llaa/llaa.html.
Cottrell, A. B. (2002) 'Educational and Occupational Choices of American Adult Third Culture Kids', in M. G. Ender (ed.), *Military Brats and Other Global Nomads: Growing Up in Organization Families*. Westport, CT: Praeger. pp 229–53.
Council of International Schools (CIS) (2003) *Guide to School Evaluation and Accreditation*, 7th Edition. Petersfield: Council of International Schools.
Council of International Schools (CIS) (2005a) *The School Board – Is There a Perfect Model?*, CIS Board Governance Newsletter, 3(1): 1–3, accessed via www.cois.org 20 January.
Council of International Schools (CIS) (2005b) *Micromanagement: Why Do Boards Do It? What Can be Done About It?* CIS Board Governance Newsletter, 3(2): 1–9, accessed via www.cois.org 20 January.
Council of International Schools (CIS) (2006) www.cois.org, accessed 30 March.
Council of International Schools (CIS)/European Council of International Schools (ECIS) (1993) *Sample Contract for Heads of International Schools*. Petersfield: Council of International Schools.
Crossley, M. and Broadfoot, P. (1992) 'Comparative and International Research in Education: scope, problems and potential', *British Educational Research Journal*, 18(2): 99–112.

Cummins, J. (2000) *Language, Power and Pedagogy*. Clevedon: Multilingual Matters.

Daignault, S. (1999) 'NAIS Leadership Through Partnership', *Leadership Forum*, Fall 1999, National Association of Independent Schools, Washington, DC.

Davis, R. P. (2001) *Wherever I Lay My Hat, That's My Home*. Unpublished dissertation for MA in Education (International Education). University of Bath.

de Mejía, A. (2002) *Power, Prestige and Bilingualism: International Perspectives on Elite Bilingual Education*. Clevedon: Multilingual Matters.

Deerfield Academy (2006) www.deerfield.edu, accessed 14 January.

Dehner, H. and Dehner, H. (2001) *Life on the Outside: Memoirs of a Nomadic Mother and Daughter*. Bangladesh: Wanderlust Press.

De Kuyper, M. H. (1998) *Trustees Handbook*. Washington, DC: National Association of Independent Schools.

Department of Education and Science (DES) (1989) *Discipline in Schools: Report of the Committee of Enquiry Chaired by Lord Elton*, London: DES.

Department for Education (DFE) (1994) *The European Schools and the European Baccalaureate: Guidance for Universities and Colleges*. London: Department for Education.

Department for Education and Skills (DfES) (2004a) *Putting the World into World-Class Education: An International Strategy for Education, Skills and Children's Services*. London: DfES.

Department for Education and Skills (DfES) (2004b) *14–19 Curriculum and Qualifications Reform: Final Report of the Working Group on 14–19 Reform*. London: DfES.

Department of Defense Education Authority (DODEA) (2006) accessed via www.dodea.edu on 4 February.

Desforges, C. with Abouchaar, A. (2003) *The Impact of Parental Involvement, Parental Support and Family Education on Pupil Achievement and Adjustment: A Literature Review*. London: DfES.

Deveney, B. (2004) 'Coming Home to Culture Shock', *Intercom* (newsletter of the Centre for the study of Education in an International Context, University of Bath), no. 20, pp 2–3.

Deveney, B. (2005) 'An Investigation into Aspects of Thai Culture and Its Impact on Thai Students in an International School in Thailand', *Journal of Research in International Education*, 4(2): 153–71.

Deveney, M. (2000) *An Investigation into the Influences on Parental Choice of an International School in Thailand*. Unpublished dissertation for MA in Education (International Education), University of Bath.

Dickens, C. (ed.) (1864) 'International Education', in *All the Year Round: A Weekly Journal*, XII, 281: pp 281–308.

Dimmock, C. and Walker, A. (2005) *Educational Leadership: Culture and Diversity*. London: Sage.

Dixon, P. G. S. (2004) *'On the Move': A Study of the Views of Primary Age Students Attending an International School, Concerning the Impact of Transition*. Unpublished dissertation for MA in Education, University of Bath.

DiYanni, R. (2006) 'Globalizing the Curriculum in US Universities and Secondary Schools', in M. C. Hayden, J. Levy and J. J. Thompson (eds), *Handbook of Research in International Education*. London: Sage.

Dobson, J. M. and Henthorne, K. (1999) *Pupil Mobility in Schools: Interim Report*. London: DfEE.

Dobson, J. M., Henthorne, K. and Lynas, Z. (2000) *Pupil Mobility in Schools: Final Report*. London: Migration Research Unit, University College London.

Drake, B. (1998) 'Pastoral Care: the Challenge for International Schools', in M. C. Hayden and J. J. Thompson (eds), *International Education: Principles and Practice*. London: Kogan Page. pp 146–70.

Drake, B. (2004) 'International Education and IB Programmes: Worldwide Expansion and Potential Cultural Dissonance, *Journal of Research in International Education*, 3(2): 189–205.

Edexcel (2006) Accessed via www.edexcel-international.org 30 March.

Eidse, F. and Sichel, N. (2004) 'Introduction', in F. Eidse and N. Sichel (eds), *Unrooted Childhoods: Memoirs of Growing Up Global.* London and Yarmouth, Maine: Nicholas Brealey Publishing. pp 1–6.

Ellison, L. and Davies, B. (1993) *Market Research in Schools*. Research Paper: Leeds Metropolitan University.

Ellwood, C. (1999) 'IGCSE and the IB Middle Years Programme; How compatible are they?', *International Schools Journal*, XIX(1): 35–44.

Ender, M. G. (ed.) (2002a) *Military Brats and Other Global Nomads: Growing Up in Organization Families*, Westport, CT and London: Praeger.

Ender, M. G. (2002b) 'Beyond Adolescence: The Experiences of Adult Children of Military Parents', in M. G. Ender (ed.), *Military Brats and Other Global Nomads: Growing Up in Organization Families*. Westport CT and London: Praeger. pp 83–99.

English Schools Foundation (ESF) (2006) www.esf.edu.hk, accessed 30 March.

European Council of International Schools (ECIS) (1992) *International Schools Directory 1992–1993*, Petersfield: ECIS.

European Council of International Schools (ECIS) (1997) *Statistical Survey 1997*. Petersfield: ECIS.

European Council of International Schools (ECIS) (2006) www.ecis.org, accessed 18 March.

Evans, E. and Evans, J. (1998) 'Relations Between Teachers and Dorm Parents', in J. M. Bowers (ed.), *Raising Resilient MKs: Resources for Caregivers, Parents, and Teachers*. Colorado Springs: Association of Christian Schools International (ACSI). pp 393–96.

Ezra, R. (2003) 'Culture, Language and Personality in the Context of the Internationally Mobile Child', *Journal of Research in International Education*, 2(2): 123–49.

Fail, H. (2002) *An Examination of the Life Histories of a Group of Former International School Students*. Unpublished PhD thesis, University of Bath.

Fail, H. Thompson, J. and Walker, G. (2004) 'Belonging, Identity and Third Culture Kids: life histories of former international school students', *Journal of Research in International Education*, 3(3): 319–38.

Fan, L. (1999) 'Applications of Arithmetic in US and Chinese Textbooks: a comparative study', in G. Kaiser, E. Luna and I. Huntley (eds), *International Comparisons in Mathematics Education*. London: Falmer.

Farley, S. (1993) 'Market Forces', *Times Educational Supplement*, 26 March.

Fast Train (2006) http://gse.gmu.edu/programs/fasttrain/index.shtml, accessed 30 March.

Fennes, H. and Hapgood, K. (1997) *Intercultural Learning in the Classroom: Crossing Borders*. London: Cassell.

Findlay, R. (ed.) (1997) *International Education Handbook*. London: Kogan Page.

Finn Jordan, K. A. (2002) 'Identity Formation and the Adult Third Culture Kid', in M. G. Ender (ed.), *Military Brats and Other Global Nomads: Growing Up in Organization Families*. Westport, CT: Praeger. pp 211–28.

FOBISSEA (2006) www.fobissea.org, accessed 18 March.

Foreman, M. M. (1982) 'Culture-Fair Testing', *International Schools Journal*, 3: 71–82.

Foreman, M. M. (1983) 'The Gifted and Talented: Part II – Research Applications', *International Schools Journal*, 5: 65–74.

Fox, E. (1998) 'The Emergence of the International Baccalaureate as an Impetus for Curriculum Reform', in M. C. Hayden and J. J. Thompson (eds), *International Education: Principles and Practice*. London: Kogan Page. pp 65–76.

Friedman, T. (2005) *The World is Flat: a Brief History of the Globalized World in the 21st Century*, New York and London: Allen Lane (Penguin).

Gamwell, B. (1999) *The Selection and Induction of Citizen Teachers to International Schools in Papua New Guinea*. Unpublished MA in Education dissertation, University of Bath.

Garner, D. (1991) 'The International School ESL Challenge', in E. Murphy (ed.), *ESL: A Handbook for Teachers and Administrators in International Schools*. Clevedon: Multilingual Matters. pp 1–10.

Garton, B. (2000) '*Recruitment of Teachers for International Education*', in M. C. Hayden and J. J. Thompson (eds), *International Schools and International Education: Improving Teaching, Management and Quality*. London: Kogan Page. pp 85–95.

Garton, B. (2002) 'International Schools and Their Wider Community: the Location Factor', in M. C. Hayden, J. J. Thompson and G. R. Walker (eds), *International Education in Practice: Dimensions for National and International Schools*. London: Kogan Page. pp 145–57.

Gellar, C. A. (1981) 'International Education: some thoughts on what it is and what it might be', *International Schools Journal*, 1: 21–6.

GEMS (2006) www.gemseducation.com, accessed 30 March.

Ginsberg, M. and Wlodkowski, R. (2000) *Creating Highly Motivating Classrooms for All Students: A Schoolwide Approach to Powerful Teaching with Diverse Learners*. San Francisco, CA: Jossey-Bass.

Gordon, E. and Jones, M. (undated) *Portable Roots: Voices of Expatriate Wives*. Maastricht: Presses Interuniversitaires Européennes.

Gould, J. (1999) *Globalisation, Culture and School Choice: a Discussion of the Issues in an International School Context*. Unpublished Assignment for EdD programme, University of Bath.

Gray, K. (2006) *The Globalisation of English*. Public lecture given at the University of Bath, 8 February.

Gray, M. R. (2003) 'Tense Conjugations: Translating Political Values into an Educational Model: the European Schools', *Journal of Research in International Education*, 2(3): 315–30.

Greider, W. (1997) *One World, Ready or Not: the Manic Logic of Global Capitalism*. New York: Simon & Schuster.

Grimshaw, T. (2006) 'Critical Perspectives on Language in International Education', in M. C. Hayden, J. Levy and J. J. Thompson, (eds) *Handbook of Research in International Education*, London: Sage.

Gullahorn, J. T. and Gullahorn, J. E. (1963) An Extension of the U-curve Hypothesis, *Journal of Social Issues*, 19(3): 33–47.

Gullahorn, J. T. and Gullahorn, J. E. (1966) 'American Students Abroad: Professional versus Personal Development', *Annals of the American Academy of Political and Social Science*, 368: 43–59.

Gunesch, K. (2004) 'Education for Cosmopolitanism? Cosmopolitanism as a Personal Cultural Identity Model for and within International Education', *Journal of Research in International Education*, 3(3): 251–75.

Haldimann, M. (1998) 'Special Learning Needs in International Schools: the Optimal Match Concept', in M. C. Hayden and J. J. Thompson (eds), *International Education: Principles and Practice*. London: Kogan Page. pp 132–45.

Haldimann, M. and Hollington, A. (2004) *Effective Learning Support in International Schools*. Great Glemham, Suffolk: Peridot.
Hall, E. T. (1989) *Beyond Culture*, New York: Anchor.
Hallinger, P. (2005) 'Foreword', in C. Dimmock and A. Walker (eds), *Educational Leadership: Culture and Diversity*. London: Sage. pp vii–xii.
Handy, C. (1991) *The Age of Unreason*. London: Arrow.
Hannerz, U. (1992) *Cultural Complexity: Studies in the Social Organisation of Meaning*. New York: Columbia University Press.
Hardman, J. (2001) 'Improving Recruitment and Retention of Quality Overseas Teachers', in S. Blandford and M. Shaw (eds), *Managing International Schools*. London: RoutledgeFalmer. pp 123–35.
Hargreaves, A. (1997) '*Series Editor's Introduction*', in P. Sikes (ed.), *Parents Who Teach: Stories from Home and from School*. London and New York: Cassell. pp xi–xiii.
Harvard Educational Review (1985) 'A Special Issue: International Education, Perspectives, Experiences and Visions in an Interdependent World', *Harvard Educational Review*, 55.
Hastings, S. (2003) 'Fun and Games', *TES Go Global Supplement*, 7 November.
Hawley, D. B. (1994) 'How Long Do International School Heads Survive? A Research Analysis (Part I)', *International Schools Journal*, XIV(1): 8–21.
Hawley, D. B. (1995) 'How Long Do International School Heads Survive? A Research Analysis (Part II)', *International Schools Journal*, XIV(2): 23–36.
Hayden, M. C. (2001) *International Education and the IB Programmes*. Unpublished paper presented to meeting of IBO Academic Advisory Committee, 5 April.
Hayden, M. C. (2006) 'The International Baccalaureate and International Education', in T. Pound (ed.), *The International Baccalaureate Diploma Programme: An Introduction for Teachers and Managers*. London and New York: Routledge. pp 25–43.
Hayden, M. C. and Thompson, J. J. (1995) 'International Schools and International Education: A Relationship Reviewed', *Oxford Review of Education*, 21(3): 327–45.
Hayes, D. (2006) 'Pupils must learn in English, says new Head of school where science is taught in Turkish', *Evening Standard*, 21 February, p 5.
Heater, D. (2002) *World Citizenship: Cosmopolitan thinking and its Opponents*. London: Continuum.
Held, D., McGrew, A., Goldblatt, D. and Perraton, J. (1998) *Global Transformations*. Cambridge: Polity.
Heyward, M. (2002) 'From International to Intercultural: Redefining the International School for a Globalized World', *Journal of Research in International Education*, 1(1): 9–32.
Hill, I. (2000) 'Internationally-Minded Schools', *International Schools Journal*, XX(1): 24–37.
Hill, I. (2006a) 'Student Types, School Types and their Combined Influence on the Development of Intercultural Understanding', *Journal of Research in International Education*, 5(1): 5–33.
Hill, I. (2006b) 'Early Stirrings in International Education Part X: school heads and governments rescue the IB project', *International Schools Journal*, XXV(2): 68–75.
Hirst, P. H. and Peters, R. S. (1970) *The Logic of Education*. London: Routledge and Kegan Paul.
Hodgson, A. (2005a) 'Introduction to the World of Governance', in A. Hodgson and M. Chuck (eds), *Governance in International Schools*, Great Glemham, Suffolk: Peridot. pp 7–11.

Hodgson, A. (2005b) 'The Board and Evaluation', in A. Hodgson and M. Chuck (eds), *Governance in International Schools*, Great Glemham, Suffolk: Peridot. pp 44–7.

Hodgson, A. and Chuck, M. (2004) *Strategic Planning in International Schools*. Great Glemham, Suffolk: Peridot.

Ilon, L. (1997) 'Educational Repercussions of a Global System of Production', in W. K. Cummings and N. F. McGinn (eds), *International Handbook of Education and Development: Preparing Schools, Students and Nations for the Twenty-first Century*. Oxford: Pergamon.

International Baccalaureate Organization (IBO) (2005) 'Fact-finding Mission in Bosnia and Herzegovina', *IB World*, 45 (November): 2.

International Baccalaureate Organization (IBO) (2006) www.ibo.org, accessed 18 March.

International Primary Curriculum (IPC) (2006) www.internationalprimarycurriculum.com, accessed 30 March.

International Schools Association (ISA) (2006) www.isaschools.org, accessed 18 March.

International Schools Services (ISS) (2006) www.isu.edu, accessed 30 March.

International Schools Theatre Association (ISTA) (2006) www.ista.co.uk, accessed 30 March 2006.

Jackson, M. (2005) 'The Role of the Host Culture as a Resource for Developing Intercultural Understanding in a Dutch International Secondary School', *Journal of Research in International Education*, 4(2): 193–209.

Jason, L. A., Weine, A. M., and Johnson, J. H. (1992) *Helping Transfer Students*, San Francisco: Jossey Bass.

Jasper, J. M. (2000) *Restless Nation* Chicago: University of Chicago Press.

Jazzar, M. (2005) Tales of Micromanagement, Part I, *American School Board Journal*, August: 31–3.

Jenkins, J. (2004) 'Beware the Natives and Their Norms', *Guardian Weekly*, Thursday 22 January: 1–2.

Jonietz, P. L. and Harris, N. D. C. (eds) (1991) *World Yearbook of Education 1991: International Schools and International Education*. London: Kogan Page.

Joslin, P. (2002) 'Teacher Relocation: Reflections in the Context of International Schools', *Journal of Research in International Education*, 1(1): 33–62.

Kachirskaia, E. (2002) 'Special Needs Provision in International Schools', *International Schools Journal*, XXI(2): 69–74.

Keats, J. A., Keats, D.M., Biddle, B.J., Bank, B.J., Hauge, G., Wan-Rafaei, R., and Valantin, S. (1983) 'Parents, Friends, Siblings and Adults: unfolding referent other importance data for adolescents', *International Journal of Psychology*, 18: 239–62.

Keenan, B. (2005) *Diplomatic Baggage: the Adventures of a Trailing Spouse*. London: John Murray.

Kelly, A. V. (2004) *The Curriculum: Theory and Practice* (5th edition). London: Sage.

Kenny, P. (2005) 'Partnerships That Develop and Sustain All Stakeholders', *IB World*, 45: 22–3.

Knight, M. (1999) *Ecolint: A Portrait of the International School of Geneva 1924–1999*. Geneva: International School of Geneva.

Koopman, J. (1991) 'State-subsidized International Schools in the Netherlands', in P. L. Jonietz and D. Harris (eds), *World Yearbook of Education 1991: International Schools and International Education*. London: Kogan Page. pp 72–81.

Kulundu, F. and Hayden, M. (2002) 'Creativity, Action, Service (CAS) Activities as Part of the International Baccalaureate Diploma Programme: a Case Study', *Pastoral Care in Education*, 20(1): 30–6.

Kusuma-Powell, O. (2004) 'Multi-lingual, But Not Making It in International Schools', *Journal of Research in International Education*, 3(2): 157–72.

Langford, M. (1998) 'Global Nomads, Third Culture Kids and International Schools', in M. C. Hayden and J. J. Thompson (eds), *International Education: Principles and Practice*. London: Kogan Page. pp 28–43.

Langford, M., Pearce, R., Rader, D. and Sears, C. (2002) *The Essential Guide for Teachers in International Schools*. Great Glemham, Suffolk: John Catt.

Lawton, D. (1989) *Education, Culture and the National Curriculum*. London: Hodder and Stoughton.

Leach, R. J. (1969) *International Schools and Their Role in the Field of International Education*. Oxford: Pergamon.

Leggate, P. M. C. and Thompson, J. J. (1997) 'The Management of Development Planning in International Schools', *International Journal of Educational Management* 11(6): 268–73.

Lester, B. Pearson College of the Pacific (1982) *Adventures in High Endeavour: People Understanding People. The Story of Lester B. Pearson College of the Pacific*. Toronto: Brownstone.

Lewis, C. W. (1993) 'The Case for the AP', *International Schools Journal*, 26: 13–18.

Lewis, J. (1993) *The Induction of Teachers Entering an International School for the First Time*. Unpublished MEd dissertation, University of Bath.

Linden, M. (1995) 'CAS: Is it to serve or is it to learn?', *Contact: the Journal of IB Teachers*, May: 18–19.

Littleford, J. (1999a) 'Leadership of Schools and the Longevity of School Heads', *International Schools Journal*, XIX(1): 23–34.

Littleford, J. (1999b) *Leadership of Schools and the Longevity of Heads*, accessed 12 January 2006 via www.jlittleford.com/articles/longevity-heads.html.

Littleford, J. (2000) *The Governance Game – Part III: What's At Risk for Independent Schools*, accessed 12 January 2006 via www.jlittleford.com/articles/governance3.html.

Littleford, J. (2002a) *Board Structure: the Plight of the International School*, accessed 12 January 2006 via www.jlittleford.com/articles/board-structure.html.

Littleford, J. (2002b) *Evaluation of Boards: Self-reflection in a Healthy School*, accessed 12 January 2006 via www.jlittleford.com/articles/board-evaluation.html.

Littleford, J. (2003) *Strong and Stable Boards: Wise, Committed and Loyal!*, accessed 12 January 2006 via www.jlittleford.com/articles/strongboards.html.

Littleford, J. (2005a) *The Role of the Chair: the Promise and the Price*, accessed 12 January 2006 via www.jlittleford.com/articles/role-chair_promise_price.html.

Littleford, J. (2005b) *Problem Trustees (and how to help them): Part II*, accessed 12 January 2006 via www.jlittleford.com/articles/problem_trustees2.html.

Littleford, J. (2005c) *Dealing with Problem Trustees (Or Their Problem Spouses)*, accessed 12 January 2006 via www.jlittleford.com/articles/problem_trustees.html.

Littleford, J. C. (2005d) *Making (or Breaking) the Chair/Head Partnership: Some Key Ingredients for Success*, www.jlittleford.com/articles/making-the-head.html, accessed 12 January 2006.

Louis, K. S. and Miles, M. (1990) *Improving the Urban High School: What Works and Why*. New York: Teachers, College Press.

Lowe, J. (2000) 'Assessment and Educational Quality: Implications for International Schools', in M. C. Hayden and J. J. Thompson (eds), *International Schools and International Education: Improving Teaching, Management and Quality*. London: Kogan Page. pp 15–28.

Luck, A. (2005) 'Trouble in Paradise', *Times Educational Supplement*, 'Friday' supplement, pp 8–10 (2 December).

Lysgaard, S. (1955) 'Adjustment in a Foreign Society: Norwegian Fulbright grantees visiting the United States', *International Social Science Bulletin*, 7(1): 45–51.

MacDonald, J. (2006) 'The International School Industry', *Journal of Research in International Education*, 5(2): 191–213.

MacKenzie, P., Hayden, M. C. and Thompson, J. J. (2001) 'The Third Constituency: Parents in International Schools', *International Schools Journal*, XX(2): 57–64.

MacKenzie, P., Hayden, M. C. and Thompson, J. J. (2003) 'Parental Priorities in the Selection of International Schools', *Oxford Review of Education*, 29(3): 299–314.

Malpass, D. (1994) 'School Boards Need Management Training', *International Schools Journal*, XIV(1): 22–8.

Marshall, H. (2006) 'The Global Education Terminology Debate: exploring some of the issues', in M. C. Hayden, J. Levy, and J. J. Thompson (eds), *Handbook of Research in International Education*. London: Sage.

Marshall, H. (2007) *Global Education in Perspective: Fostering a Global Dimension in an English Secondary School*. Cambridge Journal of Education.

Maseru English Medium Preparatory School (1990) *Maseru Prep 1890–1990: The School in the Sky*. Maseru: Maseru English Medium Preparatory School.

Mattern, W. G. (1994) *The Most Important Decision: Searching for and Selecting New Heads for International Schools*. Petersfield: European Council of International Schools.

Matthews, M. (1988) *The Ethos of International Schools*. MSc Thesis, University of Oxford.

Matthews, M. (1989) 'The Scale of International Education', *International Schools Journal*, 17: 7–17.

Matthews, M. (2001a) *Teacher Appraisal for International Schools, Report from ECIS Fellowship 2000–2001*. Petersfield: ECIS.

Matthews, M. (2001b) *Heads Appraisal in International Schools, Report from ECIS Fellowship 2000–2001*. Petersfield: ECIS.

Matthews, M. (2006) *Appraisal for Teachers and Heads in International Schools*. Great Glemham, Suffolk: John Catt.

McCaig, N. (1992) 'Birth of a Notion', *The Global Nomad Quarterly*, 1(1): 1–2.

McKenzie, M. (1998) 'Going, Going, Gone ... Global!', in M. C. Hayden and J. J. Thompson (eds), *International Education: Principles and Practice*. London: Kogan Page. pp 242–52.

McKillop-Ostrom, A. (2000) 'Student Mobility and the International Curriculum', in M. C. Hayden and J. J. Thompson (eds), *International Schools and International Education: Improving Teaching, Management and Quality*. London: Kogan Page. pp 73–84.

Meighan, M. (1995) *How to Design and Deliver Induction Training Programmes* (2nd edition), London: Kogan Page.

Meyer, B. (1996) *The Expatriate Experience: a Practical Guide to Successful Relocation*. Peterborough: Need2Know.

Middlewood, D. and Cardno, C. (eds) (2001) *Managing Teacher Appraisal and Performance: A Comparative Approach*. London: RoutledgeFalmer.

Model United Nations (MUN) (2006) www.thimun.org, accessed 18 March.

Montet, M. (2005) 'The Role of Language in Promoting International Mindedness', *IS magazine*, 7(2): 28–9.

Mulder, N. (2000) *Inside Thai Society: Religion, Everyday Life, Change*. Chiang Mai: Silkworm Books.

Murphy, E. (ed.) (1991) *ESL: A Handbook for Teachers and Administrators in International Schools*, Clevedon: Multilingual Matters.

Murphy, E. (1998) 'International School Accreditation: Who Needs It?', in M. C. Hayden and J. J. Thompson (eds), *International Education: Principles and Practice*. London: Kogan Page. pp 212–23.

Murphy, E. (2001) 'The One and the Many or life, the universe and international education', *International Schools Journal*, XX(2): 5–10.

Murphy, E. (2003) 'Monolingual International Schools and the Young Non-English-Speaking Child', *Journal of Research in International Education*, 2(1): 25–45.

Murphy-Lejeune, E. (2003) 'An Experience of Interculturality: Student Travellers Abroad', in G. Alred, M. Byram and M. Fleming (eds), *Intercultural Experience and Education*. Clevedon: Multilingual Matters. pp 101–13.

Nampota, D. C. (2005) *Relationship Between Integrated Science and University Science and Technology Programmes in Malawi*. Unpublished PhD thesis, University of Bath.

Nashman-Smith, M. and Taylor, R. (2004) 'Integrating the IBMYP and IGCSE', Report on the International Conference held in Muscat, Oman, March 10–12, *International Schools Journal*, XXIV(1): 19–25.

National Association of British Schools in Spain (NABSS) (2006) www.nabss.org, accessed 30 March.

Neihart, M. (2003) 'Social Development of Gifted Children: Fact and Fiction', in M. Haldimann and A. Hollington (eds), (2004) *Effective Learning Support in International Schools*. Great Glemham, Suffolk: Peridot.

Nelson, N. (2000) 'Strategic Planning for International Schools: a Roadmap to Excellence', in M. C. Hayden and J. J. Thompson (eds), *International Schools and International Education: Improving Teaching, Management and Quality*. London: Kogan Page. pp 169–78.

Nette, J. (2000) *Primary Age Internationally Mobile Children's Sense of Belonging and Identity: A Survey of Standard 5 and 6 Children at Four International Independent Schools in Botswana*. Unpublished MA in Education dissertation, University of Bath.

Nord Anglia (2006) www.nordanglia.com, accessed 30 March.

Osler, A. and Hussain, Z. (1995) 'Parental Choice and Schooling: Some Factors Influencing Muslim Mothers' Decisions About the Education of their Daughters', *Cambridge Journal of Education*, 25(3).

Paige, M. (1993) 'On the Nature of Intercultural Experiences and Intercultural Education', in M. Paige (ed.), *Education for the Intercultural Experience*. Yarmouth, ME: Intercultural.

Pascoe, R. (1993) *Culture Shock! Successful Living Abroad: A Parent's Guide*. Portland, OR: Graphic Arts Center.

Pasternak, M. (1998) 'Is International Education A Pipedream? A Question of Values', in M. C. Hayden and J. J. Thompson (eds), *International Education: Principles and Practice*. London: Kogan Page. pp 253–75.

Pearce, R. (1994) 'International Schools: the Multinational Enterprises' Best Friends', *CBI Relocation News*, 32: 8–9.

Pearce, R. (1998) 'Developing Cultural Identity in an International School Environment', in M. C. Hayden and J. J. Thompson (eds), *International Education: Principles and Practice*. London: Kogan Page. pp 44–62.

Pearce, R. (2002) 'Children's International Relocation and the Developmental Process', in M. G. Ender (ed.), *Military Brats and Other Global Nomads: Growing Up in Organization Families*. Westport CI and London: Praeger. pp 145–64.

Pearce, R. (2006) 'Culture and Identity: Exploring Individuals Within Groups', in M. C. Hayden, J. Levy and J. J. Thompson (eds), *Handbook of Research in International Education*. London: Sage.

Petch, A. (1986) 'Parents' Reasons for Changing Schools', in A. Stillman (ed.), *The Balancing Act of 1980: Parents, Politics and Education*. Windsor: NFER-Nelson.

Peterson, A. D. C. (1987) *Schools Across Frontiers: the Story of the International Baccalaureate and the United World Colleges*. La Salle, IL: Open Court.

Peterson, A. D. C. (2003) *Schools Across Frontiers: the Story of the International Baccalaureate and the United World Colleges* (2nd edition), La Salle, IL: Open Court.

Phillipson, R. (1992) *Linguistic Imperialism*. Oxford: Oxford University Press.

Phenix, P. H. (1964) *Realms of Meaning*. New York: McGraw Hill.

Pollock, D. (1992) 'Swans, Ducks, and Other Valid Creatures', in K. C. McCluskey (ed.), *Notes From a Traveling Childhood: Readings for Internationally Mobile Parents and Children*. Washington, DC: Foreign Service Youth Foundation. pp 72–4.

Pollock, D. (1998) 'Effective Parent-Teacher Partnerships', in J. M. Bowers (ed.), *Raising Resilient MKs: Resources for Caregivers, Parents, and Teachers*. Colorado Springs: Association of Christian Schools International (ACSI). pp 387–92.

Pollock, D. and Van Reken, R. E. (1999) *The Third Culture Kid Experience: Growing up Among Worlds*. Yarmouth, MA: Intercultural Press.

Pönisch, A. (1987) *Special Needs and the International Baccalaureate: A Study of the Need for and Development of Alternative Courses to the International Baccalaureate*. MSc thesis, University of Oxford.

Poore, P. (2005) 'School Culture: the Space Between the Bars; the Silence between the Notes', *Journal of Research in International Education*, 4(3): 351–61.

Postlethwaite, T. N. (ed.) (1988) *The Encyclopaedia of Comparative Education and National Systems of Education*. Oxford: Pergamon.

Potter, D. and Hayden, M. C. (2004) 'Parental Choice in the Buenos Aires Bilingual School Market', *Journal of Research in International Education*, 3(1): 87–111.

Powell, W. (2000) 'Professional Development and Reflective Practice', in M. C. Hayden and J. J. Thompson (eds), *International Schools and International Education: Improving Teaching, Management and Quality*. London: Kogan Page. pp 96–111.

Powell, W. (2001) 'Roles and Responsibilities: What Does a School Board Do?', in W. Powell, N. Bowley and G. Schoppert (eds), *School Board Governance Training: a Sourcebook of Case Studies*, Great Glemham, Suffolk: John Catt. pp 13–21.

Principals Training Center (PTC) for International School Leadership (2006) www.theptc.org, accessed 30 March.

Rader, D. and Sittig, L. H. (2003) *New Kid in School: Using Literature to Help Children in Transition*. New York: Teachers' College Press.

Randell, S. (1991) *Not Advancing Equally: Women in Educational Management in Australia*. Melbourne: The Council of Adult Education.

Ratté, J. (1987) 'Quis Custodiet?: The Virtuous Educator', *International Schools Journal*, (14): 7–15.

Rice, B. (1980) 'Going for the Gifted Child', *Psychology Today*, February.

Richards, N. (1998) 'The Emperor's New Clothes? The Issue of Staffing in International Schools', in M. C. Hayden and J. J. Thompson (eds), *International Education: Principles and Practice*. London: Kogan Page. pp 173–83.

Richards, N. (2002) 'Professional Development: an International Schools' Perspective', in M. C. Hayden, J. J. Thompson and G. R. Walker (eds), *International Education in Practice: Dimensions for National and International Schools*. London: Kogan Page. pp 99–111.

Rischard, J. F. (2002) *High Noon: 20 Global Problems, 20 Years to Solve Them.* New York: Basic.

Robitaille, D. (1993) *Curriculum Frameworks for Mathematics and Science: TIMMS Monograph No 1.* Vancouver: Pacific Educational.

Round Square (2006) Accessed via www.roundsquare.org 30 March.

Rugus, B. (2002) Maastricht Congress on Global Education: Welcome Address. *Maastricht Congress on Global Education,* Maastricht. Accessed via www.globaleducationeurope.net.

Sammons, P., Hillman, J. and Mortimore, P. (1997) 'Key Characteristics of Effective Schools: a Review of School Effectiveness Research', in J. White and M. Barber (eds), *Perspectives on School Effectiveness and School Improvement.* London: Institute of Education.

Sanderson, J. (1981) *International Schooling: The 'Mobile' Pupil and His Educational Needs.* MSc thesis, University of Oxford.

Schaetti, B. (1993) 'The Global Nomad Profile', in *The Global Nomad: the Benefits and Challenges of an Internationally Mobile Childhood.* Regents College Conference, London, 23 April.

Schaetti, B. (2002) 'Attachment Theory: A View Into the Global Nomad Experience', in M. G. Ender (ed.), *Military Brats and Other Global Nomads: Growing Up in Organization Families.* Westport, CT and London: Praeger. pp 103–19.

Schoppert, G. (2001a) 'The Most Important Decision: Hiring a New Head of School', in W. Powell, N. Bowley and G. Schoppert (eds), *School Board Governance Training: a Sourcebook of Case Studies.* Great Glemham, Suffolk: John Catt. pp 120–27.

Schoppert, G. (2001b) 'ECIS Board Survey Results', in W. Powell, N. Bowley and G. Schoppert (eds), *School Board Governance Training: a Sourcebook of Case Studies.* Great Glemham, Suffolk: John Catt. pp 163–70.

Schwindt, E. (2003) 'The Development of a Model for International Education with Special Reference to the Role of Host Country Nationals', *Journal of Research in International Education,* 2(1): 67–81.

Scol@gora (2006), Accessed via www.scolagora.com/ponto/Site_Web/International/OIB.htm 30 March 2006.

Search Associates (2006) www.search-associates.com, accessed 30 March.

Sears, C. (1998) *Second Language Students in Mainstream Classrooms.* Clevedon: Multilingual Matters.

Sears, C. (2006) Personal Communication.

Segal, M. W. (2002) 'Foreword', in M. G. Ender (ed.), *Military Brats and Other Global Nomads: Growing Up in Organization Families.* Westport, CT and London: Praeger. pp xvii–xix.

Service Children's Education (UK) (SCE) (2006) www.army.mod.uk/soldierwelfare, accessed 4 February.

Sewell, W. H. and Davidson, O. M. (1956) 'The Adjustment of Scandinavian Students', *Journal of Social Issues,* 12(1): 9–19.

Seyfarth, J. T. (1991) *Personnel Management for Effective Schools.* Boston, MA: Allyn and Bacon.

SGIS (2006) www.sgischools.com, accessed 18 March.

Sharples, J. and De'Ath, C. (1997) *The Complete Guide to International Schools in Thailand 1997–98.* Bangkok: Headline.

Shaw, M. (2001) 'Managing Mixed-Culture Teams in International Schools', in S. Blandford and M. Shaw (eds), *Managing International Schools.* London: RoutledgeFalmer. pp 153–72.

Shell Schools (2006) www.stichtingnob.nl, accessed 30 March.
Sikes, P. (1997) *Parents Who Teach: Stories from Home and from School*. London and New York: Cassell.
Skeats, J. (1991) *Successful Induction*. London: Kogan Page.
Sklair, L. (2001) *The Transnational Capitalist Class*. Oxford: Blackwell.
Soraci, S. A., Leggett, E. L., Dweck, C. S. and Valk, A. M. (1986) *Differential Attentional Functioning in Learned Helplessness and Mastery Oriented Children*. John F. Kennedy Center for Education and Human Development, George Peabody, Nashville, TN: College for Teachers.
Spahn, B. A. (2001) *America and the International Baccalaureate: Implementing the International Baccalaureate in the United States*. Great Glemham, Suffolk: John Catt.
Stanworth, D. (1996) 'Number One *vs* Number One', *IB World*, 12: 53–4 (August).
Stanworth, D. (1998) *An International Education at Yokohama International School: From Theory to Practice*. Unpublished MA in Education dissertation, University of Bath.
Stewart, W. A. C. (1972) *Progressives and Radicals in English Education, 1750–1970*. London: Macmillan.
Stirzaker, R. (2004) 'Staff Induction: Issues surrounding induction into international schools', *Journal of Research in International Education*, 3(1): 31–49.
Storti, C. (2001) *The Art of Crossing Cultures* (2nd edition). London: Nicholas Brealey.
Storti, C. (2003) *The Art of Coming Home*. London: Nicholas Brealey.
Stout, W. (2005a) 'Conflict and its Resolution in the Governance and Management of International Schools', *International Schools Journal*, XXV(1): 15–21.
Stout, W. (2005b) 'The Board and Managing Conflict', in A. Hodgson and M. Chuck (eds), *Governance in International Schools*. Great Glemham, Suffolk: Peridot. pp 37–43.
Sutcliffe, D. (1991) 'The United World Colleges', in P. L. Jonietz and D. Harris (eds), *World Yearbook of Education 1991: International Schools and International Education*. London: Kogan Page. pp 25–37.
Sutcliffe, D. (2006) 'Book Review: International Education and Conflict', *International Schools Journal*, XXV(2): 80–5.
Sylvester, B. (1998) 'Through the Lens of Diversity: Inclusive and Encapsulated School Missions', in M. C. Hayden and J. J. Thompson (eds), *International Education: Principles and Practice*. London: Kogan Page. pp 184–96.
Sylvester, R. (2002) 'The 'First' International School', in M. C. Hayden, J. J. Thompson and G. R. Walker (eds), *International Education in Practice: Dimensions for National and International Schools*. London: Kogan Page. pp 3–17.
Tangye, R. (2005) 'The Board and Best Practice', in A. Hodgson and M. Chuck (eds), *Governance in International Schools*. Great Glemham, Suffolk: Peridot. pp 12–16.
Terwilliger, R. I. (1972) 'International Schools – Cultural Crossroads', *The Educational Forum* XXXVI(3): 359–63.
Thearle, C. (2000) 'The Role of Women in Senior Management in International Schools', in M. C. Hayden and J. J. Thompson (eds), *International Schools and International Education: Improving Teaching, Management and Quality*. London: Kogan Page. pp 112–23.
Thomas, H. (2006) Personal Communication.
Thompson, J. J. (1988) Presentation at International Baccalaureate Seminar, University of London.
Thompson, J. J. (1998) 'Towards a Model for International Education', in M. C. Hayden and J. J. Thompson (eds), *International Education: Principles and Practice*. London: Kogan Page. pp 276–90.

Thompson, J. J. Hayden, M. C. and Cambridge, J. C. (2003) 'Towards a Structural Typology for Baccalaureate-Style Curricula', in G. Phillips and T. Pound (eds), *The Baccalaureate: a Model for Curriculum Reform.* London: Kogan Page.

Thornton, K. (1999) 'Collaboration with Community Minimal', *Times Educational Supplement, Research Focus*, 17 September.

Times Educational Supplement (TES) (2005) 'Headship', in TES Friday supplement, 14 October.

Tokuhama-Espinosa, T. (2003a) 'Third Culture Kids: A Special Case for Foreign Language Learning', in T. Tokuhama-Espinosa (ed.), *The Multilingual Mind: Issues Discussed by, for, and about People Living with Many Languages.* Westport, CT: Praeger. pp 165–69.

Tokuhama-Espinosa, T. (2003b) 'Challenges to Normal Bilingualism: Down's Syndrome, Deafness and Dyslexia', in T. Tokuhama-Espinosa (ed.), *The Multilingual Mind: Issues Discussed by, for, and about People Living with Many Languages.* Westport, CT: Praeger. pp 243–54.

UNESCO (1974) *Recommendation concerning education for international understanding, co-operation and peace and education relating to human rights and fundamental freedoms.* Paris: UNESCO.

United World Colleges (UWC) (2006) Accessed via www.uwc.org 31 March.

University of Bath (2006) www.bath.ac.uk/ceic, accessed 18 March.

Useem, R. H. (1976) 'Third Culture Kids', *Today's Education*, 65(3): 103–5.

Useem, R. H., Useem, J., Cottrell, A. B. and Finn Jordan, K. A. (1993a) 'Third Culture Kids: Focus of Major Study', *Newslinks* (the newspaper of International Schools Services), XII(1): 1 and 29 (January).

Useem, R. H., Useem, J., Cottrell, A. B. and Finn Jordan, K. A. (1993b) 'TCKs Four Times More Likely to Earn Bachelor's Degrees', *Newslinks* (the newspaper of International Schools Services), XII(5): 1, 18, 27 (May).

Useem, R. H., Useem, J., Cottrell, A. B. and Finn Jordan, K. A. (1993c) 'TCKs Experience Prolonged Adolescence', *Newslinks* (the newspaper of International Schools Services), XIII(1): 1 and 26 (September).

Vallance, E. (1991) 'Hidden Curriculum', in A. Lewy (ed.), *The International Encyclopaedia of Curriculum.* Oxford: Pergamon.

Vinge, D. (2005) 'The Board and the Head of School', in A. Hodgson and M. Chuck (eds), *Governance in International Schools.* Great Glemham, Suffolk: Peridot. pp 30–6.

Vygotsky, L. S. (1962) *Thought and Language.* Cambridge, MA: MIT Press.

Waldron, M. (1991) 'International Schools: Perspective of a Parent with a Handicapped Child', in P. L. Jonietz and D. Harris (eds), *World Yearbook of Education 1991: International Schools and International Education.* London: Kogan Page. pp 68–71.

Walford, G. (1991) 'Choice of School at the First City Technology College', *Educational Studies*, 17, 1.

Walker, G. (1996) 'Keeping the Balance', *IB World*, 11: 19–20 (April).

Walker, G. R. (1998) 'Home Sweet Home: A Study, Through Fictional Literature, of Disoriented Children and the Significance of Home', in M. C. Hayden and J. J. Thompson (eds), *International Education: Principles and Practice.* London: Kogan Page. pp 11–27.

Walker, G. R. (2004a) 'Life Together: A School's Head and its Governing Board', *IB World*, August, 40: 10–11.

Walker, G. R. (2004b) 'Trends in International Education and the IBO of the Future', in *To Educate the Nations 2: Reflections on an International Education.* Great Glemham, Suffolk: Peridot (Address to Regional Conference of IB North America, Québec City Canada, July 1999).

Walsh, P. (1999) *International Teacher Recruitment: an Empirical Investigation.* Unpublished MA in Education dissertation, University of Bath.

West, A. and Varlaam, A. (1991) 'Choosing a Secondary School: parents of junior school children', *Educational Research,* 33(1): 22–30.

Wijewardene, I. M. (1999) *What people perceive International Schools in Sri Lanka have to offer which makes them more popular than local schools for those who can afford them.* Unpublished dissertation for MA in Education, University of Bath.

Wilkin, M. (ed.) (1992) *Mentoring in Schools.* London: Kogan Page.

Wilkinson, D. (1998) 'International Education: A Question of Access', in M. C. Hayden and J. J. Thompson (eds), *International Education: Principles and Practice.* London: Kogan Page. pp 227–34.

Wilkinson, D. (2002) 'International Education and Issues of Governance', in M. C. Hayden, J. J. Thompson and G. R. Walker (eds), *International Education in Practice: Dimensions for National and International Schools.* London: Kogan Page. pp 185–96.

Wilkinson, V. (2006) *A Study of the Factors Affecting the Development of Attitudes of Students Following the International Baccalaureate Diploma Programme.* Unpublished PhD thesis, University of Bath.

Williams, K. C. and Mariglia, L. L. (2002) 'Military Brats: Issues and Associations in Adulthood', in M. G. Ender (ed.), *Military Brats and Other Global Nomads: Growing Up in Organization Families.* Westport, CT and London: Praeger. pp 67–82.

Willis, D. and Enloe, W. (1990) 'Lessons of International Schools: Global Education in the 1990s', *The Educational Forum,* 54(2): 169–83.

Willis, D. B. Enloe, W. W. and Minoura, Y. (1994) 'Transculturals, Transnationals: The New Diaspora', *International Schools Journal,* XIV(1): 29–42.

Windham International (1999) *Global Relocation Trends 1999 Survey Report.* New York: Windham International.

Yamada-Yamamoto, A. and Richards, B. J. (1998) *Japanese Children Abroad: Cultural, Educational and Language Issues.* Clevedon: Multilingual Matters.

Yamato, Y. (2003) *Education in the Market Place: Hong Kong's International Schools and their Mode of Operation.* Hong Kong: Comparative Education Research Centre, The University of Hong Kong.

Yew Chung Education Foundation (YCEF) (2006) www.ycef.com, accessed 30 March.

Yorke, D. A. and Bakewell, C. J. (1991) 'Choice of Secondary School', *International Journal of Education Management,* 5, 2.

Zilber, E. (2004) Survey on number of staff children in international schools. Conducted on list-serve of the Association for the Advancement of International Education and the Academy of International School Heads.

Zilber, E. (2005) 'International School Educators and their Children: Implications for educator-parents, colleagues, and schools', *Journal of Research in International Education,* 4(1): 5–22.

Index